The Women of Lemuria

KRYON

Monika Muranyi

With
Dr. Amber Wolf

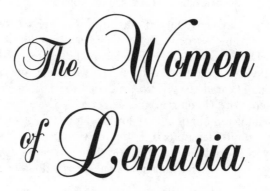

The Women
of Lemuria

Ancient Wisdom for Modern Times

The Women of Lemuria
© 2018 Ariane Books
1217, av. Bernard O., suite 101, Outremont, Quebec, Canada H2V 1V7
Phone: (1) 514-276-2949, Fax: (1) 514-276-4121
info@editions-ariane.com – www.editions-ariane.com
© 2018 Ariane Éditions Inc
www.ariane-books.com – www.editions-ariane.com

Cover design: Deborah DeLisi
Interior design: Carl Lemyre
Cover design artwork: © Christina DeHoff

Artist Christina DeHoff's description of her artwork:
The image for "The Women of Lemuria" was inspired by a photograph, taken by Frank Davey circa 1900, of Hawaiian hula dancer, Malia Kaleikoa. As I painted, a Being of Light, filled with ancient wisdom, came and sat with me in my studio. The end result is the grounded strength of Malia and the peaceful presence of a (Lemurian) messenger with a gaze in her eyes that is direct, calming, and full of intense love and guidance. Celebrating the empowered, soulful feminine is so important to me in my art. Women supporting women to shine their light brightly is the message and gift this painting gave to my heart. I hope that same energy flows into your heart.

ISBN: 978-2-89626-494-0

We acknowledge the financial support of the Government of Canada through the Canada Book Fund (CBF) for our publishing activities.
Government of Québec — Tax credit for book publishing
— Administered by SODEC

Distributed by: New Leaf
401 Thornton Rd. Lithia Springs, GA 30122-1557
Phone: 770.948.7845 – Fax: 770.944.2313
domestic@newleaf-dist.com – foreign@newleaf-dist.com.
Printed in Canada

Contents

Acknowledgements ix

Preface xi

Chapter One: Ancient Lemuria 1
The History of Lemuria 1
Lemurian Society 22
The Schools of Lemuria 40
Lemurian Health Care 48
Temple of Rejuvenation 54
Lemurian Pineal Tones 75
Lemurian Language 81
Lemuria and Atlantis 91

Chapter Two: The Women of Lemuria 97
Pleiadian Mothers 113
Pleiadian Teachers 129
Lemurian Ceremonies 163
Birth Day Ceremony 168
Winter Solstice Ceremony 172
Valentine's Day Ceremony 176
New Year Ceremony 182

Chapter Three: The Great Shift 201
Ancient Prophecy 203
The Lemurian Sisterhood and the Shift 207
The Re-emergence of Ancient Wisdom 210

Chapter Four: The Lemurian Sisterhood 219

The Akashic Awakening of Mele'ha 220

The Akashic Awakening of Women 237

The Lemurian Sisterhood Today 246

**Chapter Five: The Unexpected,
Underground "Sisterhood"** 253

Chapter Six: Rewriting the Future 271

The Task of the New Lemurian 282

The Lemuria/Hindu Connection 288

The Lemuria/Hawaiian Kahuna Connection 301

Kahuna Hale Kealohalani Makua 302

Kahuna Kalei'iliahi 306

In Closing 316

Connect with the Lemurian Sisterhood 320

About the Authors 321

In memory of...
Martine Vallée

Sid Wolf

Acknowledgements

This book is a collaboration between Monika Muranyi and Dr. Amber Wolf. Both of our lives have been profoundly touched and transformed by the channelled messages from Kryon, as given by Lee Carroll. Kryon has been a guiding light for humanity, and we would like to express our deep gratitude and thanks to Lee for bringing Kryon's messages to the world and to the sacred circles of the Lemurian Sisterhood. These messages have expanded our knowledge of Lemuria and explained the role of women on the planet.

We would like to thank our exceptional editor, Lourana Howard, and our publisher, Marc Vallée from Ariane Editions, Montreal, Canada. Our appreciation and gratitude go out to the many women awakening all across the world, especially those who have connected with the Lemurian Sisterhood. We love hearing about the positive, life-changing effects that have occurred as a result of connecting with Kryon, the Sisterhood, or both. We would like to thank you for choosing to read this book. Regardless of your gender, we wish to honor the Divine Feminine and Divine Masculine within you, and we feel blessed to be a part of your spiritual journey.

Preface

You have in your hands a book that has been birthed from many sources. The essence of what is presented actually had its original beginnings over 26,000 years ago! However, it is only since 2011 that a series of synchronicities took place that allowed the expansion and unfolding of ancient wisdom from the Women of Lemuria to come forth. These synchronicities include the Akashic awakening of Dr. Amber Wolf; the channelled messages from Kryon, as given by Lee Carroll (the original channel for Kryon); and the dedication and passion of Monika Muranyi, who writes subject-driven books based upon the teachings of Kryon.

In 2011, Dr. Amber Wolf created the first Lemurian Sisterhood gathering. Today there is a global network of Star Sisters who are part of the Lemurian Sisterhood community. The purpose of the Sisterhood is to reawaken the energy of the Divine Feminine, and to rekindle the remembrance of the original Akash, given by the Pleiadians. The intention is for women to remember their sacredness, claim it as their truth, and become a living example of compassionate mother energy.

For several years, Dr. Amber Wolf presented the Sacred Circles of the Sisterhood across North and South America and Canada. In 2014, the first Lemurian Sisterhood meeting of that year began with a special surprise. It was during this meeting that Lee Carroll offered to channel a message from Kryon. This is when Kryon revealed Amber's Lemurian name of Mele'ha, and gave some information about the Sisterhood. Since then, a wealth of information has been revealed about Ancient Lemurian, the Sisterhood, and the role of Mele'ha.

This book is a compilation by Monika Muranyi featuring Kryon's messages and teachings about Lemuria and the Lemurian Sisterhood, and includes a contribution from Dr. Amber (Mele'ha) Wolf – the Last Lemurian Priestess who made it possible for us to receive the wisdom and knowledge from our Star Mothers, the Pleiadians. In addition, Kryon has provided answers to over twenty questions relating to the topics within this book. The complete collection of Kryon channels given during the Lemurian Sisterhood meetings are available as audio files from Dr. Amber Wolf's website:

www.amberwolfphd.com/free-audio.

We hope that the wisdom, knowledge, and energetic communication presented within this book will enhance your life. It is our deepest desire that you claim your mastery, stand tall, and celebrate your life. It is no accident that you are here now on our beautiful planet Earth. Nor is it an accident that you are reading this book! We invite you to ponder some wise words from Kryon…

"When the greatest masters of this planet walked the Earth, you could see the feminine within their masculinity. They were soft and you could see it in their eyes. They reflected that which came from their mother. Emulating the sweet spirit of the feminine of the planet is the secret to peace on Earth. You know this. Know that you can be anything. This is a simple message for the women, who are the key to the softness of the planet."

Kryon Lemurian Sisterhood channelling
given in Portland, Oregon – November 22, 2014

Love and blessings,
Monika Muranyi and Amber (Mele'ha) Wolf, PhD
www.monikamuranyi.com
www.amberwolfphd.com

CHAPTER ONE

Ancient Lemuria

The History of Lemuria

Writing about the "History of Lemuria" requires some unique attributes that are vastly different than writing about the history of an ancient civilization, such as Egypt. However, it is these particular attributes that are most likely the very reason you have decided to read this book! It has to do with being an awakened *Old Soul!* What's an Old Soul? An Old Soul, according to Kryon, has nothing to do with your chronological age. Rather, it has everything to do with your Akashic age, which refers to the number of lives you've lived on the planet. As a result, most Old Souls carry a deep wisdom because they have the *most experience.*

As an Old Soul, you are more apt to desire knowledge about spiritual truths. As an Old Soul, the messages of Kryon are likely to resonate with your own Akashic remembrance. Never heard of Kryon? In simple terms, Kryon is a loving entity who gives empowering messages to humanity that are filled with profound information, teachings, and esoteric understandings. Lee Carroll is the original channel for Kryon and has been delivering Kryon's messages since 1989. The channelled messages are constantly evolving in response to the shifting energies of the planet and the evolution of Human consciousness. There is always something

1

new to discover! That's what makes it so exciting to be alive, right now, on an Earth that has graduated and is moving toward planetary peace.

Before giving a detailed history of Lemuria, it's important for you to understand the spiritual lineage of humanity. Where did we come from? Are we simply a higher form of mammal evolved from Earth? Are we the product of extra-terrestrials? How do our creation stories from various organized belief systems fit into all of this? What is your understanding about our origins? Your answers will most likely vary based on your own personal journey. However, the answer from Kryon is that we are part of a larger galactic family. Slowly, humanity is beginning to awaken to deeper truths about who we really are.

According to Kryon, our galaxy was created by the Creative Source and filled with the love of God. The physics of our galaxy is biased for completion, balance, and life. Within our galaxy, one planet at a time, the Humans have their DNA altered slightly to include a multidimensional portion of divinity (through spiritual seeding), so that a test, lasting thousands of years, would begin. The test is to see if Humans can discover the God inside themselves, their own divinity, their connection with the Creative Source – the benevolent creation system. On the planets where Humans discover their divinity, they have permission to go into *ascension status*, where physical reality melds into multidimensional reality. Eventually, this planet becomes an *ascended planet*, and is then asked to choose another planet in the galaxy, to pass on their sacred DNA to begin another test. This is the system Kryon has described. With free choice, Humans on Earth have been spiritually seeded (as part of a loving, benevolent plan), giving them the ability to embody a soul and become aware of light (an energy created as a result of high consciousness) and dark (the absence of light).

Dear Reader, we interrupt this part of the narrative to assist you with reading the channelled messages from Kryon that will follow throughout the remainder of this book. If this is your first exposure to Kryon, you may come across brand new concepts, terms, and vocabulary you have never heard before. If so, you are invited to examine the Kryon glossary found at the following link: www.kryon.com/glossary

Kryon has told us that the seeding of planet Earth was done by the *Pleiadians*, making them our spiritual parents. If we look at the creation stories of indigenous tribes, all over the planet, the majority of them refer to the Seven Sisters and the Pleiadians as our creators. So the answer to who are we, and where did we come from, is that we are a combination of an organic Human, grown from our planet Earth, melded with the sacred DNA of ascended beings, known as the Pleiadians. Here is Kryon's description of how it all began:

About 200,000 years ago, when the Pleiadians first came to Earth, humanity was a group, a variety, like all the other evolution on the planet. The mammal called Human Being had many varieties of forms. Like other mammals today, variety insured survival. Up to 26 kinds of Humans were present, but were eventually reduced to 17 kinds before the Pleiadians got here (through normal evolutionary processes). This was the puzzle for the Pleiadians, for, in the seeding of the planet back then, the DNA had to change to allow for the spiritual, Pleiadian DNA complement. Humanity needed to end up with one kind of Human Being, the kind that you have today, but also to have the "DNA of the cosmos." That kind of Human has no variety like the other mammals of Earth, as you may have noticed or not. It's the way you are today.

So you are unique, in an evolutionary way, to everything you see around you. This process created a 23-chromosome [pair] Human Being, when all around you there were the 24 of conventional mammals. So the fusing of portions of your DNA to create the 23 was the element of the Pleiadian who came in and gave you their DNA. In the process, many things happened simultaneously.

When a farmer looks at his field and decides to grow corn, he surveys it in a different way than those who would eventually eat the corn. For the eater of the corn would ask, *"When does the corn exist for consumption?"* He would then be told, *"It exists when the stalks are high and it is then collected, cooked, and provided on the table."* That would be the *story of corn* for the consumer. It starts with the collection of grown corn. But the farmer looks at it differently. He looks at the raw land that has to be plowed and fertilized, and perhaps turned over a few times with other crops to allow nitrogen in the soil until the dirt is ready. Perhaps he would plant it and then take the seedlings as they came up and turn them into the ground again; you know the story. So the farmer would have an entirely different idea of the *story of corn.*

So you have at least two questions and scenarios, don't you? When did corn begin? The eater gives you one answer and the farmer another. So which is which? It depends who's asking – the consumer of the corn or the grower of the corn. Now, there's a third question: What about the conceiver (creator) of the corn? Who made corn? When? I give you this as an example as to why the dates are different, and I'm going to give you all of them. Then I'm going to tell you what happened. I'm going to be succinct and I'm not going to draw it out.

The First Look

About 200,000 years ago is when it literally began. The concept of the "divine seeding" of planet Earth happened at that point, and the fields metaphorically started to be plowed. There is an issue and we're going to call it the *way species work with Gaia*. This is something that happened simultaneously with the *grid creation* of Gaia. For now we give you something that no one has thought about. When we speak of the *grids of the planet*, you make an assumption that these grids always existed on the planet. For the planet is old and you might say, *"Well the grids have always been there."* But I'm here to tell you that only one was always there, and that's the magnetic grid. But it was spiritually void. That is to say, it only had that which was created from the Earth's core movement. Today, when we talk about the grids of the planet, our conversation involves the consciousness of humanity, which is imbued upon the magnetic grid. We also tell you about The Crystalline Grid and about the *Grid of Gaia Consciousness*. Both of these react to Human compassion.

Now, here is the puzzle: If you don't have divine Human consciousness, then what about the grids? Do they exist without the Human Being? The answer is that they needed to be created simultaneously with the seeding of divine DNA. So what the Pleiadians did was not only to start the seeds of humanity's change into divine DNA, but they created the *conscious grids of Gaia* as well. They had to, for the conscious grids of Gaia are a confluence of humanity's decisions brought to Gaia's energy. The consciousness that we are talking about is the spiritually sanctioned Human Being that exists with a piece of God inside him, and with DNA that has 23 pairs of chromosomes instead of the common 24 that all the others have through biological evolution.

Let us back up and say it again and make it simpler, my partner [admonition to Lee to speak more plainly]. The triad of grids on this planet that we have spoken of over and over are the consciousness grids of Gaia, and were created at the same time as the seeding of humanity with Pleiadian DNA. For all the teachings we've been giving, especially about The Crystalline Grid, these grids have been reacting to Human consciousness and compassion. Therefore, the very essence of the current Gaia energy is also related to the creation of humanity.

These are the attributes of the Pleiadians' work 200,000 years ago, and it was done quantumly in ways that you have no conscious awareness of at the moment. For these things are beyond your ability to understand right now, since you are still in a single-digit dimensionality. But the result back then was "a conscious Gaia." So you might say, Gaia itself was actually created quantumly from the Seven Sisters energy, just like you.

The Gaia that existed before then was still Gaia, but not as it is now. It was a Gaia that was creating the dirt on the Earth and the energy of biological life of the Earth. It was the mother of all life on the planet, but not a Gaia that responded to Human consciousness. That's very different. So Gaia greatly expanded when the Pleiadians came, and that was by design.

It took 110,000 years for this to settle itself, and for the ground to be ready for more than 16 species of Human Beings to leave so that only one was left. When that occurred at approximately 90,000 years ago is when you can start calibrating who Humans were and who they became.

The Others

Now, what about all of those other types of Humans, and how did they leave? I'm going to give you an attribute of something that exists even today. This is difficult for my partner, for he has not heard this before. This information has not been brought in this fashion before. Go slowly, my partner.

The variety of species on this planet comes and goes accordingly as they are needed for the energy they create. So one of the tasks of Gaia is to create and eliminate species. When they are no longer needed for the purpose of Gaia's development, they cease to exist and they die out. If new life is necessary, if new concepts of life are needed, Gaia is cooperative and they are then created. The actual creation of species is something that environmentalists have not clearly seen. That is to say, the mechanics of how it works is not fully recognized as something that is strongly coordinated with your weather. But you have already seen the mechanics of some of this in your long-term studies, for you have already noted the coming and going of many species through the ages. It's ongoing.

The Appropriateness of the Elimination of Species

Now, along come Humans and they see all this coming and going of living things, but they want to save them all – all the species that exist. For in their linear mind, all species should remain and exist, since they are here. The attribute of Gaia, however, is to eliminate them, cull them out, to bring in new ones. I just gave you the mechanics of the reasons species come and go. It's appropriate and is a natural building process for new species.

When the Pleiadians started to create the grids of the planet, Gaia *cooperated* in what was to come, knew the purpose, and what was needed for survival of this new spiritual Human. Gaia knew this since the energy of Gaia had seen it before [reason given below]. So the old attribute, which needed many kinds of Human Beings, slowly died out. It was natural. There was not a war. There were no horrible plagues. There were no volcanoes or tsunamis that consumed them. Through attrition, appropriateness, and 110,000 years, they disappeared.

So approximately 110,000 years ago, there was only one kind left, and this is science, for everything that you study will bear this out, and anthropologists have already seen it and have asked, *"What happened back then at this time that would have eliminated these other kinds of Human variety?"* It's a puzzle in science that I have just answered, for science looks only for physical events as triggers. But instead, it's the marriage of Gaia consciousness that you call "Mother Nature" which facilitated this. It's the same today when you see a variety of species diminish as Humans take over a greater portion of the Earth. I'll call this "the appropriate elimination of unique life forms, which allow for the growth of global awareness and quantum evolution." Some species only exist to allow others to climb the ladder of nature, then they disappear. Gaia knows what the ladder looks like. You don't.

The Spiritual Link

So historically, this "creation of one kind of Human" also started the esoteric engine of the pattern of spiritual life on the planet, where you could then start to measure the soul energy, a quantum energy of spirituality that is allied to Gaia. It's the very work that you're

7

attempting today as you try to track the history of spirituality and what the intuition was of the Creator of that system. Human consciousness is quantum energy, and it is the *sum of all souls*.

Now we're at 90,000 years ago. We are looking at the Human Being who has 23 pairs of chromosomes ... the ones of the Seven Sisters. It then took another 50,000 years for this Human to develop into a quantum, sentient Human Being who could put together a civilization without any previous organizational model. It takes generations of trial and error for this, even though it seems normal to you today. All cooks know that it takes a very long time to cook a quality meal. Without a recipe or any training, how long would it take a Human who had never seen a kitchen or food ingredients to create a truly gourmet seven-course meal through trial and error only. It's similar, and things did not move as quickly as they do today. This was the very beginning of humanity trying to figure out how to make things work for groups of Humans together.

Wisdom is learned this way, and time is the stove of the wisdom meal. The attributes of consciousness that the Pleiadians put in place through a 23-chromosome Human Being created growth, and every single generation got wiser with time. Eventually, far beyond Lemuria, Human DNA would develop an efficiency that would allow for what you see today – the divinity inside a Human Being that is recognized and sensed almost at birth and a population of almost seven billion people, where more than eighty percent believe in the same God and even in the afterlife [today's civilization].

Lemuria's History

Now we're at 50,000 years ago. It took another 20,000 years to build the Temples of Rejuvenation and have the Old Souls begin to appear, the kind that you were part of.

Now we're at 30,000 years ago. This truly is the time frame of the Lemuria we speak of now when we say, "The civilization of Lemuria." For that's a mature Lemuria, and one that had developed spiritually far more than any civilization on the planet at that time. The island had created a pure group of spiritually seeded Humans. We've told you the rest of the story. When the bubble of the Earth's crust began to subside [which had lifted up the land], the mountain of Lemuria slowly started to sink. Lemurians scattered and took to boats, not knowing if there would be any land left.

While Lemuria was in its prime, there were thousands of years where this mountain contained an unchanging Lemuria, and it was like a pressure cooker of information, lineage, training, and experience. It never changed, and that which was learned here was different from the other places of the planet. In other areas, Humans could go forth and do whatever they wanted. All they had to do was pick up and leave! But not here [Lemuria]. So, here, they were forced to find ways to deal with the common problems of living together.

So this became the place where the Akash of humanity chose to train Old Souls. Humans would come in only one time, then go back and incarnate to another place on the planet. Therefore, there were a lot of souls who came through Lemuria within the last 20,000 years, who lived at the base of these very mountains where you are currently floating. It also explains why there are so many Lemurians on the planet now – think of it as a Pleiadian school.

Kryon live channelling "The Timing of Creation"
given in Hawaii. 11th Kryon Cruise – August 12, 2012

In summary, the Lemurians represented the relationship between Gaia and humanity, and in a spiritual way, established the energy on the Crystalline Grid. With a few exceptions, each Lemurian had only one lifetime in Lemuria. Once a soul had experienced a life expression in Lemuria, it would reincarnate to another place, and then another and another. This created an Old Soul experience. Spanning a period of thousands of years, Lemurians had DNA that was directly affected by spending time with the Pleiadian Star Mothers, who carried the wisdom and knowledge. This teaching of spiritual truths was always pure as the Pleiadians remained physically for the entire duration of

Lemurian civilization. Lemuria was a onetime experience in order to build the Akashic Record of the planet.

Lemuria was, therefore, the first isolated civilization on the planet that received continuous teachings from the Pleiadians. It was not an advanced civilization in terms of technology; but instead, it represented a culture whose consciousness and intuition was much more advanced than today's society. But exactly where was this place called Lemuria? The answer to that question is controversial. Kryon isn't the only source for information about Lemuria. Many different theories about Lemuria have been given, including the idea that it is a lost continent! It isn't.

In Kryon Book 14, *The New Human*, Lee Carroll describes the attributes of Lemuria, and gives an account of the various ways Lemuria is remembered by others. This includes the description of a lost continent called "MU" that was supposed to have existed in the middle of the Pacific Ocean. Kryon has channeled that the "Land of MU" is, in fact, Le-MU-ria. The legend of a lost continent has remained for centuries, and the reason is because it is based on historical truth, but remembered through the Akash (past-life) experience.

Instead of a lost continent, Kryon's scenario is that Lemuria was located where the present day chain of Hawaiian Islands is found, in the middle of the Pacific Ocean. In the timeline given by Kryon, the Lemurians lived on one landmass, created from a "hot spot," much like the hot spot that created Yellowstone National Park. By definition, a hot spot is a place deep within the Earth where hot magma rises to just underneath the surface, creating a bulge and volcanic activity. The chain of Hawaiian Islands is right over a fixed hot spot.

According to geologists, the Hawaiian Islands were created as the Pacific Plate slowly moved over the hot spot. However, Kryon has channeled that many thousands of years ago the movement of the Pacific Plate created a "bubble" of hot molten energy under Hawaii. This bubble of molten magma became trapped under the crust and, instead of erupting as a volcano, it began to push up the entire volcanic mountain. Over a long time, this geological process slowly pushed up the land mass into one big mountain. This means that the eight major islands of modern-day Hawaii would be represented as mountain peaks on the mini-continent of Lemuria. Now, because of the size and height of this mini-continent, not everything was pushed up in a linear fashion. The heights of the mountains today were not the heights of the mountain peaks then in proportion to one another. They sagged in the middle because of the weight.

Kryon has said that science will eventually find the glacier marks on the tops of these islands and they will know that at one point in time they were far higher than they are now. They will find evidence of altitude that they cannot explain, except for one explanation and that is that they were pushed up, in a similar manner to what happened in Yellowstone National Park.

Slowly, the bulge began to collapse and the mountain of Lemuria began to retreat back to its original position, to sit flat on the bottom of the ocean. However, it did not collapse in a linear way. The mountain collapsed in certain ways where parts of the mountain covered other parts of the mountain, like a giant earthquake that was mountain-specific. The mini-continent of Lemuria did not get pushed up as one thing and pulled down as the same thing. Geology doesn't work that way, especially because of the weight and size of the landmass. In addition, part of the release was the magma coming out of one of the volcanoes. Maui was involved and parts of the peaks collapsed, for they were even larger than they are now. The sinking mini-continent also coincided with a rise in sea-level due to the melting of ice about 15,000 years ago.

All of these things were very frightening to the Lemurians and marked the signal for them to leave the island. By divine design, it was the end of Lemuria and the beginning of work on the planet. [The work is about the puzzle of duality – where would humanity take the high level of consciousness that it was given by the

Pleiadians, with free choice]. The many years of a sinking island created a Lemurian society that became a sea-faring nation. Eventually, many Lemurians began to populate, via ships, the edges of other landmasses, such as Aotearoa (New Zealand), Rapa Nui (Easter Island), and the west coast of the Americas. Kryon also stated that some of the Lemurians started other societies (in their next incarnation) in combination with other Humans who had completely forgotten their spiritual lineage. One of these cultures was called Sumeria, in the Middle East, which eventually led to the Egyptian culture.

It can be difficult to picture Kryon's explanation of humanity's spiritual lineage and the development of the Lemurian civilization. It can also be confusing when we add known Human history onto this timeline. Therefore, a summary of this timeline is provided to help you visualize and develop clarification regarding these events.

TIMELINE OF HUMANITY

200,000 YEARS AGO   Pleiadians first came to Earth and created the *conscious grids of Gaia*. The Pleiadians also gave two new, multidimensional DNA layers to humanity and changed the number of Human chromosomes from 24 to 23. This is the beginning of a "spiritual core" to the Human Being.

90,000 YEARS AGO   All variances of Human development stopped, and only one emerged ... counterintuitive to the way evolution creates variety. Today, only one kind of Human lives on Earth, the kind who reincarnates with a spiritual soul.

50,000 YEARS AGO   Lemurian society begins to show in a primitive form.

40,000 YEARS AGO   Evidence that Aboriginal people have been living in Australia for at least 40,000 years. There is also speculation that they may have colonized Australia 65,000 years ago! They are the oldest living culture in the world.

30,000 YEARS AGO   Lemuria is in full development, representing the first Human civilization with "quantum awareness." The Lemurians also set the Akashic Record for humanity and were the only civilization to have sustained esoteric teachings by Pleiadian Star Mothers.

15,000 YEARS AGO   The bubble of magma subsides and the mini-continent begins to sink, creating the current chain of Hawaiian islands. This heralds the exodus of Lemurians from their land. Some of the places where the Lemurians recolonized include Rapa Nui (Easter Island), Aotearoa (New Zealand), and the west coast of North and South America.

12,000 YEARS AGO   Göbekli Tepe, a giant temple complex located in modern-day Turkey, is founded. This is considered to be the oldest structure in the world and is rewriting history. Its construction took place during a period of time known as the Stone Age when such buildings were not considered possible. Some scientists and researchers seem to think this site was created with spiritual, ceremonial, and astronomical significance.

5,000 YEARS AGO   Pyramids of Egypt built, and yet controversy surrounds the construction date of the Sphinx. The Sphinx Water Erosion Theory claims that the main type of weathering evident on the Sphinx enclosure walls was caused by prolonged extensive rainfall that would have pre-dated the time of the Pharaohs that built the pyramids. If construction took place during a time that experienced heavy rainfall within the area, it indicates that the Sphinx was constructed approximately 12,500 years ago.

2,000 YEARS AGO   The impact of the prophet *Christ* actually changed the calendar and marked the beginning of the B.C./A.D. dating system in which

13

B.C. stands for "before Christ" and A.D. stands for the Latin phrase *"anno domini,"* which means "in the year of our Lord." Kryon has said that prior to the arrival of Christ, we had The Dispensation of Law. The impact of the Christ reset the calendar and we moved into The Dispensation of Love. The great shift of 2012 on the planet signifies that we have moved into The Dispensation of Compassion.

THE YEAR 2012 Humanity has passed the marker, as predicted by many prophecies from the Ancients, and the Earth has moved into graduate ascension status. Kryon has said that someday this will be seen as a delineation mark from moving out of the Barbaric years, and may potentially reset our calendar again.

Now that we have identified where Lemuria was and how it was created, where is the evidence that it existed? Unfortunately, unlike the civilization of Ancient Egypt, all evidence of Lemuria has been erased – or has it? Kryon explains that:

The ocean currents under the seas are very strong; almost like rivers they surge, washing with sand and silt for eons. So there are those who say, "That means we'll never find the artifacts of Lemuria." Not only will you find some, you have already, and many are hiding them. Because when these collectors show them to science, they'll be laughed at. For there will be an oxymoron ... a contradiction within the actual artifact. It will be too old to be what it is! At least according to modern thinking, that is. What would happen if you found an automobile part that carbon-dated to 3,000 years ago? It would be an artifact that "couldn't exist." That's what the artifacts of Lemuria will be like. For they will be charts of the stars and biological information that "couldn't have been known."

And why would anyone be able to have an artifact of Lemuria? I just told you that Lemuria is washed away. It's because of the ships!

Many of them went down in storms carrying everyday Lemurian objects – artifacts. Some are waiting to be found, and some have already been found and sequestered by collectors who cannot get anyone to look at them because they don't make sense.

Kryon live channelling "The History of Humanity" given in the western Mediterranean Sea. 8th Annual Kryon Cruise – August/September 2007

What are the Lemurian objects referred to by Kryon? Have any been discovered? If discovered, how would we know the artifact is a Lemurian object? The answers to these questions are largely unknown. As of the writing of this book, Kryon has only once made reference to a Lemurian object, called a solar disc. It was in response to a question asked during a Lemurian Sisterhood meeting:

Questions have been asked this night by some of the Goddesses who are here. There is so much honor from us toward what you've been through. We speak of very, very ancient times, elementary times, and the beginning times of learning.

Here is one of the questions that were asked, which I will answer directly. Question: *When Lemuria was about to be destroyed, what of the solar disc that went to Peru?*

Answer: First, be aware that there was no *Lemurian destruction*. The whole idea about the "destruction of Lemuria" is an incorrect bias from a combination of Greek mythology and the Biblical story of Sodom and Gomorrah. The truth is that the mountain [mini-continent of Lemuria] sank in a normal geological situation as many hot spots around the planet have also experienced: It sank very slowly as the bubble of magma that had pushed it up started to diminish beneath it. The end result was that it sank to the degree where it eventually became the chain of Hawaiian Islands as you know it today.

The actual sinking took many years, as we've described before, and during those times, many typical Human things took place.

15

Number one: Mass Fear. How did Lemurians know it wouldn't simply entirely disappear into the ocean? They didn't, so if you were one of those back then, you had to leave.

Only some of you were there at this sinking time and, as I have pointed out already, you only went through one incarnation and then moved on [in subsequent incarnations] to someplace else on the planet. It's almost like Lemuria was a *core teaching area* where the learning would then be carried with you, within your Akash, to wherever else you might then reincarnate for thousands of years on the planet. Think of Lemuria as *seed-knowledge-teaching*. You didn't incarnate there again. So, those here listening [during the live channel] might have been Lemurians living at different times across the thousands of years that Lemuria existed. But – you are all Sisters of Lemuria.

Most of you didn't know each other in Lemuria, but as you sit here now, there is still something that bonds you even today, and it's the fact that you all had the same identical Akashic teaching.

Was there a solar disc? Kind of. Mythology changes apparent *remembered truth* over time, but there are seeds of truths regarding certain things that stay pure and are kept in the Akash and repeated. Some seem to be legends, perhaps, that you would then sense and talk about. When the little continent, which was MU or Le-MU-ria, started to sink and become many islands, it was slowly evacuated. Men and women took to the sea. It's easy to perceive this as a "destruction" due to the fear, but, again, it was simple geology.

The men were the ones who paddled, but even within the journey away from the sinking continent, the women had to guide the men. Why? Here's something we've mentioned before – a puzzle to some: When you took to the canoes, with the men paddling and trying their best to navigate, it didn't take long before the currents and winds took you into the Southern Hemisphere, where the stars were different. The men have always been the navigators at sea. It was men's business and their specialty when finding fishing grounds. However, how did they navigate from stars they had never seen before, with constellations that were a complete mystery to them?

The answer to this is that the women guided the boats. The women had not seen the new star configurations, either, but they had teachers from the stars all their lives, and they knew where to go, enough to advise the men who were sailing into the unknown. [This teaching was given to both genders as children, but the women studied it more as adults.]

Imagine the men willingly turning to you, yet again, for advice on when to steer toward this star or another. Combined with good sea-faring intuition from the men, and intuition from the women, many Lemurians ended up in South America, since that's where the currents and winds tended to go. This is where many of you landed. Naturally, some of you took things with you from Lemuria that were precious to you. There was not one solar disc, but many. The reason was that it was a disc that contained some of your most precious instructions from your Lemurian teachers. These were given to you and many of the teachings were etched into the disc.

It was before printing, dear ones, and it was before you could scratch onto the disc any written language as you know it today. So, what are on the discs are symbols that all the women knew, and many of the men, too (the amount that was told to them). The reason they were called "Solar Discs" was that in the middle of each one was a symbol called "The Great Sun." The other name for these discs was "The Teaching Wheel." Of all the things that could have been taken with you from your sinking mountain, this was the most common.

These were primitive times, and beautiful teachings were given to you by your Pleiadian Star Mothers. That's the solar disc. Are they existent today? Could you find them? The answer: Yes. Some are still around, and some will be found.

Kryon live channelling given during a Lemurian Sisterhood Meeting
in Tucson, Arizona – February 25, 2016

Are there any out-of-place artifacts that have been found? Possibly, many have been found, but as Kryon stated, not everything found is reported, especially if the artifact doesn't make sense to our current understanding of past history. However, here is one example of bewildering discovery. Over a hundred years ago, the unearthing of an artifact puzzled scientists from the time it was originally found. The mystery of the artifact, known as the Antikythera Mechanism, was recently solved. While it is not a Lemurian artifact, its discovery and revelations demonstrate that our understanding of ancient cultures, and the wisdom and knowledge they held, can be rewritten.

They mystery of this artifact began in the year 1900, when sponge divers came across pieces of a clock-like machine while exploring the remains of an ancient shipwreck off the tiny island of Antikythera. For decades, scientists tried to figure out how 80 fragmented pieces fit together, and what device they created. Finally, in 2006, scientists discovered that the fragments were part of the incredible workings of a 2,000-year-old astronomical calculator built by ancient Greeks. New analysis of the Antikythera Mechanism shows it to be more advanced than previously thought, and one that had nothing comparable built for another thousand years.

The research team was also able to pin down the device's construction date to 150 to 100 B.C. Further analysis revealed that the device's front dials had pointers for the sun and moon, and markings which coincided with the zodiac and solar calendars. The back dials, meanwhile, appear to have been used for predicting solar and lunar eclipses. The thorough investigation of this artifact has reframed our understanding of ancient technology and provides an example of things to come that will rewrite our history.

Source: http://www.livescience.com/1166-scientists-unravel-mystery-ancient-greek-machine.html

Questions for Kryon:

Can you provide further clarity about the "seeding" done by the Pleiadians? The creation stories from many indigenous tribes describe the Seven Sisters, but fail to mention any males.

Answer:

Dear ones, as we have described to you before, the female Pleiadians carried the show completely, and the males from Earth impregnated them. This is one of the reasons you almost never hear about male Pleiadians. This is the "seed" we speak of when we talk about your altered DNA. This altered DNA would pass on normally from any Human who then mated with any other Human who had that seed, both male and female. So both males and females who were born from a Pleiadian mother would have that alteration and would pass it on.

So, there simply were no male Pleiadians who came to Earth. Although this may sound harsh for them, it was part of the plan which they understood and was a supremely spiritual path for them. They were "starting a new sacred planet" and they knew it. What the males did was to create the systems which allowed for the actual "coming to Earth." They were the scientists, and the women were the "spiritual vessels." This is the name they used instead of Shaman. For the women carried the seeds of evolution in their eggs. Reproduction was not much different for them than for you. I have also told you that they were Humans, too, but might not actually have been classified that way in your Earth science biology due to subtle differences which unique planetary galactic evolution creates.

The Star Mothers who came to Earth did not have mates on their planets and were all volunteers. More than volunteers, they were selected out of thousands who wanted to come here. How does that make you feel?

Was there love or attachment with the Human males who were their mates on Earth? What do you think? Have you studied the principles of the Kundalini? Have you actually looked into the system whereby the mating process is more than mechanical? It was a sacred act, and beautiful, and yes – there was love. Each Star Mother had a very selective mate for the Human's lifetime. Then they selected another after that, since Humans don't live particularly long. So the process was filled with love and integrity and beauty. Birth was exceptionally special! We have discussed some of that before. But can you imagine "who" those babies were? They were the Human seeds who would then go on and pass the altered DNA to whomever they selected to be with in the future. Eventually, over time, there were no Humans left without the alteration, and the Star Mothers stopped having children and concentrated only on teaching.

Those who are trying to do the math and figure this out will ask, *"But wait, Humans who didn't have that alteration were still having babies, too. So didn't they also increase in population?"* The answer is actually quite straightforward and understandable: They were "bred out" eventually, just like in your evolution principles for lower animals on your planet. If an animal species has a remarkable shift, where some are born who are stronger or better able to survive, what happens is that the former "weaker" ones slowly diminish in numbers until they are gone. Females won't mate with those, either. It's instinct and survival.

In the case of Humans, their new intellect and consciousness actually gave them a "discernment" that kept an altered Human from joining with one with 24 pairs of chromosomes. This also tells you that Humans who had altered DNA were vastly different in many ways from those who did not.

Let's speak more about the DNA: As I mentioned before, this new DNA couldn't be "bred away" over time, since it was so powerful that it superseded anything else in your heritage or genealogy. Here's what I mean: You are used to dominant and recessive genes in the body. In the most simplistic way, eye color is an example. There are genes which will supersede others in procreation and heritage, and this is similar to the altered DNA.

Once a child of a Star Mother was born, she or he would have the apparent 23-chromosome-pair change. This was not a technical, highly scientific alteration at all. It happened naturally in the womb for the exact reason I said. The Star Mother's evolved DNA supplanted the DNA carried in the sperm of the male, and created a child who had the attributes of the mother's DNA. So in this system, the egg was the carrier of the profundity of the change.

As you study Human DNA today, you start to see the extremely interesting internal fusions and changes that are remarkably different in a Human Being with 23 pairs of chromosomes compared with the living primate species other than you with 24 pairs of chromosomes. Your science is starting to catch up enough to see the internal parts of DNA, and is starting to ask some very profound questions about how and why you are different from anything else on the planet.

This was all accomplished by Pleiadian biology, naturally. The Star Mothers' evolved DNA was programmed to create children who would have the same evolved DNA.

Are we getting closer to discovering Lemurian artifacts?

Answer:

Dear ones, regarding artifacts, the answer is yes. In fact, when they are discovered, there will be only one answer possible: *You were visited by others from the Stars.*

The problem with Lemurian artifacts is the obvious geological issues. The mountain [of Lemuria, present-day Hawaii] sank slowly, and there was destruction and the submergence by water and burying with silt over thousands of years. Then there was the incredible pressure of the deep ocean (formerly the beaches) which takes its toll. In addition, ocean creatures and chemistry do an excellent job of eventually digesting and taking apart almost anything in the ocean that is foreign. Now add to that, there was markedly uneven geological settling of the land during the slow sinking. This means the mountain sank slowly but with dramatic consequences to its shape, creating many large earthquakes. Then, on the main volcanic peak, new lava was released due to the many new fissures that opened. It was an alarming, frightening time, and the bulk of the population left soon after the hot spot below started to subside (the cause of the mountain sinking).

Everything below the current water line is gone. But you still have the peaks remaining, especially one of them. The one with the Temple of Rejuvenation was on the active volcanic peak. This is now the Big Island of Hawaii. We have given you information that would lead you to this conclusion if you figured it out: The Temple needed both extreme heat and the availability of extreme cold to work. We have given you the "whys" of this before. That would occur only on the active volcanic peak, where there was constant molten lava source at a frigid altitude of over 30,000 feet above sea level.

Let's look at timelines for a moment. What you have today regarding volcanic activity in Hawaii was also the way it was then. Plate tectonics describes the process of the "plates" of land moving slowly, over millions of years, by the convection of the planet's hot, more fluid inner layer. Lemuria was actually recent in that historical sense. So what you see happening today in Hawaii is hugely similar to what they experienced as well regarding where the lava is. Also, this Hawaiian mountain was pushed up long before Humans ever arrived. So, no Human experienced it "coming up" by the rising hot spot. But when it started to subside, humanity was there.

Lemurian Society

What was life like in Ancient Lemuria? How did society work? Who was in charge? What was the structure of society like? Before exploring the answers to these questions, let's examine the Aboriginal and Torres Strait Islander people. The Aboriginals have proven archaeological evidence of occupation in Australia for at least 40,000 years, and DNA evidence of 50,000 years.

Therefore, the Aboriginal and Torres Strait Islander people of Australia became established in a similar time frame to Lemuria.

In parts of Australia, their culture has remained unchanged and intact for over 40,000 years. Understanding their unique way of life may assist us in understanding what life might have been like in Lemuria. In Aboriginal society, everything is governed by laws and codes of behavior that are understood as being part of the Dreaming. The Dreaming is their *sacred world*. The Aboriginal *Dreamtime* is their understanding of the world, its creation, and its great stories. The *Dreamtime* is the beginning of knowledge, from which came the laws of existence. The *Dreaming* world is the old time of the Ancestor Beings.

The laws of the Dreaming tell people which animals they can hunt and when; which plants they can eat or use for medicine; which places they can go to; who they can marry; how to care for the land; and how the different groups are to treat each other. By following the Dreaming, Aboriginal people live in harmony with each other and the land, as evidenced by the thousands of years of continuous occupation. The Dreaming is deeply spiritual but it also takes care of the practical details of people's lives and is the basis for their art and culture.

Children were taught about the Dreaming all through their childhood. As they matured into young adults, their formal in-depth education of the Dreaming began. Once initiated, they would be given secret knowledge that they could only speak about with other initiated people. Knowledge about the Dreaming would continue throughout one's life, which meant the Elders were seen as particularly wise and knowledgeable. The Elders would help settle disputes or discuss how to deal with someone who had broken the law.

Gradually, the details of the laws changed across the hundreds of Aboriginal nations that existed in Australia before European settlement, but many similarities remained between all groups. Sometimes, their laws were linked through stories and ceremonies and would be reinforced at communal gatherings. In essence, the Dreaming is their creation story, the interconnectedness of all life, how to live the right way, and the teachings of unconditional love of spirit and the ancestors.

The spiritual story of Uluru (Ayers Rock) is based on the Tjukurpa of the Anangu people. Tjukurpa is frequently described as the "dreaming" or "dreamtime" but this translation is inaccurate. Tjukurpa refers to the creation period when the ancestral beings, Tjukaritja, created the world as we know it now. It is the foundation of Anangu life and society and has many complex meanings. It is also the law for relationships between people, plants, animals, and the land. It is the past, the present and the future. It is about love, spirit or soul, and the belief about creation, and the right way to live.

In 2015, there was a Kryon event held at Uluru, Australia. During the channelled messages from Kryon, startling revelations were made about the local Anangu Aboriginals. Sharing these messages with you requires a brief review on the Nodes and Nulls of Earth.

The Pleiadians created the Nodes and Nulls of Earth approximately 200,000 years ago, at the same time that they created the conscious grids of Gaia. They put themselves into a quantum state, all over the planet in various areas, and specifically they created 12 pairs of energy points. These 12 energy points are found at 24 geographical locations – a total of 24 Nodes and Nulls, where they work as a polarized pair. Each polarized pair is a time capsule that has energy set in place. Should humanity ever reach a certain consciousness, these time capsules would release information for the individual Human Being, as well as for the whole planet.

Since 2012, the Nodes and Nulls of the planet have been identified, opened, and activated. Slowly, multidimensional information is being broadcasted to the Earth's grids, allowing for higher consciousness, invention, and Human DNA evolution. The Nodes and Nulls are "hooked" into the benevolent design of the Universe. As of the writing of this book, Kryon has identified nine of the twelve matched pairs, shown in the table below:

NODES		NULLS	
1a	Maui, Hawaii	1b	Tibesti Mountains, Chad, Africa
2a	Lake Titicaca, Bolivia/Peru	2b	Mt. Kailash, Tibet
3a	Yucatan Peninsula, Mexico	3b	Mt. Kilimanjaro, Tanzania, Africa
4a	Mt. Shasta, California, USA	4b	Mt. Ararat, Turkey
5a	Uluru, Australia	5b	Mount Logan, Yukon Territories, Canada
6a	Mt. Ida and Hot Springs, Arkansas, USA	6b	Mt. Fitz Roy, Patagonia, Argentina
7a	Aoraki, (Mount Cook), New Zealand	7b	Ural Mountains, Russia
8a	Mont Blanc, French Alps, France, Italy and Switzerland	8b	Mt. Aconcagua, Argentina
9a	Glastonbury, England	9b	Gunnbjørn Fjeld, Greenland
UNMATCHED NODES		**UNMATCHED NULLS**	
10a	Rila Mountain, Bulgaria	??	Meili Snow Mountain, China
11a	Machu Picchu, Peru	??	Aneto, Pyrenees, Spain
12a	Table Mountain, South Africa	??	Victory Peak, Tian Shan Mountains, Kyrgyzstan

For further information on the Nodes and Nulls, please visit:
www.kryon.com/nodes

As evident in the previous table, Uluru is one of the 12 major nodes of the planet. So is Maui, Hawaii – the modern-day location for Ancient Lemuria. The following information from Kryon should help you connect the dots between Lemuria and the Anangu people, who still remain as the traditional owners and guardians of Uluru.

The idea that humanity might have been seeded or biologically changed by another race from somewhere else in your galaxy is often thought to be an idea from fools. It isn't. It's a beautiful and accurate creation story, shared by many of your ancient cultures, who didn't even know each other. This evidence is so consistent and abundant that it simply cannot be a coincidence. Again, I invite a study to be done by your anthropologists and researchers: Ask around to the indigenous cultures of this planet, especially around those places we call the *Nodes – ask this:* What is your creation story? [Your "Adam and Eve" story.]

They won't have an identical story, after all these years, but they will say "We came from the stars." Many of them will point to M45, the little cluster in the sky – not the brightest one – or the most obvious one, but the one that's *home.*

They celebrate that very thing here in the Red Center of Australia (Uluru) within their songlines. They know who the ones whose "names you cannot pronounce" are, and it is the same in Lemuria (Hawaii). It is the same in Shasta (Mt. Shasta). It is the same over and over in so many places all over the planet!

How could these cultures have the same kinds of stories? They even named the shapes in the sky after the mythological characters involved in the creation story itself, but these cultures never met each other!

Thousands of miles and continents apart, the same stories emerge about a smallish constellation that isn't all that obvious as you look into the sky. The only answer that you can come up with is that, perhaps, it was common sense, self-evident. Perhaps, it was something etched into the Akash of the Ancients? But, in most cases, there was a commonality of information about the Pleiadians – the Seven Sisters. It is the creation story of the planet, dear ones, and it's beautiful.

Dear ones, we are on sacred land (Uluru). It's not just sacred energy for today. It is ancient sacred energy, and remains sacred to those who live here. Much of this is because of the undisturbed energy of this particular area on this continent for so many years. Those who steward this land, called the Anangu, have kept some great secrets. However, since 1987, some of the most profound secrets of the indigenous on the planet are starting to be revealed. Some of these are being released by the Elders themselves, and some are not.

This is not an accident, for the time is right for some of these things to be known. The Anangu are not going to reveal the secrets yet, for it is not for them to do. I will not be revealing them, either, except for the ones that are appropriate with permission, and germane to this conversation. These secrets represent the beauty and the benevolence of what I teach to you. The Anangu know what I'm about to tell you.

There were twelve *Nodes* (information release centers), all seeded at the same time on this planet. Those who lived around them felt their energy and knew they were sacred. Over thousands of years, what you would expect would happen to the pure bloodlines of the stewards of these areas? Indeed, they were diluted. There was variety. There were situations that would cause the bloodline to be less pure. That's a natural occurrence – but not here.

The very blood that they carry within them, which makes them who they are today, is only one step removed from the Pleiadian – one step! No other lineage on the planet has that. Through their consciousness, if they choose to develop it, they can perform things that you cannot do, because of this. They are one step removed from their Pleiadian parents.

There are things I wish I could tell you, but I can only hint at them for reasons of honor. I stand on their land. The ones who

steward this land are seers. They can see the energy which represents the Pleiadians, but you cannot. They are watchers of the rock.
Did you ever wonder what they are watching for? Why would they
watch it for 44,000 years? Is it simply tradition? I will tell you – it's
not.

Interesting, is it not, that so many of these Nodes have anomalies.
If you find a Node that is easy to get to and there are a lot of people
who visit, there is an attribute you might be aware of: People see
things – odd things. Sometimes, there are lights in the night when
there shouldn't be. Sometimes, there are energies that are unexplain-
able. The Anangu have seen the lights. There are places in the rock
that glow and the watchers know that these represent the ones who
have never left, and the communication is still there.

The secret? They're not lights! Instead, they're the parents of the
entire race – the Pleiadians. This rock speaks to the Anangu in their
songs of creation and their dreams. They sing their songlines that no
one on the planet has but them. Indeed, they must keep it to themselves for now, for, to share it would be to dilute the truth, and they
know it.

I do not give away anything that is too precious. I tell you
instead, why the respect should be here, and I also tell you what they
know. The Earth is changing. They have prophecies they will not yet
reveal that would describe the second precession of the equinoxes as
the time of ascension. When they look at what has happened within
their own Mob (tribe), it may not occur to them that this is the
prophecy of the day.

There will come a time when the songlines of the Anangu will
only be represented within the beauty of the sound of the wind as it
sings between the rocks. It will be a time when *all that was secret*, will
be represented in the life force that is the rock itself. The time will
come when the rock which you call Uluru will be more sacred than it
is today, and regular humanity will visit in honor, and they will not
touch it, nor climb it, because they will recognize within it something
precious and beautiful and pure.

The Anangu will never leave this planet. They will become the watchers of their areas, forever. They're always here in some way within the beauty and purity and the silence of this area. They know this. They sing about it. They are the oldest Human culture, and they know that, too. They carry profound secrets about their own lineage, biologically as well. If an Anangu were to mate with any other kind of non-Anangu Human, the gifts of seeing will not be passed on to the children. Therefore, they represent, genetically, something which is unusual, pure, and special on the planet.

Science can prove that they are different. Indeed, they are seers of the Earth, one generation removed from their Star Mothers. Part of the Earth is melded with their consciousness and they are not as apart from Gaia as you are.

I want you to think about these things the next time you see a pure Anangu. I want you to understand the respect that is here and the beauty that is here. This is their home, and has been from the beginning of the star teaching. The songs that you sing in this choir [The Pineal Tones Creation Choir] are a connection to the divine. They have them, too, dear ones, long before you got them. But you share something profound: The understanding, through the song-lines, of the beauty of the Creation. This is why you're here.

Kryon live channelling "The Creation Choir"
given in Uluru, Australia – March 21, 2015

The Anangu is one of the oldest living cultures in the world and existed during the same time frame as Lemuria. Kryon has given us a glance into the lineage of the Anangu and attributes that relate to their unique consciousness. It partly explains why they have been able to live in harmony with the land and each other longer than any other civilization on the planet. Sadly, they suffered terribly with the arrival of the European settlers approximately 200 years ago. Only now, through an evolved consciousness, are we realizing how badly the indigenous from around the world have been treated. In some cases, the abuse continues, and yet, finally, there is growing recognition of the deep wisdom and knowledge held within the indigenous people.

As we compare the attributes between Lemuria and Anangu, one of the similarities we find is the role of women. The Anangu refer to it as "Women's Business," and it is taken very seriously. For example, Uluru is a sacred site for women, while nearby Kata Tjuta is a sacred site for men. The Anangu women will never visit or even look at Kata Tjuta. "Women's Business" is sacred business and it is secret business.

If Uluru really is a place for women, what happens to those visiting this site as a male? After all, thousands of tourists of both genders visit Uluru every year. While there doesn't appear to be any negative or harmful effects to males visiting Uluru, a personal story from Monika Muranyi provides a snapshot of how the energy of the Feminine Divine in Uluru affects everything around it.

"My first visit to Uluru was in 2010 with Lee Carroll. It was always on my bucket list, but I wasn't prepared for the immense beauty and ethereal aura that emanated from the rock. I was also blown away by the exhibition of women's art in one of the galleries. Every single painting was of the Seven Sisters – their creation story! This was a huge wink from Spirit, and validated what Kryon has told us about our origins.

Five years later, I was back at Uluru, only this time I was joined by 400 Old Souls who had gathered to participate in one of the Kryon Gaia Global Consciousness Retreats. An excursion to the base of Uluru was offered, in addition to the retreat, with the intention of having a Kryon channel on site, subject to the approval from the elders in charge. Thankfully, Lee Carroll was granted permission from an Anangu Elder to channel Kryon. So far, so good!

Those who follow the Kryon work know that every channelled message given by Lee is recorded, uploaded onto the Kryon website and offered for free. Something you should know about Lee is that before channelling Kryon he was an award-wining sound engineer and owned his own studio. The guy knows audio equipment like no other and the quality of the Kryon audio files is a testament to his skill and dedication to offer the best consistent quality sound possible. It is a sheer joy to listen to these recordings. Perhaps it's not something that everyone notices, but when you hear it done badly, without processing, you'll appreciate the difference (smile).

Back to the story ... there we were, at the base of the rock, preparing for the channel. Both Lee, and Kryon team member Jorge Bianchi, set their audio devices to record the channel. Unbeknownst to them, I also set my iPhone to record the channel. This is something that I never do. Why would I? Especially when there were two guys with all their professional equipment set up and ready to go, and yet my intuition was telling me to do this, so I did. Thankfully, I listened to my intuition, as both Jorge and Lee's recordings failed at the same identical minute count. What are the chances of that? How can two independent devices fail at the exact same time? Spooky stuff! The only successful recording of the Kryon channel was done by – you guessed it – me, a female! Uluru had prevented the recording being done by a male. You might think this mere coincidence, but I know better."

Here is what Kryon said:

Greetings, dear ones, I am Kryon of Magnetic Service. It is appropriate that we give messages of the Creation here [at the base of the Uluru Rock]. But before we say anything, and before we give anything, we ask permission.

There are a few places on the planet, when my partner sits to channel, where there must be an agreement with the land and the ancestors of the land – in order to proceed. My partner speaks of the fact that energetic areas often will create technical problems. That often indicates to you that undefined energy is here. It also shows you that the desire of that which is here, which you call *the dirt of the Earth* or *the rock before you*, has its own energy, purpose, and rules.

With the permission of the ancestors, let me take you on a reminder trip as you sit here literally at the base of the Creative stone.

The *red center of Australia [Uluru]* is here almost within reach of your hand. That's how close you are to history.

When we took you to Lemuria and we channelled at the volcano, you got to see pure Creation, still pumping out the lava. You saw the specter of *Pele* and she was big! Interesting, isn't it, that the Creative Source of this place has a female power figure. It's a mythology that never changed.

When we took you to that which you call Mt. Shasta, the creative energies were there and the stories were there and the Creation was there. It was all about the Seven Sisters. These two places represent *Nodes* of the planet where those who were the Creative seeds actually took their core energy and stayed there. Those who live around the volcano will swear that it is alive, and those who live at Shasta will see the lights at night, high on the mountain. They know that there is something more there than just Humans.

We are here (Uluru), almost touching the very rock of Creation. All of you had to have permission from those who are the stewards of this place (Anangu), to be here. However, did you notice that they are all women? For forty thousand years, the traditions have not changed: Women from the stars brought the light to this planet, and right here they continue, from the same place they started. This is a female area, a Creation area, and a profound teaching area. Even Kryon is a guest here. It's different here.

What is here that is not normally at the other places you might visit is a *purity of sameness* and sacredness that you might say has been *cooked well* for thousands of years. It has not changed. It has not moved off the peg of the original Creation energy, and the stories that are told about this place are pure ones. They stay pure, because they are not written down. Instead, they're passed from Human to Human in the consciousness expressed as song, and from every single Human who is born here, who is pure here, who knows the songs and knows the stories, and keeps them pure.

Now, it is not up to me to give you the rest of the story. Instead, I want to hint at it, and I want you to feel it, and I want you to understand something precious: The femininity of the songlines is on purpose. The word *Sister* is on purpose. Those who are part of the land understand something. They understand that *women's business* is sacred Creation business. Here (at the base of the rock), they actually teach what I have channelled in other places of the Earth: All civilization passes through the womb of the woman, so it is not just mythology that has the idea that the Creation energy of humanity itself is feminine. It's soft, beautiful, and it is *mother*.

It is not an accident that the Creation and teaching stories here are all about the Seven Sisters. Now, whether there were, indeed, seven or more is not your business to know. However, the seven represents divinity and the sisters represent femininity and motherhood. That is the Creation metaphor, which started here at this very rock.

Those who can track back the real history in 3D know that this place has been here untouched, as long as any other place in the recorded history of the planet. It is also a *Node*. Right now, you can turn around and almost touch it! That is how intimate we are to the rock.

Now, let me tell you a little bit of what is really here. There is an energy at this rock that is so sacred, that it represents the original seed sisters. We told you in previous channels something that I want you to remember right now, and some of you will feel it, and some of you will not. However, those who seeded you all those years ago, never left. *They never left.*

It's not in your logic or the paradigm of your Human life span to understand how such a thing could be, but it's true. Those who remain, do so in such a state that they will always be – until the end of the planet or until the end of civilization. They live on the Nodes of the planet. However, parts of this story, that the children will learn later when they're adults, are where these special ones are, and what they have to say. This is the reason for a sacred and secret songline in this continent. The creation story and the songlines are filled with profundities that you won't know about ever, because only the pure know them – but I can tell you a little.

Dear ones, those who were the seeds of this planet, and are still here, are known as *"the ones whose names you cannot pronounce."* This may be a phrase you will hear. There are places on the rock which are so sacred that no Human will go there; no photographs are allowed, either. The reason is that *those whose names you cannot pronounce* are there. Indeed, there are times, guided by the stars, where these Ancients will come out, perhaps, in a bigger way – a three-dimensional way. But those times are not scheduled or told about. They are sensed by the *grandmothers (leaders)* within the family group of Anangu.

There are lights at night that should not be here, because of these Ancient Ones. I'm not talking about a distant place. I'm talking about what's right behind me as I speak. I'm talking about a Node that you don't have to climb to observe, for it's here in front of you. There's no effort needed to feel it – not really. When this channel is over, you may turn around if you wish, and some of you will feel the profundity of it all (the listener is not facing the rock during the channelling).

This energy is not just about your creation story or the songlines of the area, but the fact that they are your seeds of existence as well. The ones who are here, seemingly hiding in the rock, represent the seeds of all humanity. This is real. It is not a fable. What a place this is!

All through history, mythology creates things that are different than how they began. This is often done for secret reasons so that there is no inappropriate knowledge spread to those who shouldn't hear it. The ones who control the stories often use the totems and the animals, and they often make giants out of things in order to make them bigger than they are. The Greeks did it, the Anangu did it, and the indigenous of the planet do it even now. It's a way of keeping secrets, using metaphors that mean other things, in order to hide the truth. To you, the information is realized as simple mythological stories. However, to the Anangu, these are the stories of their *seed* parents. The Earth has parented those who are pure

34

and the ones who are responsible are still here. This is why it is such sacred land.

Kryon live channelling "At the Rock"
given in Uluru, Australia – March 26, 2015

Kryon talks about the songlines. In each instance, the term "songline" is referring to the Seven Sisters Songline – a songline that covers more than half the width of the Australian continent, from deep in the Central Desert out to the west coast. The Seven Sisters Songline travels through many different language groups and different sections of the story are narrated and recognized in different parts of the country. Songlines are, therefore, cultural webs for the Aboriginal people. The songs follow the footsteps of our Pleiadian ancestors, and are known as the Tjukurpa Dreaming. The songlines were sung into being since the beginning of Creation and continue to be sung today.

One of the main differences between Aboriginal culture and that of most modern-day societies is that there is no concept of individual ownership of anything! Traditionally, they shared tasks, such as caring for children, making tools, hunting, and building shelters. The children considered many adults to be their parents, not just their biological mother and father. They also have an extremely complex kinship system that is an integral part of their culture. It determines how people relate to each other, their roles, obligations and responsibilities, ceremonial business, and their relationship to ancestral beings, sites, and land.

While Aboriginal people built shelters, they did not always live in one place. They lived in harmony with the land and moved from place to place in response to the availability of food and water. They truly had a sustainable lifestyle, which is the reason why they are the oldest culture on the planet today! The Aboriginal culture demonstrates advanced thinking and gives us a small glimpse into what Lemurian society might have been like. While the structure of their society may have been similar, there is one reason why Lemuria was different from any society we have had, or have today.

Kryon tells us the beginning civilization of Lemuria began 50,000 years ago. However, it took several thousands of years for Lemurian society to develop. Therefore, the peak of Lemurian civilization basically existed from 35,000 years to 15,000 years ago. The whole reason for Lemuria was to set the stage for what was to come. This is why Lemuria was a one-time experience, and then the Soul would incarnate somewhere else. So the Lemurians never had a long Akashic Record of Lemurian life. Instead, they received a profound energetic imprint of original core teachings about the God inside. Perhaps that is why specific details and experiences can't be remembered, but Kryon says if you were Lemurian, it surges through your DNA. Many who are awakening on the planet, and may never read a Kryon book, are experiencing a *return to Lemuria*. What this means is they are becoming multidimensional, which leads to a balanced life that is filled with compassion and greater wisdom. Here is more from Kryon about Lemuria:

Slowly, the first civilization on the planet was born, and it was called Lemuria. Know this: It was not an advanced civilization in the way you think about "advanced." But they had something you should know about. Their quantum DNA was at 90 percent, not 30 percent as yours is today. All the quantumness of their DNA was activated, for that is what the Pleiadians passed on to them. Lemuria was the oldest civilization on the planet, the one that was the most long-lasting, which never saw war.

It was eventually broken up only because the oceans and seas rose. As I have described to you before, they became a sea-faring people and scattered to the many parts of the Earth. Ironically, some made it to far-away continents and science sees them as actually starting there, instead of traveling from somewhere else.

Lemurians were the original Human society on the planet, and they were located where the Pleiadians originally landed, on the top of the highest mountain on Earth, as measured from the bottom to its top ... currently the largest island of Hawaii, where the Lemurian "canoes" are buried. Hawaiian elders will tell you today that this is the lineage of Hawaii, that the Pleiadians came there, for it is what they teach as how humanity began.

Lemurians had a quantum understanding of life, and they knew in their DNA all about the solar system. A quantum DNA, working at 90 percent, creates a consciousness that is *one with the Universe*. One of the most ancient of your spiritual beliefs on the planet asks you to be one with everything. It's not an accident...

...Here is some historical advice: Do not place so much attention on Atlantis. Atlantis was much, much later, and there were actually three of them, and much confusion around what was there, and what happened there. Which one do you want to talk about? Atlantis did not play near the role that those in metaphysics and esoteric teachings wish to assign upon it. Oh, it was important, but one of them is not ancient at all! It was so recent, off the Greek Isles, and was even reported within the history that you see today from the Greeks. Humans have a dramatic interest in civilizations that get destroyed quickly. It creates further mythology, creating ideas that Atlantis was one of the most advanced civilizations. It wasn't. Lemuria was, but in consciousness only.

Lemuria was not an advanced technical society, for it had no technical abilities at all. Yet they knew how to heal with magnetics. It was in their DNA, you see? It was intuitive information. Quantum DNA produces quality intuitive information. Being one with the Universe, they knew all about DNA. Doesn't everyone? [Kryon smile] They even knew the shape of it ... all without a microscope. That's what quantum DNA does.

The Ancients knew!

Lemurians knew much due to the quantum DNA they carried, thanks to the Pleiadians. They knew all about the solar system, and about the galaxy in general. They looked at the stars and understood what was there. This created a seemingly advanced society, but without any technical advancement as you now have.

Kryon live channelling "The History of DNA and the Human Race"
given in Portland, Oregon – August 29, 2009

Questions for Kryon:

Australian Aboriginal art is the oldest ongoing tradition of creative works in the world. Rock carvings, rock art, body painting, and ground designs date back to more than 30,000 years. Did the Lemurians have art within their culture? If so, will it ever be discovered?

Answer:

The Lemurians had plenty of art, and some of it was remarkably telling about the Star Mothers, and the Lemurian way of life. None of it will be found for the reasons stated in the previous answer and below.

First, most of the drawings were created on things organic and have been gone for thousands of years. Second, the more substantial carvings within the rocks were mostly done where Lemurians lived, so today, they are at great depths, covered by thousands of years of shifting silt.

However, there were also "drawings in the lava" on the volcanic island top by the Temple, but these, too, were covered long ago by more recent lava and continued flank eruptions which have opened and closed many fissures that continually reshape Hawaii. So the answer is no.

There is the possibility, however, that some artifacts will be found or petroglyphs uncovered. These are not Lemurian, but ancient Hawaiian. Ancient Hawaiian is defined by "those who arrived after the mountain had sunk."

There is often a reference to royalty within Lemurian society (see Chapter Two: The Women of Lemuria). While the concept of royalty is centuries old, it is not common among indigenous tribes. Can you please explain royalty in Lemuria, and the reasons for it?

Answer:

Royalty may not be common in the majority of indigenous tribes of the planet, but ancient Hawaiians have always had it until recently. So you might ask, is this a holdover from Lemuria? Yes, it is.

This was influenced by the Star Mothers, and is a system that works quite well for an island. There are no outside influences (others coming to conquer). The leadership is respected and allowed to continue for life, and royalty goes hand-in-hand with good community planning and law-making if the royals are wise. It's also a good system for a beginning civilization since it's absolute and has rules for royal inheritance, which create respect (more in a moment).

You may object, saying that it's not a decidedly good system at all! Look at history: The system of royalty using biological heirs is flawed by intermarriage, foolishness, unbalance, power mongering, horrible leadership, and tyrants. Ah, but you are making some assumptions. Remember this: Lemuria was the beginning of the beginning. It was not elegant and not ready for anything like what has evolved within your current ideas and evolution of government. Royalty was a good answer due to the unusual rules.

The royal Lemurian "rule of heirs" may give you a clue as to why it worked: Only the direct descendants of a Star Mother could be eligible for royalty, and I mean "out of the womb of a Star Mother." So, instead of a "next of kin" Human heir inheriting the throne, there was a system of selection that gave it to a male or female (keep reading!) who was one of the children of a Star Mother. Those children were often seen as female priestesses or male leaders.

I'm not going to give you the entire system, but it kind of goes like this: When the reigning royal ruler gets to a certain advanced age or there is a death, she/he has a ceremony of "advancement." Whether in life or death, the Queen/King is "advanced" into another respected group and a new Queen/King is selected. The rules of selection are these: (1) The new leader must be past a certain age and birthed by a Star Mother; (2) The astrology of the former or existing retiring royal, combined with the attributes of the day, were computed against the candidate heir's astrological chart. The result of this analysis determines the gender and compatibility with the mountain (the mountain compatibility refers to how the candidate matches the vibration with Gaia). So the heir was not known in advance, and not passed down as you might think. It was always a surprise.

The royal ruler could be King or Queen but they always had the direct wisdom of the Star Mother, who, after all, is the mother of them all in some way. This created good leadership, not family dysfunction. All of the royal rulers in Lemuria were good and benevolent!

Today, in certain spiritual systems, there may be an "exalted leader" for life. Even before that leader dies, the next one is selected for that post, determined by their past life experiences, astrological attributes, and that of being an Old Soul ... perhaps even a Lemurian! Where do you think that came from?

The Schools of Lemuria

Lemurian society was less technical than our society today; however, Kryon has said they were incredibly advanced. How did this advanced society function? Lemurian society functioned in ways that would appear to us like "out of the box" thinking. For example, their approach to education was vastly different to what happens today. As Kryon explains:

Let me tell you a little more about Lemuria and some attributes of their society. You might say, *"Why would you do such a thing?"* The reason is so you can start to "connect the dots" as to what else is happening on the planet. I now speak of the Lemurians way back then, in a land that was beautiful before the ocean covered it. Let me tell you about their children.

Schooling was very, very different in major Lemuria. This was before Atlantis, and it went like this: The teachers were called *elders*.

40

They were greatly respected, for they dispensed the knowledge of the culture. They were all seniors, and represented some of the highest attributes in society. Yet, they didn't run the schools as your teachers do, or have anything to do with day-to-day business. There were no administrators or administration buildings in the schools, either, and the buildings were all small, isolated, and unconnected classrooms.

There was no linear system either! Instead, the elders would get together and decide what the children should learn and know by a certain time. The parents would send their children to the local classrooms at a certain age. In a typical classroom, the children and the elder [teacher] would all decide together what had to be learned. The children would then take over and collectively decide how fast they could learn it, and report this to the elder. The teacher would be flexible and go along with the children's plans. Then the children would often choose a leader among them, or a rotation schedule of student leaders, to help with the tasks of maintenance and administration of what their goal was.

So the elder was there to dispense the knowledge and make certain the children got the appropriate knowledge. But the children had high conceptual ideas and could often conceive of the entire project of the year's learning in one day. So even without the actual knowledge, they would lay out what they felt was the best way to learn it, the quickest method, and how to best "plug it in" to their schedule in class. When they felt they'd learned it, they would request to be tested. If the class passed, they would all earn the end of the term. Then the vacation would begin (the real goal of the children at that age).

So, instead of a common term of duration, they'd start at the same time, but there were no set ending points. So, the children would determine the term's duration by how fast they'd learn. This was conceptual, and reflected their ability to understand what had to be learned, without actually knowing the information. There was no school year or grades – only the goal of certain degree of knowledge, and the goal to get it done so they could play! The children were in charge, but they absolutely understood that they had to learn what was required

Now, many might exclaim, *"No, this is too unusual and odd. It couldn't work. Human nature wouldn't allow for it!"* My reply is this: Perhaps 4D Human nature would never allow for it, but a conceptual, multidimensional child could do it easily. The reason I'm telling you this is that this is the beginning attribute of the Indigo Child that we channelled many years ago. It's very Lemurian! Even some of the "labels" of the Indigo Children were listed as multidimensional.

Back to Lemuria: If there were slow learners in the class, the children would see the situation immediately and tutor them! What you now call homework was, instead, an assignment for each student to tutor another so that they could all keep up with the class. But the only things they took home were other students! The faster they learned, the quicker the vacation. It made sense to the kids. You might say, *"Well, what about those who were troublemakers? Were there any of those in this great land of Lemuria?"* Of course. Make no judgments as I reveal how this was handled.

The children would handle the discipline themselves – oh, not by the bully system, for that's not in the consciousness of a conceptually-minded child. Remember, in this type of consciousness, the overview is the goal of the group, not individual power. The children would handle it logically. If there was another student getting in the way of their vacation, they would tutor them in the best way they could. If some didn't respond, or were troublemakers, eventually the students would cast them out. Anyone who was cast out of school by a consensus of the class could never rejoin that class. Instead, they had to go to other classes that were not in major Lemuria. This (of course) created another complete society, one which was dishonored and often didn't live long, since they didn't earn the right to go to the Temple of Rejuvenation, which was a huge part of the health system of Lemuria.

Harsh, you might say? Indeed. Within the evolved standards of today, perhaps it was. But this is how the schools worked. Your society has progressed in ways that they did not, because you've worked on other parts of your enlightenment.

These explanations may help you understand why school is so difficult for the current Indigo, for the Crystal, and for all children of the new Earth energy. For, within them is a layer of DNA that's activated and ready to work. And it *remembers*. I'm going to tell you about that in just a moment.

Kryon live channelling "The Lemurian Connection"
given in Mt. Shasta, California – June 20, 2004

How do you feel about what you just read? Perhaps you have children or grandchildren in school. What are their experiences? It can be incredibly challenging to navigate parenthood today, but, at the same time, a bright future is coming. Slowly, education will change to meet the needs of our children. It is truly uplifting to discover that some schools are resorting to meditation instead of detention and the results demonstrate the positive benefits from adopting this approach. The following links are examples of this new concept occurring at a school in Baltimore, USA:

Source: http://www.newsweek.com/education-meditation-after-school-program-holistic-life-504747

http://www.cnn.com/2016/11/04/health/meditation-in-schools-baltimore/

http://www.parents.com/toddlers-preschoolers/everything-kids/what-we-can-learn-from-the-school-that-replaced-detention-with/

It is extremely encouraging to know that there are educational institutes taking new approaches that are designed to empower children. What about the children? Is there any evidence that their consciousness is shifting? Yes … and Kryon tells us to watch for changes in children. One heartwarming example comes from Boston, Massachusetts, where several boys took positive action to stand up for a boy who was being bullied.

Danny, a first grader, is a water boy for his school's football team. Sadly, Danny was being bullied because of his speech impediment and his love of wearing a shirt and tie. When the football team he supports found out about the bullying, they decided to send a message in a positive way. Instead of responding to the bullies or trying to intimidate them, they simply stood in unity with Danny. The boys on the football team all dressed up in suits and ties of their own! Their message was clear: They loved Danny for who he was. You may wish to see the story on YouTube on the following link:

https://www.youtube.com/watch?v=DNvOcK6Uslc

Another example also shows the reaction of a group of boys who noticed that a classmate with a learning disability was getting teased and bullied. They decided to take action, and that action was to band together and include him as part of their circle of friends. Such genuine compassionate action transformed the life of a once shy, reluctant boy to someone who couldn't wait to get to school. You may wish to see the story on YouTube on the following link:

https://www.youtube.com/watch?v=xdeuivQYnas

These videos represent the new paradigm of Human nature – one of unity, love and compassion instead of separation, fear, and hatred. Kryon has also said that a new paradigm of education is coming. This new paradigm has a strong correlation with how the schools of Lemuria operated!

Dear ones, there is going to come a time when the education for your children is going to be revamped from top to bottom. It will become totally and completely different from anything that exists on the planet right now. This concept creates comment: There will be those of you who say, *"Well, I expect that could happen, but the challenge of making it happen is almost insurmountable because an old*

Human nature will not let you change things." The opposition to this whole idea is enormous.

If you start changing the way children are taught, you'll have opposition from those parents who say, *"Look, we know how to teach our own children, so don't tell us something different."* You'll encounter the opposition of ego, of seeming common sense of the way it used to be, what people have tried and failed to do, and many of the things that we have told you, which don't apply any longer in your new energy.

Dear ones, there has to be a new system, and it will reveal itself so profoundly by the results it creates in the children, that there will be no question that the old system no longer is viable. It's not going to happen all at once, and it may not happen here first [referring to the United States].

Here we go [Kryon's way of saying that this is controversial]! There will be schools starting up that will be revolutionary in their methods, but doing everything that children of a new consciousness relate to and love. The results of these schools will be profound for the students, as measured by educators. Everything will be different from the very beginning of their learning to the end – pre-school to graduation.

Listen to these attributes: The children will decide for themselves how fast they can learn, what they are going to learn first, and how long it should take. This vastly new paradigm will feature agreements between the children and teachers, instead of a hierarchy of educators in other cities deciding what it should be.

It will be a system completely and totally designed, built, and run by those who actually have to learn in the chairs, instead of a set system for all. It involves a cooperation between the children and the teachers, because they'll have the current consciousness and wisdom to know what they can do and how fast they can do it at that time. They will have the ability to cast out things they already know, or already have the concepts of, and instead, concentrate on learning what they don't understand yet. Each group will be different, all over the country.

There will always be outcasts. These might be slower students or ones who may not belong with the group because of discipline reasons, or ones having older-energy Human nature. In the past, these students would often drag down the others. However, in the new paradigm, these students would immediately be recognized by the children as those who might not fit in with the consciousness, and might, indeed, slow them down. They will then be sorted out by the children, and not by a principal or a counselor. The outcasts will understand it was peers that decided, and not parents or the rules of the school. The result will be much, much different than today's remedial efforts, in that the outcast children may then have a desire to move with the others, instead of simply dropping out.

The teaching itself will be something that is a cooperative effort, instead of totally from the teacher. There will be an alliance of knowledge, a celebration of things learned, and a party given when the tests are passed. All of these things are completely and totally opposite from what happens now. Imagine school being a place where everyone cares about everyone else. The reason? It's fun, and it rises to the level and intelligence of the students who are in each class. What do you think?

I ask you to think about this. Is this a doable deal? Most of you will say, *"No. It's just too fraught with problems of Human nature."* That is correct! The old Human nature will never allow it. It's the new Human nature that will gradually put this in place.

What will cause the great "aha" is when these special school students start graduating, and they test way above anything you've ever seen in education. They'll pass tests that children can't pass today! They'll qualify for jobs that are not even testing to their level today. Governments and cities will look at that and say, *"We must have this!"* That's how it works. You know it does. The few will affect the many, and the forerunners will capture the imagination of the future.

This will be "taking advantage of what elegant Human nature is going to become." And this is where you get into trouble. People will tell you, *"This is impossible!"* You'll call a friend and say, *"You've got to hear Kryon's channel, because he's talking about a change in thinking, and I know that's what you're interested in."* Then they will listen to this channelling and say, *"This is actually funny. Good luck with that."*

Listen, dear ones, I'll talk to you in fifty years, and we'll see what you're doing, because you'll laugh and say, *"Well, I didn't believe it could happen, but now I see it."* Perhaps it might happen before that, dear ones? How fast do you want to move? That's up to you completely.

Old Souls, unite! Unite in wisdom and balance. Old Souls unite! Start balancing. Start getting out of fear and things will start to take on a whole different way of life! It's how you treat others and how you react to things that old Human nature told you how Humans are supposed to react – and you don't. Suddenly, you're shamanic in the way you act; you have wisdom with things that people say, and you can report; *"I have peace in my heart with who I am and what's going on, on the planet. I sleep better and I'm going to live longer."* This is the New Human. That's the message for tonight.

Kryon live channelling "New Paradigms"
given in Minneapolis, Minnesota – July 22, 2017

The future of education, as presented by Kryon, is truly inspiring. However, some individuals aren't waiting for the future. Instead, they are making education fun again and the results are spectacular. New Zealand-born Hamish Brewer describes himself as an "educational disruptor" who makes his decisions based on one fundamental question, "Was I better for kids today?" His infectious energy and unique leadership approach transformed a struggling school with low test scores into one of the best schools in the state of Virginia. His journey with two schools is shown in the following YouTube video:

https://www.youtube.com/watch?v=VKt9CslbVsg

Lemurian Health Care

Before we discuss Lemurian health care, let's take a look at some of the healing practices of the Australian Aboriginals – a culture that existed at the same time as the Lemurian society. Traditional Aboriginal healing is a body of knowledge and wisdom based on the resources of the land and the teachings from the ancestors (Pleiadians). The Anangu Elders who are regarded as healers are called Ngangkari, a Pitjantjatjara word that literally means "traditional healer." Ngangkari are born from a family lineage and the knowledge is passed down from one generation to the next. Becoming a Ngangkari can begin as a toddler if the family sees signs of them being a natural healer.

Traditional Aboriginal healing is entirely holistic, incorporating mind, body, and spirit. Spirit is the ultimate wisdom because, if the spirit is well, the body will be well. This is why they heal the spirit through the body. Connecting with Spirit requires deep intuitive awareness through dreams, visions, signs, and symbols. It also involves becoming intuitively aware of everything around a person's life because of the interconnectedness between all living things. If someone had a pain in the stomach, which is the center of digestion, the healer may ask, "What are you not digesting?" If a woman is suffering period pain, the healer may ask about their creative outlet needs because a woman's reproductive organs are the center of feminine creativity.

Despite the origins of the Ngangkari being over 40,000 years ago, the art of healing is still being practiced today. In 2012, a group of Ngangkari came together to form ANTAC, Anangu Ngangkari Tjutaku Aboriginal Corporation. Since their formation, the healers have begun outreach work that has taken them to several Australian towns and cities. You can connect with this nonprofit organization on Facebook:

https://m.facebook.com/antac.ngangkari/

In observing the ancient art of healing used by Traditional Aboriginals it is evident that consciousness plays a significant role in creating balance within the mind, body, and spirit. These principles are being rediscovered in modern science and medicine, such as Biological Decoding, Neuro-Linguistic Programming, and BioReprogramming.

What about the Lemurians? Kryon hasn't revealed detailed information about healers, but instead, we have been told about the Lemurians recognizing the importance of having everyone healthy. Here is what we know from Kryon:

I'd like to tell you about the Lemurian health-care system. You know, Lemurians didn't have tremendously high science. They didn't have the computers you do. Instead, they had highly developed, multidimensional intuition. Those of you who know what a medical intuitive is will understand this. All of them had this kind of intuitive knowledge. The body is smart. Lemurian bodies, depending on how far back you go, were far larger than yours. But as we said, they devolved ... became smaller and shorter. They were aware that this was happening. That also might give you information that Pleiadians are larger than you are. They still are.

Here is what the Lemurian society decided to do about health care. Most of the resources of Lemuria were spent making sure that all were as healthy as they could be. There were no health-care payments, since they were a conceptual culture. They had a far better evolved intuition about the entire picture, rather than an individual Human one. The Lemurian society intuitively realized that the healthier the population, the more it helped the economy. There was land ownership, but of a very different kind. It was group ownership. Therefore, it always involved group decision.

If you had one who was sick all the time, then they weren't able to share their load. This hurt the whole, so they found out very quickly that if everyone was healthy, they had a far better economy.

Now, again, I'll discuss the reason I take you to Lemurian history. It's because this very thing is about to happen once more on your planet. Suddenly, the realization that Human Beings who aren't sick can buy land and pay taxes will create a revolutionary idea ... if a government can heal its population, it can have an abundant society. What an idea! Watch for a shift of funds, resources, and focus regarding this. How can we cure the most for the least amount of money? How can we take from one financial focus and apply it to another? Did you ever wonder how you're going to cure the diseases of the planet? Many have complained: *"Humanity will never reach the point of enlightenment where they'll dedicate enough funds to heal the masses."* You're right! So another method, which makes far more sense to your current Human nature, will! Do not make any judgments about this, but be aware that you're about to face a new idea that's all about "economic healing." How else would the Earth provide something so needed at this time? The answer: Find a way to fit this into the agendas of those with the biggest amount of money to invest. Healing will become an investment in global health. How will the investors get their return? They'll take a portion of the GNP of the governments they work with, as measured by the "cure rate" of the country. Watch for this. It's inevitable, and under way at this moment.

Kryon live channelling "The Lemurian Connection"
given in Mt. Shasta, California – June 20, 2004

What a magnificent concept! Here we have a wonderful example from the Lemurians that demonstrates how a healthy economy is based on having everyone healthy. What would stop this kind of high-level thinking? The answer is low-level consciousness. Signs of a low-level of consciousness include fear, war, drama, and decisions made for profit and greed instead of compassion and integrity. Perhaps it may appear that our global situation will never change (don't watch the news!), but Kryon assures us that the balance of light and dark has shifted on the planet. A new paradigm is slowly beginning to emerge that demands integrity and compassion in all aspects of society. Kryon has even given a prediction...

Big Pharma [the drug companies of America] are going to have to change or they will collapse. When you have an industry that keeps people sick for money, it cannot survive in the new consciousness.

The big money that is involved in this closed circle is immense, and the lack of integrity is going to be revealed, slowly. The lives "lost for profit" will be counted, and there are going to be embarrassed faces, and even a suicide or two. To think of an industry that's supposed to cure people, keeping them sick on purpose will be a wound in the very fabric of what is correct for humanity.

So they will fall and you'll know their names and they're going to have to scramble to keep up with the rest of the world who may not have the proclivities from greed that made these fall. This may also change the perception of what countries have the best health inventions and solutions, and many in this country may turn to overseas answers for their health needs.

That's the prediction. When it starts to happen, dear ones, and perhaps the movie starts it [the one that's in the works that is a secret], I want you to remember where you heard it first. Perhaps this information, given in advance, will solidify that this is real – that the channelling you hear today comes from the source that we say it does, the one inside you.

> *Kryon live channelling "The Recalibration of Light and Dark"*
> *given in San Antonio, Texas – February 25, 2012*

The Lemurian health care system was filled with integrity, and showed the wisdom of a high-consciousness society. Watch for these changes to begin as Human nature and consciousness begins to shift. In fact, there is already one Canadian city that has adopted this new paradigm of health care and it's all due to thinking out of the box.

The Canadian town of Medicine Hat, Alberta, introduced a radical "Housing First" policy, which pledges to give any person who spends ten days on the street a home. The thinking behind the policy was attributed to the solution being the cheapest and most humane way to treat people. The reason is because of the results of a study that found many homeless people fell into cycles of drug use and poverty, leading them to emergency rooms, hospitals, detention centers and shelters – all things that cost tax money.

Since implementing the "Housing First" policy, hospital emergency room visits and interactions with police have dropped. So have the costs. Estimates indicate that it costs $20,000 to house a homeless person for the year compared with $100,000 when they are on the street. It's also encouraging to know that a similar policy has been introduced elsewhere with the same results.

Sources: http://aplus.com/a/canada-solves-homelessness-problems?
no_monetization=true
http://sus.org/canadian-city-ends-its-homelessness-problem/

Questions for Kryon:

A Traditional Aboriginal Healer comes from a lineage of healers. The wisdom and knowledge are passed down from generation to generation. What can you tell us about the healers in Lemuria? When a Lemurian was sick or injured, where did they go and how were they healed?

Answer:

Dear ones, the answer to this should be obvious. The women of Lemuria were the shamanic healers, and guides for the entire group. They had the lineage. It wasn't passed down, but rather, taught to each generation.

The Lemurian Teaching Wheel attributes should give you a hint as to the fact that the advanced teaching for the women had to include how to accomplish effective healing for them all, using what they had on the mountain. So, you might say, all the women were healers, but some were better at it than others, depending on their herbal skills.

Imagine a society where each family had many trained healers! Even today, you may hear, *"The old wives remedies are the best."* It's a phrase that means the common sense of the mothers have the best common sense advice with uncommon substances for healing. Many times, those remedies work better than those from the doctor! That phrase came from Lemuria.

However, also note this: Most of the healing in Lemuria was for those who fell, were cut, or who had the normal accidents of life. No diseases, snake or animal bites, or a vast amount of other things you have today, were ever treated since they didn't yet exist. All that came later, and had to be learned by the "healers of the day" as humanity ventured out into places that were more dangerous.

What were the major causes of death in Lemuria? Was it common that children died, or that mothers died during childbirth?

Answer:

Dear ones, childbirth in Lemuria was not normally life-threatening, and remember, Lemurians were all pure descendants from Star Mothers. They were all "fresh" and new descendants from the seed source. For this reason, there was a "purity of the 23," or a biology that was exceptionally resistant to dysfunctional birth or deformities. There was also no disease yet. Lemurians, in general, lived exceptionally healthy lives and had good life spans for the day. In fact, the direct children of the Star Mothers were so pure that they lived up to three times as long as their own children! Also, remember that I told you "The beginning consciousness for humanity at the start was far higher than it is now!"

What you don't realize is that almost all the things that take your lives today have been "bred" into you. Let me state something, yet again, that is radically controversial to your current thinking: Your state of consciousness creates your biological state. Those who think in a low consciousness way have immune systems that are far weaker, for they mirror the consciousness of the host. A low consciousness humanity will be one that is ripe for plagues, disease, early death, and even be accident-prone.

Part of an evolved consciousness will result in better resistance to life in general and diseases of all kinds, even the worst ones you have today. When you start to see a great reduction of cancer in your civilization, there will be medical historians who will scratch their heads and say, *"Well, that was just something that ran its course."* In actuality, it simply can't attach itself as well to a humanity that won't allow it to. Consciousness is the key to so many things that you don't connect it to right now. Remember, disease is often alive. Would that mean it has a consciousness of sorts? Can a virus or a growing cancer have that?

Your science of today will never admit that disease may have a consciousness of its own. It's just not a logical possibility. However, through profoundly convincing evidence coming in the future, it may have to. Then things will start to change.

Temple of Rejuvenation

Kryon first began describing the Temple of Rejuvenation in the early 1990s. Just like the name suggests, it was a temple that rejuvenated the body and stopped the aging process for approximately three years. How awesome is that! This leads to a very important question. Does the Temple of Rejuvenation exist today? Kryon tells us the answer is YES! But it's not a building. Instead, it is the individual Human's capability to change their DNA from within, with the new abilities granted by a new grid system and a new spiritual reality on Earth. Kryon has given several channels about consciousness controlling physics. Eventually, this is the direction medicine will take, instead of relying on chemistry.

Kryon tells us we will start to understand and develop new medical physics and that medi-physics is going to *speak* to our cellular structure and give it instructions, without one chemical involved. There are also those working with stem cells, using physics to guide the stem cells to a specific destination in the body to repair failing systems. The future of health and healing is consciousness and physics based. These solutions are the elegant replacements for what the Temple of Rejuvenation did.

PLEASE NOTE: Within some of the channelled messages that follow, Kryon gets very technical and discusses magnetics, DNA, entanglement, physics, and high science. For some spiritual seekers that have chosen to read this book based on their interest in the Women of Lemuria, their eyes may begin to glaze over as they re-read the same paragraph over and over, trying to understand what Kryon is saying. If that is you – relax! It's not important that you completely understand everything. Perhaps, you even prefer to skip this section entirely. Maybe you'll read it sometime later. Please feel free to skip ahead and keep reading!

Understanding about the Temple of Rejuvenation demonstrates to us how quantum the Lemurians were. They had a dimensional perception given to them by the Pleiadians that allowed them to "know" and "see" things. The Temple of Rejuvenation used magnetics to alter the body clock. Here is how it worked, as described by Kryon:

I take you to the Temple of Rejuvenation ... a time before the ice. A time that some of you do not wish to experience again, a time when some of you died. But during this time, there was great science. How ironic that it would now "raise its head" again. For, now you get to have the same science, but this time without the fear of termination. Pass this fear, for it is a phantom! Visit with me again, the beautiful Temple of Rejuvenation. See the Temple clearly in all its beauty, and understand the celebration involved in its use.

Here is where the Humans are repolarized! Here is the description. As you stand off at a distance and view this Temple, you see a spire pointing to the sky, and spire pointing to the Earth. It is girded in the mid-point and held up with five legs at an incline. The color is black. The reason? Most of the walls are made up of a composition that cannot be magnetized. There is not metal as you know it. In addition, most of the composition is made from crushed crystals. Remember this composition, for this is the same material which will shield you in flight (*space travel*).

The five legs are hollow. They are inclined to the center area where the work is done, and attached there. The first leg contains the power, running from the ground up into the apparatus. The second leg is hollow, and contains the entrance and exit for the facilitators. The third leg contains the entrance and the exit for the priest that day. The fourth leg contains the ENTRANCE ONLY for the one TO BE healed and rebalanced. The fifth leg contains the EXIT ONLY of the one who HAS BEEN rebalanced and healed. You have heard me channel the message that Spirit enjoys ceremony. Spirit enjoys ceremony for reasons you are not aware of. Spirit does not wish to be worshipped ... hardly! Spirit knows your humanness, and ceremony breeds repetition. You see, the truth is the truth and is static. It works the same, over and over. It is unchanging. Ceremony is the partner to repetition. (*It overcomes the Human trait to always want something new. It helps provide for the same needed process to be repeated accurately each time. It often cloaks accurate, truthful processes in the veil of religion. If you had to think about your own breathing, you would have given it up long ago.*)

There is symbolism in the entrance and exit only of the one to be healed, for the entrance represents ascension, and is the color of death. The tube coming back down, which is the exit from the chamber, back down to Earth, represents the rebirth, and also is of the appropriate color. Ceremony and symbolism at its finest (*more cosmic humor*).

I take you now to the inner chamber. Whereas before, I gave you the view of what was taking place, I will now tell you HOW it is taking place. There are two tables, both of them are rotating. You will now see that both tables are in perfect synchronization. That is to say that when one turns in one direction, the other does as well. They also turn at the same speed. At one table, I told you previously, there is a crowd of facilitators surrounding the table with their hands on something. I also told you that the target Human, the one to be rebalanced, is on a table alone with only one facilitator. Now I will clearly show you what is taking place. At the table with the crowd there is one who stands out. She has her hands on two globes (*she is the priest*). The globes are connected to the machinery, which is humming with great activity above and below, housed in the spires. The spires represent the dipole of the machinery – that is to say, the positive and the negative. The machinery is measuring the one who has her hands on the globes. There are indentations in the globes for her fingers. Those who stand around her have more balance, for the same reasons that those assembled here as a group provide more balance for each other than any one can do alone. The Priest for the day is the one who has the highest balance available … as measured by the machine. The machine measures the balanced organs of the Human (*including all the correct polarities*), interprets it, and flows the information into the giant machinery above and below the target Human … thereby rebalancing the polarity of the target Human's organs. Do you have this picture? Do you see how the polarity works? Do you understand what is happening? A balanced Human, with the correct polarity, will not allow disease. A balanced Human will live a very long time. This is why they called it rejuvenation.

The table which contains the target Human goes into many physical planes – vertical, horizontal, and also tipped at an incline (*yawed*). The one who stands next to the target Human is a worker, who is only there for the Human's comfort, *and to make certain that the Human stays firmly in the table's containment system*. The work is being done with three-dimensional science, with the interaction of the machine and the Human balanced Priest giving the machine information to balance the target Human. When the rejuvenation is finished, the target Human arises from the table, and there is great celebration. All in the room are filled with joy, and applaud the process. There is ceremony, and a special robe is worn, and then the Human descends down the tube of rebirth to Earth. (*The robe is worn for three days to let all know and celebrate with the Human.*) Now you know what has taken place in that Temple. It is, indeed, a Temple with a Priest … and it is pure science (*biology and mechanics in partnership with intelligence*).

Some of these things sound silly. The truth will remain the truth, regardless of your level to understand it.

Kryon live channelling "Attributes of Health & Healing"
given in Kryon Book 2, Don't Think Like a Human – August 17, 1994

In Kryon Book Three, *Alchemy of the Human Spirit*, the following question was asked about the Temple of Rejuvenation:

Dear Kryon: In regard to the three-year program of refreshment and rejuvenation, what aspects of the program were there, if any, that did not require the technology of the Temple that conceivably could be implemented now? Also, why did it take three years? Did the processes taking place in the Temple require periodic visits as opposed to one grand process at the end of the program?

Answer:
The actual "program" is less than a day. The results of the program lasted only three years, and then a revisit was necessary. Although the technology exists now to duplicate the Temple, the knowledge of biology does not. It may be some time before you decide to build this device, and there are more advanced rejuvenation possibilities that make the Temple of Rejuvenation seem like a dinosaur to you! Dear ones, there is a great deal of information hiding in the information given regarding the Temple of Rejuvenation.

The first question all of you should ask is, *"Why do Humans need rejuvenating at all?"* Your bodies are designed to rejuvenate themselves! Why isn't the biology more efficient to rejuvenate 100% of what is lost? What is the process?

The real answer is spiritual. Your biology in this cosmic energy is flawed, and therefore creates death. It wasn't actually designed this way, but became this way over time, thereby allowing the birth-death-birth-death attribute that has become the important "engine of karma" and has allowed you to raise the vibration of the planet. Long before any Human of any kind set foot on this planet, the bio-

58

logical energy ratio was less than 100%, meaning that all biology was destined to only last a short time, then be renewed by reincarnation.

The science answer may surprise you, for the machinery of the body reacts to an energy quotient of the cosmos. As that energy reduced over eons of time within your universe, those internal machines became less efficient (with less energy present). It is, therefore, no accident that your planet and your biology was set up at a time when this energy quotient was inefficient. Otherwise, you would all live forever, and the karmic work that is the work of the entire planet would never be able to be done.

Now, the exciting news is this: the tools have always existed to give your individual biology that extra 10% "push" to allow for true rejuvenation. True rejuvenation is 100% internal body rejuvenation, where the biology actually is able to keep up totally with all loss due to Human living. In the days of Atlantis and Lemuria, the "push" was done with magnetics. Those, in the day, understood the magnetics of Earth and the Human body. They were able to give the biology an outside "tune-up" to allow the magnetic DNA structure around the biological one to operate at full potential for at least three years without deterioration. During that time, the biology kept up with the deterioration, and the immune system was 100% effective. As the magnetics of the DNA slowly returned to reflect the current energy quotient of the cosmos, aging again set in and another trip to the Temple was in order. This pure science healing was wrapped in ceremony and kept close to those with power.

What you should know is that the entire channelling regarding the Temple was to give you insight into what is actually going on inside you. The information for your health science is this: there are at least three ways to accomplish total and complete rejuvenation potential for Humans in this time that is well within your capacity to produce. One is magnetic, one is biological, and one is spiritual. Does it surprise you that again you have the team of physical, biological, and mental (spiritual)?

(1) The magnetic method deals with the Temple of Rejuvenation. The science of your time will allow you to recreate this Temple at a fraction of its original size if you wish. Those who have worked with this information already have recognized this fact. (2) The biological method is just now being discovered, and uses live essence medicines. It will cause great controversy within your medical community. The controversy will be around the fact that the information will challenge the very basics of how the Human body works at the cellular level. (3) The spiritual method is ascension technology, which many of you are working on daily.

One of the aspects of the Temple of Rejuvenation is that it was located on top of the mountain, which Kryon tells us was 33,000 feet high! Mt. Everest is approximately 29,000 feet and those who attempt to climb this summit are well aware of the extreme weather and the small window of opportunity where they can make the ascent. In addition, at that altitude, the available oxygen is 33% of that at sea level. This is why the majority of climbers use supplemental oxygen when attempting to climb mountains at high altitude. The Lemurians didn't have supplemental oxygen – or did they? Kryon has revealed the practical details about how the Lemurians climbed the mountain:

When you see Mt. Everest, it is known for something, dear ones: ferocious weather! It's known for weather that changes dramatically from hour to hour, so that climbing the mountain is treacherous. Climbers must be ready at any time to stay for days, simply waiting for the weather to shift.

So, would you then practically apply this same attribute to a mountain that's much higher than Everest, in the middle of the Pacific during Lemurian times? No. You see, there wasn't ferocious weather around the mountain of Lemuria. The Himalayas, and the place where they are, create their own weather issues. However, in the middle of the Pacific, you didn't have major weather issues simply due to a mountain's height. In fact, there were very few winds. Only the strong trade winds, like the ones you have today, would be there. There was no ferocious weather. The mountain was easily climbable, without having weather be an issue, but like Everest, it was cold. It was cold simply because it's cold at high altitude.

We've told you that at the top of this mountain called Lemuria, there was something called the *Temple of Rejuvenation*. Lemurians did not live on the actual mountain; rather, they mostly lived near the shore. They were a tropical bunch, except for the few who climbed the mountain to service the Temple of Rejuvenation.

As I have told you about this Temple in the past, and have told you what took place there, many have been confused. They would say, *"How is it possible that, in those days, you could have a Human Being living at 28,000 feet? First of all, where did they get their heat? There's no real wood to burn since trees don't grow at that height. Even if you had some wood brought up, you'd run out of it quickly because you would need to burn it constantly. And where did they get their oxygen? You cannot live that high without constant oxygen."*

So let me tell you about both things. One of them is totally understandable, and one of them is not. First of all, remember the island was volcanic, just as it is today. There was plenty of heat. It had a caldera, much like today, and, like today, lava continued to flow. Even before this mountain began to slowly subside, it was still a volcano. So there were many steam vents, and there was plenty of lava all of the time. So there is the heat source needed at the top of the mountain. So, now you understand why someone could live in that cold, and perhaps even support a small community working at the Temple of Rejuvenation. That's the heat. The oxygen? That's very different.

Here is something that someday you'll discover and know more about. How do I tell you this, dear ones? How do I give you information which sounds fantastic today? Here it is: When the mountain was pushed up by the bubble, it exposed a great deal of ancient sediment. In that sediment was a discovery: Rocks were discovered that

61

actually stored and contained oxygen. They were easily seen and identified and used. You see, when those rocks were melted, they gave off oxygen!

So these rocks were found, and were delivered to the top – very slowly. However, the rocks had to be melted! How do you melt a rock? Simple: You need natural molten "other rocks" for the heat ... Lava! [Kryon smile]. So what I'm telling you is that the rocks were melted in a confined area using existing molten lava, releasing oxygen.

Is it a difficult thing for you to imagine ... something you haven't seen yet, where formations on the planet actually would trap oxygen before they solidified? That is how they got their oxygen at the top of the mountain. There will be science someday, that will come along and discover this and then you will know that there is validity in what I tell you.

So, Lemuria was different than you might think: There was no ferocious weather around the mountain – one even higher than Mt. Everest. There was plenty of snow, fire, ice, and a beautiful Temple of Rejuvenation.

Kryon live channelling given at the Kopan Nunnery
in Kathmandu, Nepal – October 16, 2017

Is there any evidence of the "oxygen rocks" described by Kryon? Yes, but in an interesting twist, the evidence was first discovered on the moon! Brian Handwerk has written an article titled, *"Oxygen-Rich Moon Minerals May Help Astronauts Breathe"* for the National Geographic News. Here is an extract of the article:

"The Hubble Space Telescope has detected oxygen-rich minerals on the moon that might someday help astronauts become more self-sufficient in space.

The first high-resolution ultraviolet (UV) images ever taken of the moon have identified several promising deposits of ilmenite. The mineral could provide a crucial oxygen source for future manned lunar missions.

Ilmenite is composed of titanium and iron oxide, or rust, and contains oxygen that is relatively easy to extract.

Titanium oxide is found on Earth in mountain ranges and sedimentary deposits. On the moon, the compound could be converted for use in breathing apparatus and for producing power sources such as rocket fuel.

Speaking at a press conference today, Jim Garvin, chief scientist at NASA's Goddard Space Flight Center in Greenbelt, Maryland, said, 'Our initial findings support the potential existence of some unique varieties of oxygen-rich glassy soils [in certain lunar regions].'

'They could be well-suited for visits by robots and human explorers in efforts to learn how to live off the land on the moon,' he added.

Oxygen Mining

Because the moon has no atmosphere, astronauts or robots searching for oxygen must find it within the surrounding rock and soil of the dusty lunar surface.

There are several ways to extract oxygen from ilmenite. Researchers have used electric current, heat, and other gasses.

Scientists don't yet know which method might prove most effective in the lunar environment, but say the possibilities are exciting.

The presence of ilmenite is only the first in what scientists hope will be many new revelations provided by the UV images."

Note : Original link removed. Similar information can be found in the following links: https://www.nasa.gov/vision/universe/solarsystem/hubble_moon.html https://ww.newscientist.com/article/dn12305-hubble-space-telescope-maps-minerals-on-the-moon/

NASA has begun field-testing instruments and equipment that may one day be used by astronauts to extract oxygen. The irony is that these experiments are taking place on Hawaii's Mauna Kea volcano due to the volcanic terrain, soil and remote environmental location. Perhaps in the future, scientists will also discover the "oxygen rocks" on Hawaii that Kryon describes.

Source: https://www.space.com/6294-moon-dust-yield-oxygen-fuel-water.html

Another attribute of the Temple of Rejuvenation was that it was cold, due to the altitude. The cold temperature was absolutely essential to the rejuvenation process. The reason is because the cold was needed in combination with the magnetics. When certain materials become super-cold they become super-conductors and so the Temple of Rejuvenation was utilizing the principles of cryomagnetics. Exactly how did the cold and the magnetics rejuvenate the body? The answers are revealed in the following channel from Kryon, featuring a conversation with Dr. Todd Ovokaitys, who Kryon calls Yawee:

The Temple of Rejuvenation

As Yawee, Todd ran something called the *Temple of Rejuvenation* in Lemuria. There were attempts to recreate it in Atlantis much, much later, but that didn't work because Yawee wasn't there. Yawee had an attribute that the Lemurians knew was unusual, and that was that he lived three times the life span that they did. So he had within him some secrets about energy, and specifically, DNA. In the Temple of Rejuvenation, he had discovered something that is in the works of being discovered right now. I don't have a clock. How soon? You'll see.

So I address Yawee now in order to continue the teaching: Good morning, Yawee. [Note that the time of day is irrelevant, seeing as how this meeting was approaching 5 p.m. Many never noticed this. It's Kryon humor.]

Todd: Good day, Magnetic Master.

We've spoken before. We've done it like this and we've done it in private. You're not being put on the spot, for we always give these discussions in appropriate love, just in order to perhaps press issues that are already there, so they match your clock [again, speaking of the 4D time we have]. What do you remember about the Temple of Rejuvenation that comes to you in certain aspects? Do you remember what the energies were there?

Todd: There was the use of the intrinsic magnetic core of the Earth that was especially concentrated in certain areas and was further augmented by altitude.

You remember, dear ones listening to this and reading this, that the Temple of Rejuvenation rested on the top of Lemuria's mountain. Lemuria is the highest mountain on the planet. To this day, it remains the highest mountain, but today it is submerged. It is called Hawaii. The Islands of Hawaii are only the mountaintops of one giant mountain. Measured from the bottom to the top, it is the largest on the planet. There is snow at the top, even now. Can you imagine it 20,000 feet higher? Can you imagine what it looked like observable from space? This is the one that the Pleiadians chose to come to first. Obvious, it was.

Yawee, you might remember, you were always cold. Always cold. For, you couldn't have a heater in the Temple because then it didn't work! When you saw that which is being done in science today on the screen that my partner brought [a video that Lee showed earlier on macro-entanglement], did you see anything interesting that you might remember?

We speak of temperature. We speak of cold that is so cold that it actually creates less resistance to the flow of energy. This is actually the catalyst for increasing that which is magnetic by 10,000 times, even 1,000-fold, depending on the temperature. Without technical machinery, it was one of the attributes that allowed you to do what you did in that Temple.

I want to ask you this. How much do you remember about the physical apparatus that was necessary for this? I ask you these things only of interest to see what your Akash is up to. We have said there was something called the target Human.

Todd: In this moment, the key attribute is a magnetic driver with a particular geometry both above and below the so-called target Human.

So, there was both magnetics – there was the no-zone point that creates the entanglement and there was the importance of a counter rotation and counter spin.

Very good. Impressive. Now, the big question. So the Human is entangled, is it? With what is the Human quantumly entangled? Do you remember? Let me ask you this. How many Humans are in the room?

Todd: About 10.

Indeed. And is there a special one?

Todd: The template Human.

Correct! Ah, indeed. Do you remember any other attribute about the template Human that would be noticeable if you saw them? You're not there yet. And that is what we're going to jog in your memory today, if it's all right with you.

Todd: Sure.

I'll get back to you, Yawee, but for now, I have to go through a process for all of you to understand what is happening. In the process, there is revelation. I now take you to basic atomic structure. I've done this before, but I've never taken you to this stage. I want you to look at an electron with me, as though you are there and as small as it is. Now, go slowly, my partner, for you've had no training in this and it's important that you get the message as presented and don't enhance it [Kryon speaking to Lee].

Physicists say that electrons spin. They don't, and they can't. There's no surface on an electron, since they are energy. They don't spin, but instead have an electronic potential. Every single particle on this planet, everything you can see, all things in this Universe are created with polarity. This is new information now. All things are created with polarity, and they're designed to be self-balancing. And because of the polarity of what you would call plus and minus, they move and try to balance themselves within a field – all things, both physical and other.

However, all polarities are prone to be biased by what I will call *peer pressure*. Electrons that carry (or *spin* with a polarity of) what you would call a certain kind of charge – we'll call it positive – are drawn to those that are negative so that they will null themselves out. They seek each other out to create the null of balance. They seek to be balanced, and if they are not, they are not *happy*. I use this word only to emphasize the condition of a particle of physics that does not find its balance. Even the unscientific can appreciate this.

But even with atoms, there are not always matched pairs of electrons, since there is no atomic rule that says that electrons will always be created in even numbers. So there will often be what I will call the *odd one out* and when that happens, the entire atom will then be charged positively or negatively, depending upon the odd one out. When this happens, this atom will seek out another atom, which has an odd one out of an opposite charge. That has a name: Magnetism. I've just explained magnetism. Now, science knows part of that already. What they have not realized yet, however, is that all things have a duality. They suspect it and there are theories that will show it soon enough, and I've given it to you today because it always has existed in someone's mind.

So from the very smallest to the very biggest, even the galaxy has duality. At the center of your galaxy, what you call the black hole, is a quantum push/pull engine, and I'm going to tell you in a minute why it's that way.

Here is a big question and I will answer it right now. Why does everything have a polarity? Why would it be created this way, even down to the electron? The smallest thing, even to what you call the Higgs Boson [God Particle] and the quarks, they all have polarity. There isn't a piece of nature that you're going to find that doesn't have polarity. Why? I will tell you why: Physicists will laugh. Not in ridicule, but in agreement. If it were not this way, the Universe would be a dull, boring place to be. Because, by creating a duality in every single particle, you create an active Universe that is self-balancing and is never at rest. If it were not this way, it would be static, unchanging, and non-creative. Therefore, without polarity, there would be no life. Life is created by having a duality, a polarity in atomic particles. Life is that which is necessary for the Universe to exist. There's no reason for physics without life – and you thought it was the other way around, didn't you? Life was an accident on one planet. Oh, how 3D of you! Life *is* the DESIGN.

Let's continue the discussion, for it's going someplace. Yawee, you just described the process of creating macro-entanglement in the Temple. What you described was magnetics and null points. Very good! Do you perhaps understand that magnetics and null points are even at the center of your galaxy?

Todd: Of course.

So that means the galaxy is an entangled state with itself. This now explains why all the constellations and solar systems are not following Newtonian movement. Instead, they all move together as one around the center because they are entangled. I've just given the reason for it, and science will start to understand that soon. It has been a mystery so far, but now you know.

So you have macro-entanglement. The largest thing you can imagine, the galaxy, is entangled with itself. Is it possible there are other entanglement issues that you don't see or recognize or know about in every single day of life? And the answer's yes. So here we go.

Oh, dear Human Being, what I'm going to give you next is beautiful, and it has to do with DNA and Yawee knew it. He knew how to do something magical.

The blueprint for DNA is perfect. The good doctor will tell you that in his current incarnation [as Todd]. I've told you that before. It's perfect inside you, yet you sit here with DNA that doesn't work well. It seems to be a dichotomy, since it is perfect and designed for extended life, yet it does some things that are counter-intuitive to that.

DNA is designed as an informational source to receive the energy of that which is around it, created by the consciousness of humanity. It then postures itself in an appropriate reaction to the energy it is in. In other words, if the planet has low energy, it will, too. It's a quantum engine, and if the quantum energy created by Human consciousness is low, it works poorly.

I want to define life for you – not biological life, but *spiritual life.* So, for all those intellectuals, just hold on, for many won't like this. Spiritual life, as measured by Spirit, is when a Human has free choice. When is that? It's when they take their first breath. Not in utero. There will be those who will say, *"That's wrong, that's wrong. The soul in the woman's body is alive!"* Just wait. I'm talking about spiritually. That which Spirit sees, and it's when you come from the other side of the veil and take your first breath.

A child with the mother has no free choice. That child is linked to the choice of the mother until it is born. It is, indeed, a soul in preparation for free choice, and there are many attributes that are spiritual that we have discussed before about how that soul reacts. But now I'm discussing life with polarity [duality], free choice.

But let's discuss that "child inside" for a moment, for there is a process I want you to know about. I want to talk about 240 days into the pregnancy. At about that time, the child has *perfect DNA.* It hasn't taken its first breath. The DNA hasn't measured the energy of the planet yet, since it is contained. Did you realize that? Inside the womb is a perfect child. The child's DNA has all the attributes of the Akash and also the parent, but it's different in a way you have not been told. The DNA is 100% as designed.

The quantum instructions within the DNA are all talking to the biology of the child, getting ready for the first breath. Now, I reveal to you, Todd, Yawee, what you already know.

Explanation of the Temple of Rejuvenation

The Temple of Rejuvenation has two Human Beings quantumly entangled. One is the target. The other one is the "template." Life extension, through the knowledge of DNA that Yawee had, was to entangle the target with the template and transfer certain attributes from the one to the other.

The only way this could ever work is if DNA had a quantum attribute, and it does. All our teaching for more than 10 years has told you that the 90 percent of DNA that is non-encoded and considered "junk" is a quantum instruction set. Therefore, the DNA molecule must have some quantum attributes yet to be discovered, but they are very real and have to do with instructions to the chemistry of more than three billion parts of the DNA molecule. This is especially true to the gene-producing chemistry of the protein-encoded parts. For simplicity, I tell you that DNA is actively dynamic and can change the reality of everything you think of as "normal."

Yawee, you explained very well the attributes of the target creating an entangled state with the template Human. Now we reveal that the template was (1) a woman (2) who is pregnant. You have...

Todd interrupting: ...the source of the perfect DNA template!

That is correct! So the secret of the Temple of Rejuvenation is twofold: (1) DNA is perfect on Earth within an unborn child and you can transfer some of the attributes of that perfection before it assimilates the energy of the planet. (2) You can extend life and healing through a quantum communication with the DNA molecule. Do you see the implications? The wise, divine feminine who is with child is the only one who could be on the template table. Are you starting to understand the beauty of this, the implications of this and where it's going?

There are several things that are going to happen in mainstream science. First, you're going to find some secrets of DNA and they're going to be embryonic. Start watching scientists discover the embryonic cells and the magic within them. You already know that unusual stem cells exist in the placenta. You also know that the pre-programmed adult stem cells are still there in the body. But what about the DNA of the unborn? (Intellectuals, please keep reading, for to stop now will create unrest.) Second, your work today, Yawee, will represent "the perfect template" without using what you did in Lemuria. That's why you're the Human who will do this. It's an extension of why you came here, and is perfect for 2012 and beyond.

These embryonic cells of the unborn are untouchable by society, and they might as well be on Mars, for no science is going to try to use these cells in a 3D manner, which is all you know how to do at

70

this point. If they try, it won't work anyway. There are quantum processes you are learning about that are not only non-invasive, but actually helpful and that can transfer attributes from one biological cell to another and from one Human to another. Think "wireless" [Kryon humor again]. What you thought would take wires over 1,000 miles long is now done with satellites. It's an analogy that shows you that you are moving into totally new understandings of the transfer of energy. Let's discuss the mother in that Temple for a moment.

The woman on the table back then, who is the "template," won the "Lemurian lottery" [Kryon being funny], for she knows that her baby, being entangled with another Human, no matter how old or how sick, creates an enhancement of who that baby will be. This is complicated, but the process of helping the other will be etched into the baby's Akash, and the child will be born with an attribute of the healer. There is complexity and controversy and over-intellectual thinking in all this, for your 3D brains will race to find things wrong with this. All I can tell you is that a quantum system is not a linear one, and your logic will fall on the floor if you try to analyze these things. Can you imagine time in a circle? Can you see being in two places at the same time, or even of changing your molecular structure at will to be part of another object? If you can't do that, then you are not allowed to comment reasonably. For all those things are part of quantum possibilities of DNA. If you don't believe me, ask a Pleiadian [more cryptic Kryon humor].

Now, Yawee, are you understanding what you were doing back then? Do you need any more answers?

Todd: Well, I could say, do I? Yes!

[Laughter]

Yawee, what is it that you dream about? What is it that you dream about that you don't know and want to?

Todd: I dream about recalibration of the DNA and the coherent alignment that allows us to move freely, I guess, as the Pleiadians do in a quantum state from one place to another.

71

Of course you would ask that, since you see a much larger picture based on what your Akash has seen and remembers. You also know it's possible.

Meanwhile, all those in here are asking about the same thing about what they just heard: *"Where can we find a pregnant woman and do this now?"*

[Laughter]

It's way beyond that, and the Pleiadians knew it. All this information originally came from them and passed to you, Yawee. It was for then, not now. The Pleiadians don't need a pregnant woman in order for them to do what they do today. They have DNA, too, but it's in a fully developed quantum state – a state that is the potential for the Human race.

I would remind you that my partner has given you messages in the past about the *attitude* of physics. Now we are right back to the polarity discussion that started this channelling. This "attitude," Yawee, is imbued into the natural invention that you have discovered. Physics is active and seeks balance. That is to say, that every field you have created with your process has the attributes – are you ready? – of perfect DNA. It already sees the attributes of the blueprint of the unborn. You don't need a pregnant woman. The attributes can be passed to the Human and received by that Human in whatever posture that his/her cellular structure is able to absorb.

What you have done in your work is to create a quantum field with those Pleiadian attributes, and the cells *listen* when they are exposed to them. It's not finely tuned yet, but you will discover how, eventually. When you do, you will have the regeneration engine of the future, without a "template Human," but instead, with the attributes of the template Human.

This process and others will be seen by science also. You won't be alone. It is not appropriate that you would have the secret of life exclusively, so there will be others. Embryonic studies with animals are going to start to reveal that which gives the ability to grow back limbs for Humans, and many of the other things we have talked about for 23 years.

Kryon live channelling "The Recalibration of Knowledge"
given in Boulder, Colorado – January 14, 2012

Questions for Kryon:

The Temple of Rejuvenation was located at such a high elevation because the cold was needed. Evidence of Lemuria is mostly beneath the sea; however, because of the Temple's location, it should theoretically still be above sea level, somewhere in Hawaii. The description of the Temple's physical structure would suggest the Pleiadians designed it. Did they also remove it? If not, will the Temple ever be found? Can you tell us more about this?

Answer:

Let me tell you about the Temple of Rejuvenation. It never submerged, so you might think that some of it can be found. First, know this: The Temple of Rejuvenation was real, and Pleiadian technology was used for its design. However, a select few Lemurians did the construction over many years. It was an interesting time, for those who did it had to work in an environment that was artificially created, using some devices that they had never seen (for lifting), and constructing the Temple piece by piece from instructions recorded much earlier by Pleiadian males. The select few who created it were there for life and had families on the mountaintop. How could that be? Too cold! No oxygen! The answer is yes. [Kryon humor, which means, "I'm not answering that one."]

It was elegant above anything that could be designed by the Lemurian civilization, and it was built from materials that were synthesized through advanced physics – something you will actually be able to do at some point.

So can anything be found? Yes. Will it be found? The answer requires two things to happen. (1) Funding for the research on the Big Island of Hawaii. Not everyone will agree that this is worth looking for.

(2) New technology that allows you to clearly "see" things within the mountain that have been buried deep into the lava for thousands of years.

What is in the "field of potentials" is this: The funding will only come about from an accidental discovery. This discovery will ironically come from the space observatories that are also on this peak. New technology, meant for one thing, will discover another. The artifact materials used in the Temple will "stick out" and be totally out of place within the lava. I have said enough. As usual, Humans must do this on their own.

What was the true purpose of the Temple of Rejuvenation? Was it simply to extend life, or was there something else?

Answer:

Because you never asked, what has never been revealed is that the structure on the top of the mountain simply contained the *Temple of Rejuvenation*. The full structure was much larger, and only a portion was for the Lemurians' Temple. Most of it was for the use of the Pleiadian Star Mothers.

First, the Lemurian rejuvenation portion was called a "Temple" to create the idea that it was sacred. The sacredness of it was because it was using processes that honored the elements of embryonic life, to extend *adult* life. It also used processes that were purely from the stars, but available, even today, to Earth science.

Next, the Pleiadian Star Mothers needed a type of rejuvenation, too, but it was "communication and solace" from home. This structure was called "The Compassion House," by the Pleiadians and a portion contained the Temple. This Compassion House provided the way they were able to speak to the home planets, thereby feeding their desire to be connected to loved ones, and to participate virtually in many things that brought them closer to home. Remember, they were Humans just like you. They didn't just "leave home" and were unconnected. They needed solace, compassion, and love from others just like them. They were on a low consciousness planet, existing as high consciousness, evolved Humans. Can you imagine?

Next, the technology they used to power these buildings was completely done with small units they called "strip mag units" (in their language). Using magnetic power, they could generate the equivalent of electricity indefinitely and pull oxygen from the thinner air of high altitude. The heat from lava and the use of "oxygen rocks" (as we have reported to you earlier) were only used for the Lemurians. No off-world processes were allowed for Earth-based projects unless they were actually used by the child of a Pleiadian. This guaranteed that these higher technologies that were needed back then, would eventually die out and not be used inappropriately by a low consciousness Human nature in the coming Earth history.

Next (and the biggest revelation) is that these structures were present in every Pleiadian node on the planet. There were twelve, but all were only temporary until the time when all the Pleiadians moved from a corporeal form to a "consciousness package" form.

Finally, every one of these structures was bio-degradable and had a half-life of at least 10,000 years. This was designed so that they would not be found in the rubble of history. Even in that, there are traces of them that might remain due to the fact that not 100% of everything could dissolve. Parts of the strip mag units remain, but they hide by virtue of the fact that many rocks are magnetic also, so they fit right in with what is buried deep within the planet, which future sensors could pick up.

Only sensors looking for "designed magnetics" would be able to see them, and this, too, is by design. For when those kinds of sensors are available to Humans, you will be fully aware that those from the stars had been here, and it will simply be more validation, instead of revelation.

Lemurian Pineal Tones

The Lemurian Pineal Tones first emerged in 2001 when Dr. Todd Ovokaitys developed the Pineal Toning Technique™. Over the next few years, these tones were taught to thousands of individuals for personal growth and healing. Many individuals singing the tones reported their experiences, which included visions, healings, and a vast expansion of their consciousness. Toning can be briefly described as the creation of an extended vocal sound from one single vowel. There are no melodies, no words, no rhythm, it is simply the sound of vibrating breath. Toning synchronizes the brainwaves, helps relieve tension, and restores balance and harmony to the mind and body. During these early days of teaching the tones, Dr. Todd was unaware of just how profound they were and the role they would play in planetary esoterics.

In November of 2010, Kryon provided further information about the tones and gave instructions to Dr. Todd [Yawee] about what he should do with them. The tones were to be sung in pairs to create coherence. One half of the tone is the carrier, while the other half is the modulator. The paired tones, therefore, create quantum communication that talks to the pineal. The pineal becomes a quantum transmitter that is entangled with the galaxy. The energy created by the tones can be seen by Gaia, the Pleiadians, and any civilization in the galaxy that has quantum sight.

Yawee's instructions were to create a Lemurian Choir that would sing a specific combination of tones. He was instructed that the choir had to sing at either Hawaii or Mt. Shasta on December 21, 2012. Perhaps you were there in Hawaii and felt the energy of this amazing event. Or perhaps you were participating in an equally energetic event somewhere else on the planet. Regardless of where you were and what you were doing, the collective consciousness of humanity on this significant date fulfilled an ancient prophecy about the Eagle and the Condor (which will be discussed later in this book). Kryon described Yawee's remembrance of the Pineal Tone combinations of the 2012 Lemurian Choir as "shockingly accurate." But why did Kryon instruct him to sing the Lemurian Pineal Tones on a specific date and time? The answer is intrinsically linked to Ancient Lemuria.

In Lemuria, once a year, on December 21 [the solstice], Human Beings got together and they sang the 12 sets of Pineal Tones. They activated all of that which is in the pineal from all of them, and you had hundreds of Human quantum transmitters all going at once. Each one of them, from a Human Being, put together something that one Human Being could not do ... a mass consciousness quantum signal. And the signal was sent through the galaxy for anyone to hear, but, dear ones, there was only one set of *ears* listening. These were the seed planters, the Seven Sisters, the Pleiadians.

You might say it was calling home [Kryon smile]. And once a year, the Lemurians, remembering those elders who planted the seeds of enlightenment on Earth, and who lived among them from the start, were giving a message to the home planet. It was a thank you for all of the years of their teachings, a thank you for planting the seeds that you and I know today as the divinity within your DNA. Once a year, this message went out to say, "We are well and thankful for all you did." The message was, "We are here, and we know who you are. We love you. We thank you for giving us these elders who still walk among us."

The message stopped some time ago, and hasn't been given for a very long time. Now you are about to give it again, for the first time in more than 26,000 years [referring to the 2012 Lemurian Choir, which took place in Maui, Hawaii].

It took 12 sets of Pineals in order to "spell," if you want to say that, the myriad of frequencies that gave the message to the Seven Sisters. It only worked on December 21 in Lemuria [and in their time zone]. It doesn't work in Australia at that time since it's a day later! Only in Lemuria on December 21. Indeed, Humans can broadcast from almost anywhere, but the truth is that there is only one place that it was ever done ... Lemuria. The time center for the Earth is there, not in London [new Kryon information indicating that GMT or UT is only a product of culture and maritime designation, and not the true "center time" of the planet].

In 2012, that day represents the galactic alignment, which slowly moves the wobble of the Earth [precession] through the equinoxes. It's all there, and that's when they listen. The profundity of this is that they have not heard from humanity in 26,000 years ... until now.

Yawee's house will be complete in 2012 [referring to the Lemurian Choir] and for those of you who sit there in that energy and vibrate in that energy, I want you to feel it: that the pineal will be activated, the transmission will be sent, and there's going to be a lot of rejoicing in that constellation called the Seven Sisters. It's going to activate other beings on the planet who have been waiting for this; for this transmission says, "We remember who you are! We remember who we are! We are ready to move forward to do what we came for." What is that? We are planting the seeds of peace on Earth so that this planet will eventually be able to foster yet another planet someday, as they fostered you and, in a quantum state, go somewhere else and begin to plant the seeds.

Kryon live channelling "Lemurian Choir Rehearsal Seminar"
given in Sedona, Arizona – June 14, 2011

Hopefully, you now have an appreciation of the significance of the 2012 Lemurian Choir. What about the significance of the tones? What are the mechanics behind them? Before discussing the Lemurian Pineal Tones, as developed by Dr. Todd, let's continue the discussion of toning. Toning can be described as the universal language of sound. Unlike a melody with words, rhythm, and harmony, a tone is an extended non-verbal sound, often a vocal sound on a single vowel. When you tone, you align with the sacred energies of healing sounds, creating a highly transformative and expansive experience. The vibration of the Human voice is a powerful healing force that stimulates our entire physical system. Toning can awaken and deepen your sense of self.

The power of toning lies in the vowels (and personal intent) rather than the "pitch" (high or low). Each vowel is a unique experience in energy, emotion and effect. The act of toning heightens our awareness and tunes us into our own inner energies and vibrations. Toning is a highly intuitive experience and most of us have been doing this since birth. One of the wonderful things about toning is that no two people tone in exactly the same way. The point of toning is not the quality of sound but your experience of the vibration produced and the effects on your body. There is, therefore, no right or wrong way to tone, which means everyone can do it!

Regarding the Lemurian Pineal Tones, Kryon has said:

Esoterically, it is believed that the tonalities have a multidimensional overtone structure that creates light within your DNA field and a patterning which can be seen by a quantum engine. This is correct, and is the definition that Yawee is aware of.

But it's even more than that. It is the return to the most basic communications you have ever known. Some of the tones seem funny. How many tones can the doctor [Todd] make? How many funny noises are there? How fast can you do it? And to the 3D observer, it's very odd. That's all they can see and hear: Funny noises and motions.

Take a beautiful rainbow in the sun, with a mist occurring so that it glows ... and the colors are beautiful, almost surreal. Now take away color sight and you're looking at it in shades of gray. Now take away most of the shades of gray and it appears as one black line. The 3D Human Being looks at the one black line and says, *"I don't understand it, but it feels okay. I don't know what's there, but somehow it reminds me of something else."*

So I want to tell you what you are really looking at metaphorically: You're looking at a rainbow with infinite colors you cannot imagine, that only the quantum sight of God can see fully. When you involve yourself with intent for the handshake that is there, in communication with these quantum noises and sounds and rhythms, you are awakening your remembrance within your own quantum DNA. Eventually, this remembrance will flood through the very fabric of the quantum parts of your body, and the Lemurian in you will be reawak-ened.

Now, what does that mean to you, Old Soul? Let's start with some basic cellular-level information. When structure is balanced and snaps into place, you live longer. And if that weren't good enough, you live longer with a better attitude, because the balance starts to reawaken the core information of why you are here. Mothers become better mothers and fathers become better fathers. There's no limit to what can be improved in your life. Compassion increases.

I wish to take you back in time. Only thirty thousand years ago. Lemuria was still high, and the water had not yet come up [The bub-ble in the crust of the Earth at the hot spot called Hawaii had not sub-sided]. I take you into a stadium, Yawee. It is filled with almost 800 people. They are selected to be there, selected for their voices and their knowledge. I want to take you there to feel this ... four hundred are on one side facing the four hundred on the other side. You, Yawee, are in the middle, and they are singing pairs of pineal tones, creating quantum magic.

There are twenty-four individually matched tones that pair to cre-ate twelve energies when sung together. This becomes a language, and that is why some of them are sound, some of them are buzzing, and some of them even seem like spitting. They are not any of those things, for the overtones are rich, like punctuation marks within the others which are sung in a tonality way.

I want to show you something before I close. There was a Lemurian who made a movie* and many of you saw it, and his name was Steven Spielberg. Within the story, space creatures were called down from the sky with tones. Do you remember the movie? Now, do you remember what happened? Not only did they have tonal sequences, which meant communications to those in the skies, but when they came down, they started playing the tones with each other. That is to say, that one would play, and then the other would play, and then you had a duality, did you not? A duet. You had a pair

---

* *The movie described by Kryon is* **Close Encounters of the Third Kind.**

of energies. And if you remember the film, and the intuition of the one who wrote it, it wasn't just sequences of tones. Instead, they became faster and faster and faster, did they not? This continued until they had one large blasting tone, which was all encompassing of the others. The Lemurian remembered, didn't he? That's what you are learning as well, and remembering. Does this sound familiar?

Now, why would Lemurians sit, 400 on one side, 400 on the other? It wouldn't matter if there were only 200 and 200 ... but why would they sit and tone together in these pairs that we tell you go together? Now I will tell you: Not only does it activate the DNA inside, *it activates the Pleiadian part of the DNA*. It activates that which is the most sacred seed given to you, Human Being, at the onset of that which you would call Creation, which gave you the pieces and the parts in your DNA which could sing with God. It starts a process that is communication with the Creator's purpose.

Kryon live channelling "Pineal Tone Information"
given in San Diego, California – November 2010

Since the 2012 Lemurian Choir, Dr. Todd has assembled many other choirs at significant locations around the world (mostly corresponding with the Nodes and Nulls of the planet). If you are interested in obtaining an audio recording of the choirs, or accessing further information about the Pineal Tones, please visit:

www.pinealtones.com

Lemurian Language

Regarding the Lemurian language, Kryon has said that the Lemurians ...

...were here long enough for their language to evolve and change grandly and greatly and provide the seeds of some of the most profound languages that you know today ... of the Egyptians, the Israelis [Hebrews], and the Polynesians ... all derivatives of what we'll call the original language of Solara Maru. In these languages were contained basic truths that even today you grapple with, and it's due to something the Lemurians had, but that you don't.

What the Lemurians had was an added dimension of perception. They walked upon this Earth with a dimensional quality that had attributes way beyond what we have today.

The Lemurians understood multidimensionality. Over time, they were exceptionally aware that there was a *devolution* occurring (an expression that means the opposite of evolution), and that they were losing certain abilities. In addition, they were also aware that their time on the planet was limited, as they realized their island was sinking. Many Lemurians became sea-faring and reestablished themselves in other places, but not all of them did. Some continued to stay on the island, while others transformed and became a multidimensional part of Gaia. How can such a thing happen? Kryon explains how:

There have been those who have asked how physical beings like Humans, back then [in Lemuria], could suddenly decide to become multidimensional and enter a mountain and stay there with the attributes of a time capsule [the Lemurian story of Telos and Shasta]. That is too unbelievable! It's not something that you can conceive, and it becomes eye-rolling information to those who hear it. Truly, it's because the Lemurians had a perception, given to them by the Pleiadians, that was equivalent to *one more dimension* than you have.

Let's back up for a moment and do some disclosure. We know that talking about a race of beginning Humans who had extra-dimensional perception is a wild idea. But there's some evidence, and I will now give you something to think about: The closest ancient race that you have artifacts for are the *Sumerians*. Now, the Sumerians were far removed from the Lemurians in time, but they still possessed a bit of the awareness that the Lemurians provided in their culture. All these things happened over thousands of years. The challenge: Go take a look at the Sumerian artifacts. First of all, you'll see that their computations were all base-6 (a derivative of base-12 math, and a staple of nature and real physics). Next, the artifact known as *The Berlin Seal* clearly shows that they knew all about your solar system! They knew of the motion of your planets, and even that some had rings ... all without any evidence of this culture having telescopes.

Your science would laugh at this and completely dismiss the idea that they could know any of these things. They'll tell you that this society must have featured *lucky guesses*. But the odds of a lucky guess that would depict an accurate solar system, even showing the rings of Saturn, would be farfetched indeed. Let me remind you that your own science has postulated that atomic structure is all multidimensional, and that your idea of reality as a Human is less than half of what's actually there. They've also told you that when you start to study the other dimensions, both time and distance are almost completely voided, entangled, and in a quantum state.

Now, I take you back to the Sumerians. They didn't have telescopes, yet they knew all about the cosmos. This is due to the fact that "multidimensional sight" gave them this. It was absolutely intuitive within their perception to "know" what was around them. Neither time nor distance was a factor in "seeing" the solar system. So what you need [modern] technology for, they did intuitively. The same is true of the Lemurians, only more so. The Lemurians not only had this ability, but also intuitive knowledge of the multidimensional DNA. This was what led them to easily build the Temple of Rejuvenation, and allow them to use magnetics to alter their body clocks.

So, understand that none of these Sumerian revelations needed high science, as you might say they would, but rather only a simple perception that they had, but you do not. It would be like a sightless society stumbling upon one that could see. If the culture had been blind for centuries, it would seem to them amazing to find an ancient one that had sight. In the sightless reality, they had to go and discover what a mountain far away was like, but you could "see" it from a distance! This is a very similar situation: one perception versus another.

Kryon live channelling "The Lemurian Connection"
given in Mt. Shasta, California – June 20, 2004

Can you see how an extra-dimensional perception would create a unique Lemurian language? It also explains why the Lemurian Pineal Tones are a form of quantum communication.

Further evidence of Lemurian language can be discovered in Kryon Book 12, *The Twelve Layers of DNA*. This book provides a detailed explanation of the twelve layers, or multidimensional energies of DNA. What does DNA have to do with anything? Not much – if we only examine the chemistry. Beyond the 3D chemistry, DNA is the crossroads of God and Human, the mixture of quantum and non-quantum, and it vibrates with the essence of the truth of the Universe. It carries with it all the history of creation, including the galaxy within which you sit.

As part of the esoteric teaching of DNA, Kryon assigned the energies of the DNA layers to our existing numbers one through twelve. To further understand how the twelve layers work together, Kryon presented four groups of three layers each. Layers Seven, Eight, and Nine make up DNA Group Three – The Lemurian Layers! Why Lemurian? Because as the other kinds of Humans died out on the planet, the ones with Pleiadian DNA survived and created their own culture. In discussing the Lemurian Layers, Kryon revealed that:

The language of Lemuria has been lost, but it survives in a modified core fashion with the "ancestral language of Hawaii," for this is their lineage, and that of those who left the *big mountain* due to rising water and fanned out in all directions to eventually seed the Earth. They first went where the currents took them naturally, then later, sailed against the wind.

Many have asked, *"Kryon, does the current Hawaiian language, therefore, sound like Lemurian?"* Somewhat, but not as much as you would think. As is the way of things, language morphs with time and much is added and subtracted. This is not unusual and the time needed for all this to happen was considerable [to a Human]. So today, you really have nothing that sounds like full Lemurian. If I had to give you the closest current languages, however, it would be a combination of Japanese and Hawaiian. As the Lemurian population scattered, it created many new cultures and eventually contributed to many languages of Earth.

"Kryon, science does not acknowledge Lemuria, and says that the seat of Human civilization came out of the Middle East. What do you say?" I say the truth is the truth. As I described, the Pleiadian seed was planted on all continents. So it's what science has discovered that creates their facts. As discoveries shift, their facts shift. Science will continue to change with discovery. The truth stays the same – that in the middle of the north Pacific Ocean was the most advanced and oldest stable Human civilization in history.

Let's make something else clear. Before the Pleiadians did their work with you all over this planet, there was no divinity inside the Human structure. You had no Creator inside, and the system of your divine coming and going did not exist. You were the same as much of the other life in the Universe, for there is an assumption by Humans that all life is the same. It isn't. There is only a fraction of life in the Universe that is "allied with the divinity of the Creator," and you are one of them. Thanks to your brothers and sisters who helped put this in place, you are part of their lineage and part of their planet's purpose. By the way, this means that at some point, there was a "first" – the first Human who embodied the Creator inside. It wasn't easy and those around him were not yet ready. It took centuries to bring all humanity into focus and to give them the DNA ...

...The Pleiadians were following the intuition and synchronicity of Spirit to come to Earth and seed one kind of Human with their spiritual quantum DNA attribute. You simply did not have it before they got here.

Because these energies [layers] seven and eight are labeled "Lemurian Layers One and Two," they are very special in the scheme of Human spiritual history. For this reason, I will actually give you not only the Hebrew names for them, but also the full Lemurian names and meanings. For to me, Lemurian is still a language.

Author's note: only the Lemurian names and meanings will be presented here – please see Kryon Book 12, *The Twelve Layers of DNA*, for the entire channelled message.

HOA YAWEE MARU is the Lemurian language name for layer seven. The Lemurian meaning of Hoa Yawee Maru is "revealed divinity." Without it, you have darkness, but with it, you have a reason to be here. It is the end of the age of innocence and so this is the equivalent of the realization of God. It is the exposure of the concepts of light and dark, of the consciousness of integrity versus non-integrity, and of what others [might say] is good and evil.

AKEE YAWEE FRACTUS is the Lemurian language name for layer eight, and it means "wisdom and responsibility." This is very Lemurian, for here is the first large society in existence who knew they were different, somehow spiritual, quantumly endowed [multidimensionally aware], and responsible for finding spiritual purpose. It is these who gave wisdom to the others, and who planted the seed of knowledge that would eventually spread all over the Earth.

Today, most Humans on Earth eventually search for the Creator as soon as they are old enough to do so. This is an attribute that is caused from "missing the other side." You know intuitively that you are part of God, that your soul essence isn't just biology. It causes even the atheist to cry out to God the instant before he leaves the Earth on his deathbed – sometimes in solitude, sometimes not. For it is imprinted in his DNA, within the 12 energies, that God is inside and is related to him ...

... *Akee Yawee Fractus* sounds a bit like a formula, does it not? It actually is, for in Lemurian, it represents a saying that they had. The saying they had was posted above the Temple of Rejuvenation, a place where they were able to extend life with the magnetics of the geology around them. The saying was: *"The solution to your problems lay at the feet of practical things."* This saying is not that elegant, for remember, this civilization was not yet that wise itself. But the saying was an axiom of wisdom that encouraged those who saw it to take care of the practical things in life before esoteric things.

It is the forerunner to many of the ideas of today that indicate that if you "know yourself" first, then all will be well. This is not high-minded, esoteric thinking, but rather, it is practical thinking that contains the idea to "look inward to solve outward issues" and was one of the core beliefs of the Lemurians. It also pushed them into action and invention quicker than other societies to follow, for they viewed the practical as something very much aligned with spiritual values.

In Lemurian, the word *Yawee* appears in both of the Lemurian layers. This is because it was a placeholder for the word "wisdom" in their language. Anytime it occurred, it meant that whatever followed would have wisdom connected to it. It was also an honoring of the great Lemurian scientist, Yawee, who gave them the technical design for almost everything that healed them.

The Lemurian language was a combination of linear words with a syntax construct [as you are reading now], combined with "word symbols" such as Yawee. Therefore, you couldn't read it in a linear way, as you are doing now. It was more conceptual. Eventually, the word symbols became only marks, almost like shorthand of sorts, and Yawee was one of those marks. There are languages you use today that continue to use the Yawee mark. Look for them, and smile at the revelation of where the mark came from...

... In Lemuria, they had something you do not. They were "fresh" from the seeding of the Pleiadian culture. Multidimensionality was a way of life, and they had no problem understanding something in a quantum state of seeming randomness. Were they advanced scientifically? No. They had no computers or telescopes. Yet they knew about DNA! They knew about the solar system and even of the galaxy. Did you ever wonder how so many of the ancients knew of galactic motion, yet when modern men with modern tools started traveling, they were afraid they would fall off the edge of the Earth? There was not even the acknowledgement that the Earth was round! Seemingly, humanity had lost everything they knew about the stars and were starting over – and you might say, that's exactly what happened.

As modern men became more scientific, they became more 3D. The ideas of quantum thought became separated into religion and spirituality. Some of it split off to become occult and even witchcraft. But the truth is that it was not seen as being solid science, for it wasn't predictable, couldn't be seen, and didn't make 3D linear sense. The ironic twist is upon you, for it is science that is discovering the quantum state, where particles behave in a random fashion and can be in two places at once. It is science that has discovered that the Universe seems to be "biased for life," against all odds. It is science that will eventually discover the elegance of multidimensional energy, ironically, with the help of those who are esoterically based, and who have spent years working with it.

So the Lemurians had their Temples of Rejuvenation. The "machines" in those places were not really machines as you know it, but rather "places of enhanced conscious thought." Isn't it interesting they called them temples? For later in history, you define a temple as a place of worship, but the Lemurians were not worshipping; they were dealing with the "temple inside." These were places of incredible, enhanced energy and information, all done with Human consciousness and magnetics in a process designed by a famous Lemurian scientist who outlived most of them.

Kryon channelling "DNA Group Three Layers Seven, Eight, and Nine" given in
Kryon Book 12, The Twelve Layers of DNA – 2010

Isn't it interesting that Yawee is a placeholder word for wisdom? What a coincidence that it is also the name given to Dr. Todd Ovokaitys by Kryon. Regarding the Lemurian name of

Yawee, it is actually composed of nine glyphs. The Lemurian writing, much like Sumerian, which became part of the Asian culture and the Indus culture, was glyph writing. The letters themselves had meaning. They were concepts, and not just sound. Nine of them comprised the name of Yawee.

Questions for Kryon:

It has previously been stated that female Pleiadians had a muscle in the vocal cord that allowed them to create sounds that Humans cannot. This leads to an assumption that the Pleiadian language is different than the Lemurian language. Perhaps this explains why the Anangu of Australia refers to the Pleiadians as the "ones whose names cannot be pronounced." What were the dynamics of communication between the Pleiadians and Humans?

Answer:

Everything you have derived from these past communications is correct. All over the galaxy, the humanoid form is the one that contains the "image of God" as you do. This also explains why your Human body is far, far beyond anything that the random chance of evolution could produce. It was designed, and has been the basic vehicle of intelligent life on awakening planets for millions of Earth years. You might say that the Human is an interplanetary design, and not from Earth at all. You simply didn't come from anything here (on the Earth).

Planet to planet, the part that evolution played created the subtle differences in looks and function for them all. Some of the humanoids on other planets started with one kind of functioning organ, and when it wasn't needed, it was discarded. Others have better or worse oxygen processing due to the subtly different atmospheres; but, in general, the planets are all in "the zone" of the attributes of your Earth. The humanoids are all carbon-based, with DNA, and they exist with other living animals from their own planetary evolutions.

The vocal cord differences were developed on the original home planet within the nine-star-system that they have. Of your star family lineage, only the Pleiadian has this attribute. The original home planet for them is in the solar system of what they called Star One (of course). It also has a name, but it can't be easily written here. As they developed space travel, and later, corporeal-consciousness travel (which they call "phasic displacement"), they did not find any other humanoid life on any of the other planets within their star cluster. Over more than a thousand years, they ended up populating the few other planets that could sustain life in the "zone" around the other stars in their neighborhood.

Their language can't be duplicated with an Earth Human's ability to speak. It requires sounding two tones at the same time, and their vocabulary was complex with these sounds. Interestingly, this, then, caused a written language that was almost completely conceptual, rather than one which sounded out groups of letters. Therefore, they used symbols which contained concepts, and still do. You will not find letters in the Pleiadian language writings.

Earlier it was mentioned that the language of the Egyptians, Israelis, and Polynesians were all derivatives of the original language of Solara Maru. Can you tell us more about this language?

Answer:
Continuing the last answer: Yes, the conceptual language of the Pleiadians then became the evolved symbol-based conceptual languages of your planet. So any language that uses mostly symbols to communicate are the ones we speak of. Also, some of these Earth languages became hybrid languages, with a little of both – conceptual symbols and sound-based letter-groups.

Take a look at the reasoning behind this: On all of the Pleiadian planets, the exact same thing happened over time to their language, which happened on Earth. When you separate cultures for long amounts of time, they become unique and the language then changes. Accents change and even new words are born. This happened to them as well. In order to keep a baseline for communication, the conceptual symbol-based language was developed so that no matter what happened within the many Pleiadian languages, they would still be able to fully communicate using the written one. That worked, but with the addition of a few special conceptual "letters" for each culture, which other cultures also learned as they needed. It also meant that instruction manuals, equipment, and teaching could all use the same symbols. It also meant that all labeling of anything would be understandable. You are actually discovering this with your "icons" for international understanding of some processes or signs.

Lemuria and Atlantis

Not everyone has heard about Lemuria, but almost everyone has heard about Atlantis. Atlantis is known beyond the metaphysical community. In fact, the mythical island of Atlantis has created a popular culture, and enjoys legendary status within mainstream film and literature. In addition, many Humans from around the world believe they had a past life in Atlantis. Why is Atlantis remembered so well, while Lemuria is shrouded in seeming obscurity by comparison? The answer is complex and attributed to several factors.

One of the significant reasons why Atlantis is remembered so well is attributed to the way our Akash works. Within our Akash is a soup of all our past, present, and future experiences. Our Akashic memories are felt and experienced energetically, not in a linear fashion. For example, you may remember a past life in Ancient Egypt, but the details, such as your name, the names of family members, the exact year, the precise location, and intricate details of everything that happened, are not evident. Within our Human bias of singularity, our Akash sees the significant events we have experienced as "one past and one history." It became *one perceived event* in our cellular structure remembrance, which Lee Carroll and Kryon have described as the "Sinking Island Syndrome."

Many Old Souls have had multiple "sinking island" experiences. What would create this pattern? The answer is attributed to the profound effect of the one-time Lemurian experience. The imprint of living in Lemuria created an Akashic drive for the reincarnated soul to be on an island with others of like mind. With free choice, the reincarnated Lemurians would often search for an island with an enlightened society. Given the dynamic nature of islands and their susceptibility to natural disasters, the continual desire to live in these locations greatly increased the potential of a "sinking island" experience. This is the reason why Kryon tells us that there was more than one civilization known as Atlantis, spread across a vast time frame.

Earlier we discussed how the mini-continent of Lemuria slowly sank, and how the Lemurians became a sea-faring nation (see Chapter One: Ancient Lemuria: The History of Lemuria). During several Lemurian Sisterhood meetings, Kryon revealed more information about the feeling of remembrance that Old Souls have with Lemuria and Atlantis. The following channelled messages from Kryon reinforces Lemuria's unique role in setting the Akash for the planet, and the connection to Atlantis.

Dear ones, Lemuria has a very rich history, and it's different from, perhaps, the other time capsules [NODES] that were on the planet where civilization and the seeding of the Human race began. I'm speaking about the creation of the Human Being who has the knowledge of light and dark. These are ancient places, tens of thousands of years old. But Lemuria was different from the rest.

My partner [Lee] speaks about Lemuria, and something that has not been proven geologically. However, I will tell you that, eventually, you will find evidence that the geological hot spot underneath Hawaii pushed up that mountain so high that it was the highest on the Earth. It expanded the size so this mountain could be considered a mini-continent. Now, this bubble of the hot spot is something we have told you about before. What we didn't tell you is that, in geological terms, it took a long time to be pushed up and a long time to sink.

It was fully pushed up when the Pleiadians got here, dear ones. When it went down, however, it didn't completely sink. It only sank to the tips of the mountain range, and that resulted in the chain of Hawaiian Islands that are there today. So the part of Lemuria that I will call the "sinking years" spanned many lifetimes. These lifetimes were frightening to many because the island continued to sink. It was obvious to many, however, that they had time. But "the sinking years" also created something new for the Akash of those who were there.

In the beginning, Lemuria was a *launching pad* for the Akash of the Human. What I mean by this is that you only had one life [incarnation] in Lemuria, and you came back somewhere else on the planet. Perhaps you now understand why the Temple of Rejuvenation was so important? You understood reincarnation and this special Akashic process in Lemuria back then. This is because you were carefully taught about it. This teaching was given to everyone.

Dear ones, this idea of the Akash is intuitive to all humanity. The first organized spiritual belief systems on this planet believed in reincarnation because they knew it at a cellular level. It was only later, in *modern* spiritual days, where you were talked out of it. So it's a *first intuitive* kind of thought. The Pleiadian teachers told you, literally, about this Akashic launching system. Again, this was a system where you only had one lifetime within Lemuria, and the subsequent lifetimes were experienced in other parts of the planet.

Lemuria was a *pressure cooker* of wisdom. No one could leave the island and no one could come because it was isolated by water; you didn't meet anybody new, and the traditions survived a very long time. The only thing you have that even came close to it on this planet is in Australia with the Aborigine culture. Thousands and thousands of years of one culture builds wisdom, and you were part of that.

So the time frame that we are talking about is the sinking years of Lemuria, and the lifetimes that were lived there. You were not all there at the same time, dear ones, but you participated in the same kinds of rituals and honorings and birth ceremonies, because they never changed. So what I talk to you about now is not about family camaraderie, where you were all together in one spot. I talk about the fact that you were all participating in the same kinds of things in the lifetime you spent there.

Now, you knew about this reincarnation: A Human life would come in, a soul would be launched from Lemuria, and it would have no Akash at all until it got somewhere else. Now listen: Many would reincarnate in Europe, and they would have an Akash of "a sinking island"! Welcome to *"the sinking island syndrome"* – which would then become the legend of "Atlantis" of today. This is why so many Humans place Atlantis in the Pacific, when actually it may have really been in the Atlantic. The actual places called Atlantis (there were three of them) were all in different locations. However, they echoed the *sinking island Akash* of the Lemurians.

That which is *Atlantis* is complex, for it actually responds to *many* Akashic energies that you combine into one feeling called Atlantis. However, all this actually started in Lemuria. So the Lemurians who lived during the "sinking times" had an influence that many of you now carry in your Akash: a memory of what you feel is Atlantis.

When we speak about the traditions, who you were, and what you did, I want you to know that these laid the groundwork for who you are today. Perhaps you didn't understand that? Dear ladies, when you understand that you were the Akashic launching pad of the Earth in those years, it was all about reproduction. Every child you ever had, would never have another life in Lemuria, and neither would you. It changed how you taught, and how you looked at your own life. Some of these things shape who you are today, and why you might be here listening to [and reading] this today.

Kryon live channelling given during a Lemurian Sisterhood Meeting in Calgary, Canada – May 23, 2015

Question for Kryon:

Kryon Book 13, The Recalibration of Humanity, was about the beginning of a New Earth, a result of the recalibration of self, of the planetary grids, and dark and light. As we begin to recalibrate and rewrite our future, how will this change the Akashic remembrance of the sinking island events?

Answer:

You must understand a basic concept that we have tried to give you since we started talking about DNA. Here it is: As goes the degree of functionality of DNA, goes the degree of functionality of everything around you, including Gaia (nature). We will call this "The Awakening Principle."

This means that, as you evolve, so do some of the processes and attributes around you that you never thought were related to you. Already, this planet has rid itself of plague. Think about it: More people living together within a seeming runaway population increase, should logically create a greater hotbed for biological mutation, and the far greater ability for microbes to develop that would also create runaway plague and disease. Yet it didn't and won't. Being cleaner didn't eliminate this from your culture – your consciousness did.

As you continue to evolve and there is more light than dark, Gaia will respond to this Human growth in other ways as well. You will have better growth of food, and insects won't be as interested (you will see). Disease will not be as deadly or virulent, and even the most aggressive types of cancers will diminish from your societies.

The Crystalline Grid will start delivering better remembrances and so will your Akash. The "sinking island syndrome" is a metaphor for Lemurians only remembering the horror and frustration of their sinking island, and an Akash that only remembers bad things. This is changing.

Does all this stretch your belief? If it does, remember the profound ideas from those involved in the original intuitive spiritual system on the planet: "oneness with everything" was the idea, and without a prophet. This is a core truth concept, and an accurate one.

The reason for this planet is for Humans to have a test of light and dark, for the greater evolvement of the galaxy. Planet after planet has done this. First, the inhabitants of these planets are seeded (DNA change) and they learn about the Creator and realize that they are not alone. Then, they understand about the one God instead of many. Next, they either destroy each other because they disagree about resources or about how the "one God" works, or they start understanding the oneness of it all. Finally, if they get through the war stage, they start to awaken to the idea that they are part of a larger galactic family and start to evolve as a planet.

Through all this, they also begin to understand the Awakening Principle and begin to expect an Akash that delivers supremely benevolent help for them. We taught you the concept of "Mining the Akash" so you would understand the "Awakening Principle" and you would understand the true reason for the Akashic Record.

The true reason the Akashic Record exists is to let Humans remember the experience and wisdom from one life to another. This allows Humans to grow during lifetimes instead of wallow in dysfunction and war, starting over each time they arrive and trying to work puzzles again and again that end up terminating their civilizations. What if each birthday you forgot everything and had to start over in reading, in school, and in learning life? This is what it has been like, with Humans only having an Akash that sat there in mystery, with occasional remembrances that were negative. This is due to very low functioning DNA, in which your Akash is stored.

Now you know. Your Akash is awakening and will start bringing you good memories and help you to use what you earned – lifetimes of knowledge, wisdom and Human know-how.

CHAPTER TWO

The Women of Lemuria

The women of Lemuria represented the society's spiritual consciousness. Similar to the Anangu at Uluru, it was the Lemurian women who were the Shamans and gave guidance to their community. This shamanic knowledge was well known, deeply respected, and absolutely necessary for daily survival. The men counted on this. The children depended on this, and it was simply the way things were done. The women were the spiritual center and the connection to the Creative Source.

In addition, the Lemurians understood they were part of the Earth. Each day, they honored and greeted Gaia, for this was the basic training from the Pleiadians. They understood that Gaia reflected back the honoring it was given. The men counted on the women's connection with Gaia. They counted on the women for predicting and changing the weather through their quantum awareness. They depended upon the women for counsel and guidance on where to fish and hunt. The men understood the shamanic energies held by the women and counted on it for everything.

The divine guidance that was received intuitively by the women allowed them to take care of the men. With the men's agreement, the women were the spiritual guides because they had the intuition and the connection with the Creative Source. It was absolutely natural and normal in the exact same reasoning and logic as to why women gave birth, not men. They had the "equipment" for it. If you were to ask a Lemurian man about the women being the spiritual guides, his reply would be, "Isn't it this way everywhere?" Gender-specific tasks were known and understood by Lemurian society.

Today, the shamanic teachings of the Lemurian women are being re-established, thanks to the Akashic awakening of Mele'ha (see Chapter Four: The Lemurian Sisterhood). Mele'ha is Dr. Amber Wolf's Lemurian name, identified by Kryon, and it has been revealed that Mele'ha was a teacher and leader of women in Ancient Lemuria during the last 500 years of Lemurian civilization. In 2011, Dr. Amber (Mele'ha) Wolf founded the Lemurian Sisterhood, as the modern-day representation of the ancient teachings from the Pleiadian Star Mothers. When Dr. Amber asked Lee Carroll about the Lemurian Sisterhood, here is what Kryon said:

The original Lemurian Sisterhood was practiced within all parts of Lemuria, both the mother mountain (Hawaii), and the descendant islands and mainland settlements (such as Rapa Nui, New Zealand, and Mt. Shasta). It lasted far past the "Akashic growth centuries" and continued to spread around the Earth, until it was all but forgotten due to survival attributes and the beginning of the conquering eras of your history.

It outlasted the "exclusive expression" attributes of the original Lemuria and made it into some of the most secret societies all over the Earth. It was renamed and even denied by those women who kept it dear, but eventually, the Priestesses themselves perished due to the unbalance that was rolling over humanity. But it never left the Akash of the Old Soul. Like the whispers of a past love, it was always ready to re-emerge and rekindle itself with the fire of compassion for all of humanity.

The marker has been passed, and the new calendars are being prepared. It's now time to remember and resurrect the sacred balancing methods of the past, and push them into the future.

Throughout several channelled messages, Kryon often refers to the Sisterhood of Lemuria. However, in subsequent channels, we discover that the term "Lemurian Sisterhood" was never used in that culture. Kryon is honoring the Akashic remembrance of Mele'ha, and recognizes that the modern Lemuria Sisterhood and the sisterhood in Ancient Lemuria really is one and the same. Kryon has revealed much about Lemuria, especially the role of women, during the Lemurian Sisterhood meetings. Your interest in reading about the "Women of Lemuria" is very telling about who you are, and what you wish to create for yourself in this life. The whole purpose of the original Sisterhood was to allow those who participated in it to retain and hold a specific energy so that, in future incarnation's, feminine wisdom would be passed on to others. Kryon explains:

You are Old Souls and have come to this meeting now rekindling some old memories because you feel it deep within. Your Akash rings with it – the truth of it, and the beauty of it. We have told you that the Sisterhood is unique. It has to do with the culture of Lemuria, but more than that, it has to do with the beginning, the posturing of Human nature itself. In the beginning, and in some of the indigenous even today, there is an acknowledgement that those who would give birth would also carry the spiritual center of the tribe. This attitude is about the giving of life, which then gives an *edge*, perhaps, to the female, a consciousness that would have the ability to produce and understand life. So the spiritual part of living within Lemuria often passed to you, not completely, but to set the stage. In Lemuria, that's what you did. You gave spiritual balance to the whole.

Extending the information earlier tonight, the ceremonies that you did back then were very primitive. They lasted a great amount of time, and they were the beginning. This is an age where we ask you to rekindle the intent and the purpose, the spirituality, and the beauty. The planet is becoming more mother-like. It is more caring, more compassionate, and the entire Earth needs this intent and grounding that you are accomplishing. However, you are doing this in a new fashion. At this time, it is being tailor-made in this new energy by Mele'ha, who is a modern woman with an ancient remembrance. Now, Mele'ha existed [lived] through many life spans of others in Lemuria, and we haven't really discussed this before.

She lived a very long time as Mele'ha in society. She lived literally three times longer than most of you lived. This was accomplished by her association at the top of the mountain at the Temple of Rejuvenation. This is where the elite were asked to come, right or wrong, in a system that, indeed, was socially primitive. But there had to be Human teachers who remained through a number of generations, and she was one of those who were taught from the original Pleiadian source. This gave her the ability to be rejuvenated, and she was. So, she was a teacher for a very long time and there were many, many women who passed under her tutelage. She taught that which was the original intent, not just the ceremonies, but wisdom. There was wisdom in Mele'ha. Her teacher was full Pleiadian. Only one generation of humanity received this association, then incarnated into other places.

Now I want to give you information that makes you appreciate what happened in the Sisterhood. Throw away the idea that you were a number of women that just came together socially for a time of ceremony to help the tribe, to help Lemuria. Instead, this was your life purpose. Not all women were in the Sisterhood, right or wrong. There was a system of who could, and who could not, be included. I will not go into that now. It was a circle of women who felt a certain way and who carried that which was the searching energy of how to proceed with the wisdom of life.

The whole purpose of the Sisterhood was to allow you to retain and hold that specific energy in later incarnations and continue passing on this feminine wisdom to others. It would be a soft wisdom that would then affect everyone around you. Now, this was the intent, but with free choice, Earth could go any way it wanted.

However, you had the ability to plant the seeds for many generations to come, and you did. You might say you were trained for this.

What is your individual remembrance? Can you picture a group of women at sea level [next to the ocean] having wonderful, beautiful ceremonies? Can you feel the soft trade winds blowing as the sun sets, and then remember the moon coming out without cold evenings? What do you picture? Are you aware that you were dark-skinned with black hair? All of you Lemurians were the precursor to the Hawaiians.

Now, what I want to tell you goes beyond ceremony and spirituality, and has to do with feminine bonding. You will appreciate this. In Lemuria, the Sisterhood encompassed everything important to you. Everything in your life, and the things that I have not told you about, were beautiful experiences beyond comprehension. Imagine, the Sisterhood was there when you gave birth to your first child. All of you had children unless you were barren. This was simply the way of life in a primitive culture. You all gave birth, and when you did, there was a protocol. The Sisters were there. Every child born on the small continent of Lemuria had the Sisterhood around it. Imagine the child's awakening and the consciousness with all of the women participating! You would touch the hands or the body of the one giving birth. You were there through her cries or her pain or perhaps even her death. If there were complications, the Sisterhood was there.

Each of you knew that you had this support. If there were birth issues, or in case you didn't make it and your child did, the Sisterhood would be there. The Sisterhood would be responsible for raising the child – the ones who were of feminine energy and were compassionate and had the spiritual seed. If you died, it would be in peace, not in frustration. But that was the exception, for most were very healthy and had wonderful, experienced help during these moments.

Imagine giving birth and having the joy of this profound event with the Sisters, instead of the way it is now. Each one of you had the hand of another in a circle, holding hands, culminating in the hands being held by the one giving birth. If it were not possible to hold the hand for some reason, then you would touch the body. It was always a circle. At the moment of birth, the circle was complete and you did something unusual, very unusual and spectacular. When the child was born, at the first cry, you would release your hands and applaud and sing, "Welcome to Earth!" That was the first sound that the child heard – the Sisterhood applauding and singing as the child took its first breath.

When a Sister passed over and you knew it was eminent, and if it was possible, she went out the same way she came in – holding her hands and singing. It was a joyful, compassionate event – a goodbye ceremony with the Sisterhood.

It's not just about spirituality, but about compassionate cama-raderie – life and death, purpose and beauty. If you later could pass that to the planet, can you imagine how soft it would be? The honor-ing of birth in this way, the honoring of death in this way, was the lesson for all. It's about life itself being soft, compassionate, and beau-tiful. This is the Sisterhood in all that it encompasses; this is the Sisterhood and I was there.

In your mind right now, feel the breeze blowing through your long, black hair as you sit with your feet in the water, as you did before, remembering what it was like.

Kryon live channelling given during a Lemurian Sisterhood Meeting
in Atlanta, Georgia – February 14, 2015

What a beautiful way of honoring birth and death. What about the birthing process? In Lemuria, the women had a water birth. In Ancient Egypt, some rock carvings are rumored to depict the water births of pharaohs. Similarly, the Minoan civilization on the island of Crete created temples for the women to give birth in water. Within the Hawaiian Islands, it is believed that thousands of generations have been birthed in the water. Water birth is also found to have occurred in many other indigenous cultures. In the next channel, Kryon further explains about our Pleiadian Mothers and the celebration of birth.

The Pleiadians were the teachers in Lemuria, and it was often hard to tell the difference between them and the Humans back then. This was because many of them were what you would call *hybrids*, whose mothers were from the stars but the fathers were not. That would be similar to Yawee. He had a direct parent who was Pleiadian. This represented some of the first Human souls on the planet to have a mother and a father who were truly from different worlds. This, indeed, was actually part of the Human "seeding" process, where DNA was changed for all future generations. The Pleiadian DNA influence was "gene dominant" in your biology. This was the process in every place the Pleiadians had come on the planet.

Further information: Last week, we described a circle of Lemurian sisters that were together celebrating birth and death. At that channelling, my partner did not recognize the significance of what was actually happening, so we will extend this information now. As he channels, sometimes he does not have your consciousness, so he reports that which he sees as it goes through his filters. He saw you around a birthing pond and he did not see the significance of an underwater birth. This is the way it worked in Lemuria, for at the time, as it is now, the water was warm. An underwater birth is symbolic for many things, and was also very healthy for the child. The salt water was healing; it is the right temperature, and being born into it simply extends being part of the fluid of the mother. The child is comfortable with the birth, and is suspended in the water until it is time to cut the cord. Then it is pulled up and its first cry is heard. It is a more gentle experience and you were part of it.

It is interesting, perhaps, to you to also know that not all females in Lemuria were part of the Sisterhood. Right or wrong, the civilization and the society was structured as a *beginning consciousness*. It would, therefore, be an "unevolved" society to you now. You were elected to the Sisterhood by the various families to represent them in the Sisterhood, so the Sisterhood actually became those who would later become elders. It would be a special group in training for later eldership.

Indeed, spirituality was "women's business," but whereas perhaps you thought you were simply part of all of the women, you were not. Lemuria was larger than you think, and the population grew even larger. Yet, the Sisterhood did not, so you see, it was an elite group, a selected group, and an elected group. The election was by those who were the most representative of the female Pleiadians.

The models were there of consciousness [The Pleiadians], and you reveled in their angelicness and their compassion and their benevolence to you – a long-lasting female template.

Kryon live channelling given during a Lemurian Sisterhood Meeting
in Sacramento, California – February 21, 2015

How did the "Sisterhood" of Lemurian women work? What were the roles of the women and men? Who was in charge? Kryon explains:

Lemuria was one of the first civilizations of humanity to have any teachers from the stars. It was original, new, and it was basic. However, what you had was an acknowledgment of what the gender-specific tasks were for your culture. There was no vote about what you did. Instead, it was innate understanding, intuitive, and common sense to all of you.

The women gave the men advice from the stars. They had the intuition to do that. No one ever questioned whether the women should do what they did, just like no man ever questioned whether the women should give birth – and this isn't necessarily about the biology of a woman. It's totally about how the brain was *wired*.

The woman's brain is the one that was nurturing, caring, and intuitive. She was wired to raise the children, and was "connected." The men's tasks were clear as well, and their responsibilities were in other areas, but they needed the women a great deal in the Lemurian culture. The women actually did more work then, than they do now, due to their expanded spiritual intuition.

The women were tasked with knowing the potentials of what might happen. They had intuition of when the weather would be right, when the oceans would be right for fish, and more. I've painted this picture before, but where it differs from what you might think is what I'm going to tell you now.

You live in an elegant society and one that is enabled. It's enabled with history and experience and the sophistication of years of practice. In Lemuria, you're dealing with a very, very basic society. First, it had no history at all. There was no experimentation with anything even close to democracy. Democracy is an evolved idea, from years of living with other systems. None of those things were there that you feel are "normal" today. In fact, the Lemurian culture was extremely linear, as you might expect from anything that is elementary, or "a beginning."

Women's meetings: You may find this funny, but there was no circle when it came to the Sisterhood. The only time they worked in a circle was when they assisted with underwater birth. That's the only time. Every single meeting was done with the women sitting in a straight line seating arrangement. The elders sat in the front row, and the younger ones sat in back. There was one leader of the group, and that leader was the only one who was allowed to speak – ever. The idea that some women would stand up and give their opinion was several thousand years too soon!

The same thing happened with the men. The elders were in charge, and the younger ones sat in back. The younger ones were always in training and they weren't even considered part of the group until they sat in the front row. This front row seat had to be "earned" from years of being a good, efficient provider and builder for the culture.

These are the things you face with elementary societies. So, the very first thing I tell you is that what you have now is much, much grander and elegant. You can steer things in this, your modern circle, in ways that they never could in Lemuria. So we don't ask you to emulate them or what you remember. We don't ask you to try and return to a less elegant time. What we ask you to do is to graduate from what was, to what is.

So the whole idea of a Lemurian Sisterhood is to create a resurgence of appropriate shamanship within women of the Earth. It's a gentle resurgence, dear ladies, not a revolution. It is one where men would be attracted, because of what you do and what you have that is exceptional and different. The gentleness of it will attract the men. That's different than you might expect. You might say, *"Well, who was in charge in the Sisterhood?"* In this linear society, it was always the main leader. So there was no leader of this area or that area. There was "the leader," and the leader did the work of deciding much of what happened in the culture. In the timeline that we have spoken of, Mele'ha did all the work of leadership.

You might ask, *"Well, how were the women involved? Did they influence Mele'ha's decisions? She couldn't do absolutely everything"* Yes. They didn't vote, but rather, they "influenced." It's an interesting way they made decisions: Only the front row was involved and they did it through hand signals of who was, and who was not in a certain mind to do a certain thing. Remember, this was basic and simple. There would be a collective reaction only from the front row elders, and Mele'ha could override any of them. This was not a democracy. Rather, it was truly a very basic cultural behavior. Later, it became what you saw with a queen and her court, where very subtle signals were given to the leader, as to what the women had in mind.

It isn't that way today. Today you have an opportunity to carry into your Sisterhood that which you have earned: The enablement, the decision-making, the softness, and the equality you feel. But here's what I really wanted to tell you: In that original culture, the women took their power and the men liked it, needed it, and expected it. It was the specialty of women to do this.

If you asked any woman then, how did that feel? They would say, *"What do you mean? How does it feel to eat with your mouth? It feels correct normal, it is right. Why do you ask something so unusual?"* No one was afraid of being a Shaman ... but you are, today. So that's the next step, ladies: Accepting the mantle of the past. Accepting that mantle of a wise and mature advisor.

So if you're going to emulate this Lemurian past, I want you to try and remember what it's like to feel full empowerment, and to know that you belong here, doing what you're doing. Remember that it will not "upset the applecart" for you to find mastery. Listen: What women have that men don't, is natural mastery and elegance. When someone has a beautiful countenance, and is a beautiful example of caring, love, and compassion – They can win over anything and anyone on this planet. You know I'm right!

Women, take your power! Because the power we speak of is the same one we talk about all the time. It's love, compassion, and the sense to use it with wisdom and gentleness.

Kryon live channelling given during a Lemurian Sisterhood Meeting
in Phoenix, Arizona – January 16, 2016

One of the attributes of the Lemurian Women is the power of love. Their love is based on compassionate action, caring, kindness, patience, tolerance, and wisdom. These attributes are going to be noticed by others, regardless of gender. These attributes are also available, whether you experienced a life in Lemuria or not. What about other aspects of Lemuria and the teachings given by the Shamans? Were all women involved? Was there an initiation for women? These questions and more are answered by Kryon in the following channel:

We speak now of profound feminine wisdom, which was a collective event in Lemuria. What that means is that it was something that was above anything you would normally now find anywhere on the planet. Lemuria was different from anywhere you might study in current history.

Last night we said that this "Land of Mu" was the *launching pad of the Akash*. What this means is that, as the souls were birthed

107

through your loins, you were always aware that you were delivering "first time souls" to Earth (the first time that a soul came to this planet). These were also souls who would not be returning to Lemuria in any future lifetime. You were helping to give them an original imprint of humanism, which they would remember first when they reincarnated to other places on the planet. It would be their "starting consciousness" when they arrived again in a future life.

In past channellings, we have given you some of the minutiae of what it was like in this place called Lemuria. We've also told you that, as you sit here listening, you don't necessarily represent one family or one group that was in Lemuria at the same time. The Sisterhood was practiced in Lemuria over many generations, but we tend to concentrate on the last few hundred years, since these were the most developed. So, together, you are remembering many Sisterhoods, or the Akashic energy of being together in that way. The Akashic Record is like that: It remembers energy, and not a timeline. So you actually are participating in something that was spread over a great deal of time, which was sacred, and which never changed.

There is much to discuss about your time in Lemuria, and you might find the history to be interesting. In fact, some of it may resound to you, and you might actually *remember* things. However, tonight we're going to do something that is different to start: We are going to interact in channel with Mele'ha, child of a Star Mother, sister to Yawee, and one of the last priestesses to exist in Lemuria. It is through her Akashic awakening that this meeting even exists at this time. I'm going to ask her what she would like to talk about in these few moments we have, and let that guide the direction of this particular short message we will have for you.

Mele'ha: I feel the questions of the ones who sit before us: Was I there? Wasn't I there? What did I do? What was it like? Who were we, as Sisters? Did we teach? Did we learn? Where were our children? What was the progress like as women having one life in Lemuria?

Kryon: It is a good direction to go; however, there are many questions here that we will not address at this time, but we will supply you with some answers from the most asked questions in this group, about what you actually did in that land of "one lifetime."

Dear ones, the Sisterhood was extracurricular. You were women in a society that operated similarly to most societies. It was not a culture that was sacred to the degree that everyone went around wearing the same color, or bowing to leaders, or watching what they said and did. It was a good life with normal kinds of living.

Where were your children? They were being taken care of by women who were not in the Sisterhood. You were busy! We just gave you new information: The Sisterhood did not necessarily contain all the females in the villages. If you haven't gleaned this fact yet from the many channellings, age was profoundly respected in both genders and given a great deal of honor. I want you to stop for a moment and think about something: In most indigenous societies today, the emphasis is on the ancestors and the elders. In Lemuria, there were no ancient ancestors, but rather, only a generational family tree. So, past lineages didn't carry the emphasis of the kinds of ancient ancestors that indigenous have and look to today. So, the only place of real honor and wisdom was given to those at various stages of life.

The younger females would not be in the Sisterhood until a certain age. You might have guessed that it revolved around menses, the first one. That event initiated them into an honored reproductive cycle that you respected more than just *a potential childbearing female.* It represented a responsibility for bringing in new souls with the new Star Mother DNA of life for humanity (the 23 pairs of chromosomes). Everyone knew this, for it was taught, even to children, as one of the spokes of the Lemurian Teaching Wheel.

After first menses, there were some years of training and childbearing, and only after that was there a time when these younger women could be "Sisters in training." You may have guessed that the true Sisterhood in Lemuria was made of advanced shamanic-trained women, all of whom were being taught their final lessons by both the Star Mothers and the direct female children of the Star Mothers (like Mele'ha).

Dear ones, all women who were able gave birth to children seasonally (as the culture dictated) for as long as they could during their lives. They didn't have one child a year, but rested their biology for two to three years between children. There were also years when children were not conceived at all due to various reasons: shortages of existing resources, or extremely severe weather. These were things that influenced the quality of life, or the future quality of life. For instance, you also had years of no children to keep the population down, intuitively knowing about the quantity of sustainable resources for the future, or a cycle of weather that would last a few seasons. Still, this created many children for the village. Even as "Elder" women in the Sisterhood, you continued to have children. Over your childbearing lifetime, you may have averaged up to eight births each. However, as "Sisterhood members," your children were mostly cared for daily by the younger women.

The ladies who are here (in the room), all of you, are not accidentally involved in this meeting. What is it that drew you to the chair tonight? City after city, Mele'ha gives an invitation for any women to attend, who might *resound* to the Sisterhood. So it's not necessarily against all odds that all of you were part of this group of Lemurians, because she is collecting Old Souls in these meetings. Old Souls who are females in this lifetime are that gender by design. The design, dear ones, is that you would hear the words, feel the energy, and *remember*, if you wished to. This is not accidental.

Those of you who answered this esoteric call to be here were part of this history. So I just answered that question of, *"Was I involved?"* Yes. This weekend, you were in the right place at the right time to experience this Akashic calling.

The other thing that gives this idea credibility is that, throughout centuries, there were thousands of you involved in Lemuria. So, many are resounding to it. All of you here were part of a Lemurian lifetime, over many years. All of you here tonight were part of a Sisterhood group within the last Pachakuti (500 years) in Lemuria. That's not such a stretch of logic.

Again, I want you to know that, unlike your societies of today, the traditions were quite static. That is to say, that they didn't change much at all. There was not the kind of energy around newness or the evolution of the desire to have things different, which permeates your culture today. So, for generations, there was sameness, and it was kept that way by the Star Mothers, who knew emphatically that Lemuria was an Akashic school, and that the core truths did not change over time. This means that, collectively, you all remember the same kinds of things, and the same kinds of energies.

One of the questions was, "What were you doing all day?" You were doing what women have done in society forever. Yet, as members of the Sisterhood, there were specific ceremonies and activities that you were part of, which may surprise you. What were your men doing? What do you think they were doing? They were fishermen. In Hawaii (Lemuria), fish was the main food source. Did you know that as early in the morning as you could imagine, the men got up to prepare for the hunt for fish and other edible sea life, and the Sisterhood was involved in sending them off! Why? This was part of the wisdom that you women were known for: Bringing life and food to their nets.

You were an active part of all of the societal elements, even those which involved the men. There were no demeaning positions for either gender. The men would fish and bring you the catch, and you would prepare the food around the fish (which included some harvesting, preparation, and storage). The men would cook the fish, and were proud of this task. Cooking the fish was done collectively, and not individually for a family unit. The "fish pits" for cooking were special and the men knew this craft, which was passed down from their grandfathers. This had been the way of it for generations. You never were allowed near those cooking pits. It was just for men.

The ceremonies that you had were extracurricular, and you had plenty to do. From dawn to dusk, you worked in a society that had to feed itself, and work the issues of life. In Lemuria, a great deal of these issues needed your advice and intuition. The Sisterhood was tasked with guidance for the society, and this included all things spiritual. But we haven't even gotten to the fun part yet.

There were special social times that involved the men, but which you introduced with ceremony. There was dancing, a lot of it, and music, a lot of it. You would be interested to know that all of these things started with the blessings from the Sisterhood. This was how this society saw you, as the women of Lemuria.

There was a full and complete acknowledgment within the society of the importance of the wisdom of the feminine. The women were the ones who would bear and care for the children, harvest and store the greens, prepare the meals, and advise the entire culture. This idea of women's intuitive guidance was shared by the men, totally and completely. There was a confluence of consciousness that knew who the Sisterhood was.

The society knew the roles of men and women, and honored the talents of who did what, the best. The men counted on you to set the energy of the day, to be the gentle ones they loved, and to birth the children at the pools with honor and healthy wisdom. You cared for the little ones properly and correctly, got them to the Teaching Wheel schools, and even had the wisdom to know when to give birth and when not to (as discussed). However, you should know that the men cooperated fully with that, too. They understood that this kind of advice would create a better life for all, and women had this gift of "knowing."

You were the ones who advised the men not to fish when unseen storms were coming. You were the ones to know where the fish were, from day to day, and the men loved this! You created a wisdom within a society that kept everyone alive, and gave honor to the core truths of the Creator. The whole of Lemuria depended upon you for ceremony in birth, fun, marriage, sacredness, food, and even in death. You were the priestesses of the Akash.

Kryon live channelling given during a Lemurian Sisterhood Meeting
in Regina, Canada – May 24, 2015

Pleiadian Mothers

At a certain point in time, when humanity was ready, the Pleiadians came to Earth to give Humans divinity. According to Kryon this happened 200,000 years ago, when the female Pleiadians came to mate and reproduce with the male Humans on Earth. Such a statement sounds fantastic, almost like an elaborate plot in a science fiction movie, and yet, this is the creation story as given by Kryon and many indigenous tribes all over the planet. Is there any proof of this intervention?

Internationally renowned scientist Gregg Braden has provided compelling science on what might possibly be evidence of our spiritual seeding. His latest book, *Human by Design*, documents startling discoveries about our DNA, in particular, Human Chromosome 2. This chromosome is responsible for our enlarged brain; our capacity for emotion, sympathy, empathy, compassion; and our memory and learning processes. What makes Chromosome 2 so mysterious is that it's a relic of an *ancient telomere to telomere fusion* of two ancestral chromosomes. Gregg Braden tells us that the timing, precision, and result of this ancient DNA fusion suggest something beyond evolution as we know it.

When did this ancient DNA fusion occur? You guessed it – 200,000 years ago. The female Pleiadians carried out the seeding of divinity, altering our DNA in the process. They came to Earth and needed the males to impregnate them. This is one of the reasons you almost never hear about male Pleiadians. The creation stories relating to the Pleiades always refer to the Seven Sisters. The seeding process was totally accomplished by the females and it lasted for many, many generations. The Pleiadian women had many children over a great deal of time, and in the process, taught the Human women about sacred birth, and Pleiadian consciousness. Those born from Pleiadian Mothers, male or female, then had the divine "seed" and would pass it on through normal Human to Human reproduction. For many, this concept is difficult to believe, but, indeed, it has happened many times throughout the galaxy with one ascended planet seeding another – one at a time.

The Lemurian experience was special and the "most pure" experience because it was sequestered to the mini-continent (of MU) in the Pacific. Much happened in Lemuria that could not have happened in any of the other creative seeding places. This is because there was no dispersion of Humans "leaving town" and starting a new settlement elsewhere. This created generations of Lemurians that had the same original (Pleiadian) information and the same culture. The Pleiadian Mothers and teachers physically remained in Lemuria for an uncommonly long time, and in a multidimensional state, they are still there! The one-lifetime Lemurian experience, therefore, created profoundly important, sacred information and remembrance within the Akash. Here is what Kryon tells us about the ones who did the original *seeding*.

I want to talk about the Pleiadians. This subject may seem so far removed from the reality of today, but it is no farther removed than when we speak of Lemuria. You carry within you the seeds of the Pleiadians, and it changed your DNA. I have said this before. I have also told you that it would be foolish for one moment for you to think that your expressions [lifetimes] on Earth are the only ones that you have had in this galaxy! For many of you have been on other planets, and almost all of you have been Pleiadian. So I would like to tickle the Akash this evening and see if you can relate to anything I'm saying.

The ancients reported the landings of the Seven Sisters, and like so much of history, there is a confluence of stories that were intermingled together to create one seeming mythology. As expected, the facts are not quite right and the timing is compressed. History does this repeatedly; it keeps the essence of what took place, but the actual stories are enhanced. In the case of the story of the landing of the Seven Sisters, the stories are not exactly as it was. But the part that is totally and completely accurate and true is that these travelers were female.

Let me tell you a little bit about the Pleiadian consciousness. With their DNA working at greater than 80 percent of maximum efficiency, they had mastered what I would call *the consciousness of physics.* Through their consciousness, they were able to supply things for themselves, create the energy they needed, and have a society that was peaceful. Indeed, they were explorers. However, they had also learned that *consciousness at 80 percent* creates the ability to do some things that are not in your reality whatsoever! Your Human consciousness created television. But show it to an ancient and it would be magic. But it's not magic; it's just you, creating things with normal physics, only with a higher consciousness of invention. This is how you must perceive the Pleiadians.

The ability of having a Shadow-Self, what I would call *being in two places at the same time,* is one of these things. You see, Pleiadians are corporeal, just like you are. Now, that's simple biology, and it never really changed. They are still corporeal. However, through their spiritual evolution, their bodies became better and healthier. This explains why it is that they are always reported as taller than you are. The height comes from nutrition perfection of balance to bone structure. There are no overweight Pleiadians. Now, your health issues come with your Akash, dear female [Light]worker. You might want to think about that. It comes with consciousness, not diet. Is it possible that even on this planet today, hidden in your Akash, are the secrets of good health? You do not have here on Earth what they ate, but in Lemuria you had the healthy consciousness that was applied to your own systems. Follow the dots: You can create a perfect body with your mind. Eventually, you can even be in two places at the same time.

Pleiadians, in general, are fair-skinned. The reason is that they do not have the attributes that you have with your sun. On their planets, and there were three, the sun is a little more distant than yours. They also are a little colder than you are most of the time. You will find that the experience that the Aborigines had with the Seven Sisters was different than reported. This is mainly because it was very uncomfortable for the women from the stars. It was simply too hot. But, indeed, these voyagers were female.

What you carry here is the tradition of the Seven Sisters. All over the planet, it was the females who came. Much like today, where you may send mainly men, they did the opposite, for exploration and spiritual encounter was women's work. They were corporeal, not their shadow selves. Their travel was not difficult. It was what you would call "entangled object reality." They, indeed, had crafts and some *machines*, but they were females.

The society of the Pleiadians had a very high consciousness. There was firm understanding and intuitive recognition of the part that females would play in higher consciousness. Even in your wisdom, you have had the saying, *"If women ran the world, they would never send their sons to war."* This is not exactly true, since there have been many women who were queens and leaders and who sent their countries to war. However, the basic premise is still true for the same reasons that the Pleiadian visitors were women. They hold the creation biology and, therefore, are seen as closer to God. This is a real holdover from a truism [basic truth] and the Pleiadians knew it.

You might ask how they could carry seed biology for the planet if the men weren't here for the process of reproduction, for their biological reproduction is very similar to yours. The answer is this: The originals, the ones who came first, the ones who met you, were the ones who had to be female. It's because of what they carried with them, which was the DNA alteration that you needed. Your future children would be a combination of Human and Pleiadian.

Later came the males. In their society, in a higher consciousness, they recognized the evolved role played between the female and the male. Higher consciousness was always a softer one, and it was always the female who led. Today, in your corporeal body, the brain hemispheres are connected differently for the female than the male. It was for theirs, as well. There's a connection between lobes for you that the males do not have. The connection gives you better insight to raise children, and the raising of the children is the issue. The females were first to land here as an honoring to the seeding of Earth. The mothers came first. Now, let's be clear – there are those in the room who have not given birth this time around, so what I tell you next, not all will relate to as much. However, all of you have given birth in your [Akashic] history.

There is an energy of giving birth that is unique to females, and which no male can ever understand or appreciate. Even if he is standing next to the bed, he can't feel it. It doesn't have to do with the joy or with the pain. Instead, it has to do with *giving birth*. From your loins comes your own biology! There is nothing like it and you know what I mean, ladies. There is nothing like it. So this is the ceremony, the reasoning, that the Seven Sisters constellation was actually named *The Seven Sisters*. Without any knowledge of the true creation story, astronomers clearly saw the feminine when they named the stars.

The profound energy of birth and rebirth, completely and totally, has been carried all the way through from the seeding ceremony to Lemuria to today. What you're going to do this evening as you gather around, metaphoric as it might be, is all about rebirthing the energy of Earth. Returning it, perhaps, to the original intent of free choice, where the females arrive first and have the ceremonies, paving the way with the softness of the love of Spirit and the Creative Source. It sets the intent of the land of a new planet so it would carry the softness and understanding of the birth of a child.

There's something interesting you should know. Woman might ask, *"As the Pleiadians progressed in their evolution, did they ever come to a place where they could have painless childbirth?"* The answer was, surprisingly, yes, but in their wisdom, they discarded it and returned to the natural way. They realized that all of the technology that cancelled the pain within the process of childbirth also changed the experience. It wasn't the same. A higher consciousness was able to eliminate chemical problems, but it changed the experience. The pain, they decided, was necessary. It gives you thought before you impregnate, and carries with it a real biological effect. *Do you want to do it?* It makes the intent stronger and the experience, although

117

painful, more profound. You may shake your heads in disbelief of this, but this really defines wisdom.

Your planet is going through pain right now as it births a new energy. The ceremonies you perform with only females are appropriate and correct for this time, for you supply the energy that only females know about – what it's like to give birth. Not the pain, but the love connection.

The biology of creation is yours. It continues to be yours as the new Human and the new energy is born. Listen: The new consciousness of this planet will come from the loins of the female Old Soul. I think you understand what I mean.

Kryon live channelling given during a Lemurian Sisterhood Meeting
in Madison, Wisconsin – July 26, 2014

Kryon discusses the difference between genders regarding the connection of our right and left brain hemispheres. This is referring to the corpus callosum, which is Latin for "tough body" because it is the largest connective pathway in the brain, and is made up of more than 200 million nerve fibers. Women are often regarded to be better at multi-tasking than men. Many tout the reason for this is due to women having a larger corpus callosum compared to men. Several scientists, however, refute these claims.

Is there any evidence that the connections in women's brains are different to men? The answer appears to be obvious in an article titled *"How Men's Brains Are Wired Differently than Women's"* found on the Live Science website. The article states that:

"The research, which involved imaging the brains of nearly 1,000 adolescents, found that male brains had more connections within hemispheres, whereas female brains were more connected between hemispheres. The results, which apply to the population as a whole and not individuals, suggest that male brains may be optimized for motor skills, and female brains may be optimized for combining analytical and intuitive thinking."

Source: https://www.livescience.com/41619-male-female-brains-wired-differently.html

The article cautioned about applying the results to individual men and women. It should be viewed as a generalization, not as a definitive truth. This is because scientists can't quantify how much an individual has male-or-female-like patterns of brain connectivity. If you are a male and reading this, it is highly likely that you have a strong level of connectivity between hemispheres. This may explain why females, as a gender, are the first to embrace spirituality, but some men, as individuals, can be highly spiritual and intuitive.

Kryon really invites us to ponder the energy of the divine feminine in a new way. The emergence of a new energy on our planet can be seen and felt as the *mother energy of compassion*. As we enter this new paradigm, the role of mothers is even more critical than ever before. The nurturing care, love, support, and guidance of mothers will determine the speed of the evolution of consciousness. Kryon emphasized all of these attributes in several Lemurian Sisterhood meetings, especially in the next two channels that follow:

This is a very special time. I want you to take a deep breath and relax. I am aware of who is here and what you would call a gender-specific group. I would like to review with you what I have said in the past about how reincarnation works with gender, because it is going to paint a picture for you of tonight and beyond.

When you come into this planet, lifetime after lifetime, how do you know what gender will be next? Does it matter? The answer is yes. Specifically, the female gender on the planet is the gentle one. It is the one that gives birth. All humanity is taught by the mother. It is important. Now, I have given the explanation of reincarnation and gender, and I'm going to give it again. Indeed, you take turns being both genders, but there is reasoning which gender you are, when you are, and also how many times you are.

The Human system calls for the same gender many times in a row. Every single one in the room has been female the last two times, and you know it and feel it. When you arrived this time, you were comfortable with your gender and in this, it is important you understand. If you were not comfortable with your body, at least you knew what you wanted, based on a past consciousness as a woman. All of this is to say that you are right where you belong as female energy this time around. Now, I have said that before, but what I have not said is that all of you are in the process of a *series* of being female. The next life will be, and the one after that will be. So this is a system, and you *own* this gender for a while. It truly has to do with the times, with what we have taught and what we are teaching today about a planet that is becoming more mother energy. Therefore, your task should be obvious.

What you do today may influence what happens the next time around, and even the next time. It's because this carryover is not just of gender, but of consciousness. This carryover of altered consciousness and grander, softer wisdom was given to be remembered by you. The changes you make today will also be remembered, and you will awaken again in the gender that you prefer, the one that you are used to, the one you desire, and the one that makes sense to your countenance – female. You will awaken into it with a greater comfort even than you did this time.

Now, depending on what you do next in this meeting will affect *you* many years from now, and even affect your next incarnation. What are you going to tell your *Innate* [smart body] tonight? I want to give you some hints. I want you to think about the concept of limitlessness. Whatever you want and whatever you think you want, I want you to think of it as ten-fold. You tend to limit yourselves to what you think you can be, based upon the past lives you have been. It reflects the countenance of the consciousness of the differences of male and female today. Let me reword that: You limit yourself because you have a bias of who you are within the culture you think you belong to.

How many filters are here within you that would put a limit of what you think you can do, based upon what a female is expected to do in your culture? If you approach it from that standpoint, it's not good enough. It just isn't good enough. The female carries the perfectness of birth. Every Human on the planet has come from your womb. Every Human! Don't forget that! It's not just that you are a female and that's what you do. Instead, you carry in your body and transfer to your baby the consciousness of who you are. It is the *consciousness engram programming* of every Human Being from now on who is born on Earth.

So, what is it that you are going to transfer this time and next time to those around you? What do you give to babies to come, if any? It's potentially the idea of limitless consciousness to the men and women who will be your children. It's the idea of who you can be, and what it means to be a Human Being. Just when you thought you were done with mothering! Now, this is not just the birth process, for you might be done with that this time around. It's the mothering of compassion. You can *mother* your family, you can *mother* your neighbor. It's about having compassion for everyone you are around – true compassion with action attached.

When the greatest masters of this planet walked the Earth, you could see the feminine within their masculinity. They were soft and you could see it in their eyes. They reflected that which came from their mother. Emulating the sweet spirit of the feminine of the planet is the secret to peace on Earth. You know this. Don't limit yourself within the affirmations to come in the ceremonies you are about to do. Know that you can be anything. This is a simple message for the women, who are the key to the softness of the planet.

Kryon live channelling given during a Lemurian Sisterhood Meeting
in Portland, Oregon – November 22, 2014

First this: The last time we were with you, we made a comment. I want to review it. We wanted to remind you that all of humanity passes through your womb. Some would say, *"This is not a big deal. It's simply animal energy and is simply the way it works."* Indeed, you might have said this eons ago, but in a sacred energy, it's different.

When the Pleiadians seeded this planet, they depended upon a process that you lost. The process was through the womb. That is to say, that as the Pleiadians populated the planet with the hybrids that they needed, who eventually became Human with new DNA, they depended on a process you have lost. Let me tell you what it was: When the Human fetus spends nine months in the womb, it shares your bloodstream. In the process, these pre-Humans are also existing within your Merkabah. In the process, they are also sitting in whatever soft, gentle energy it is that you have as a woman, which radiates from your DNA in a quantum field.

In those times, it was needed that these things be enhanced so that when children were born, they'd be different from past humanity. This was how the planet was seeded completely and is your creation story – general awareness of light and dark. The Sisters were responsible not just for the actual birth, but also of passing on that which was Pleiadian consciousness to humanity at that time. It was most successfully done in Lemuria.

Now, what I want to tell you is an extension of what I told you earlier today. New processes are starting to be part of real Human life. There's going to be a partial return to the Lemurian attitude. Listen, what is it that is missing on the planet right now? I speak to you now as a genderless piece of God. What is it that is missing? The answer: The compassion of mother energy. The planet still reeks with bravado and chest pounding.

But what you know is that if the Humans on the planet had more compassion, they would never kill each other! Indeed, they would never send their sons to war. This is what is balancing on the planet, and this is what we have told my partner to teach. But there's another thing that is beginning to change. There's going to be a return to a process. It's the process of how wisdom is passed to the child, and it's going to happen before birth. It's going to happen in the womb. It happens with the Old Souls who are female. There is a lot more work for you and that which you are going to be responsible for, women. It is the passing of the consciousness that you have into the child, no matter what gender it is. The children are going to receive it because they share your bloodstream, because they are there for nine months looking at your consciousness, the field that is you, which you call the sacred Merkabah. It's going to affect the fetus.

This is one of the attributes of soul-sharing, and we have talked about this attribute before. Did you wonder, perhaps, what the process was of spiritual evolution? It's going to come from mom! This is the reason for this meeting, it's the reason why there is a Lemurian Sisterhood. It's the same reason why there was one in Lemuria. These are the kinds of things that perhaps humanity will not believe at first, but they'll start to see later.

For Christians, a tremendous emphasis today is put upon the mother of Christ – more, perhaps, than what others would want to see. We speak of this now just so you'll know why. It's because, even within the system of organized religion with all male masters, you had to have the feminine energy! It was Christ's mother that helped pass to him who he was!

So this is the beginning, perhaps, of something that is completely new. You won't see it this time around, and you know that. Many of you, if not most, are not bearing children anymore. But when you come back, almost all of you will be female again. This is an honoring, and we have talked about this before. It is no accident that you are a female now. When you return, you will be female yet again. This is the plan, and there is comfort in this. So you know what it feels like to bear children. It's the other reason that you get together in meetings like this, to celebrate a new kind of impact you are going to have on all of humanity.

If you can think past your own Human death, if you can look at yourselves as eternal, then you understand you're going to be here a long time! In this perception, you're going to be passing wisdom to all humanity who passes through your womb. Humanity is ready for what you are going to give them! Blessed are you who have accepted this task and are here today, knowing that I'm telling you the truth.

Kryon live channelling given during a Lemurian Sisterhood Meeting in San Rafael, California – December 13, 2014

Kryon gives us new insights about the transference of energy, consciousness, and wisdom, which takes place during pregnancy. We have discovered that births in Lemuria were water births, accompanied by the Sisterhood surrounding the mother in a circle. Was there anything else unique to how the Pleiadians and Lemurians gave birth in Ancient Lemuria? The answer is yes, and Kryon explains further:

I want to tell you some things that I've never broached before, and my partner has no idea where this is going.

I want to talk about the importance of your reproduction. I want to talk about the honoring of it, and just briefly to speak of a couple of the attributes that perhaps you would not expect.

Birth was very, very special. It was because of what the Pleiadians had given you in your DNA, and the traditions of what it represented with a "first time Akash" on the planet. Ladies, unlike today, you totally controlled it with a wise and beautiful common sense system.

Birth in Lemuria was done seasonally. Reproduction was not 24/7 as it is here. It was seasonal. Taking an instinctual clue, perhaps, from the animal kingdom, it was done seasonally. The reason wasn't for food, for fish was the staple and it was plentiful. Instead, the plan was intuitive, and it kept the population in check and made sense for the whole culture.

Imagine, wise reproduction! This was something that the men cooperated with fully, for they understood the same things the women did. However, let me tell you something that you don't know. I want to talk about something, and again I tell you that my partner has no clue about this. In fact, he's stepped aside. I want to talk about menses.

There are places today within certain kinds of societies that will not let women "in a certain condition" into a certain place – because of this! In time, the attitudes regarding menses became archaic and ignorant compared to the way they were in Lemuria. You see, part of the woman's mystic was the privilege of menses! Remember: Reproduction was highly respected and given an especially high role in how the culture thought.

Ladies, when you were in that condition, you were raised above Goddesses! You sat in the front row with the elders! You wore a royal color and everyone knew it. It would indicate your status at the moment. Even when you were in seasons that were not correct for a seasonal birth, it was still hugely important. Can you see why? Do you understand this? Reproduction was important.

Lemuria was the launching pad for the Akash of humanity, and you were careful and honored it. So honored was it, Mele'ha, that this is one of the chief reasons for the Temple of Rejuvenation. It was so you'd always be young and have menses. So, life extension was not just because you wanted to live longer. It was to continue menses! It's a little different now, isn't it? I want you to think of this. I want you to think about honoring the feminine, and beyond.

Kryon live channelling given during a Lemurian Sisterhood Meeting
in Calgary, Canada – May 23, 2015

The suspension of pregnancy due to limited resources was also a practice adopted by the Anangu women living in Uluru. What an elegant solution to only have a baby when the environment around you supports its survival. Many cultures around the world today continue to face family planning issues. However, an evolved consciousness will eventually result in an elegant society that has wisdom around family planning.

The Pleiadian women in Lemuria were not only mothers, they were teachers, and what they taught created a profound energy within the Akash of those they taught in Lemuria. It is the reason why so many women have come together in one of today's

Lemurian Sisterhood meeting. It is the reason why you are reading this book. The gathering of women together is more than just
sharing the same gender. **It is about unifying the Akashic
remembrance of the Pleiadian Mothers**.

In Lemuria, over the periods of time that you were there, the ones
who were with you were your teachers. Dear ones, there was nothing
like it. On Earth, there was nothing like it. The Pleiadian Mothers
taught the Lemurian mothers. We told you in the past that Yawee,
the male who is here, the doctor who is here, had a Pleiadian Mother
who used to sing him lullabies. However, as teachers, the Pleiadian
Mothers taught women. So there's a strong differentiation between
being the child of a Pleiadian Mother, and being a student. Not all of
you were babies of Pleiadian Mothers. Most of you here were daugh-
ters of Lemurian mothers.

So let's get this straight. The Pleiadians were teachers and some
of them also bore children. Either way, these Pleiadian Mothers did
the master teaching, apart from the actual cultural teaching in
Lemuria.

However, what's in your Akash is the memory of sitting in front of
a Pleiadian Mother teacher and hearing that voice, which was unique
and special. It was not Human, but beautiful, and you were hearing
instructions for life from that voice.

I told you before that you carried the spiritual attributes of
humanity. You were the everyday Shamans. Everyday life shamanship
is what you were taught.

Now, we want to refer to the channelled message we gave earlier,
and some of you were here for it. It was called "The Great Escape." I
want to talk more about your *filters*. If you could remember those initial instructions, what about that Pleiadian voice? How many years
ago was that? How many lifetimes ago? Is it possible that this
remembrance might still be with you? And the answer is: Do you
remember your mother's voice from this lifetime? You can! It's in
there. It's in the Akash. Even if she's gone, you'll never forget it and

you will not forget the Pleiadian Mother teacher, either. That voice is still there, too.

She sang songs, even to her students, and that singing voice is still there, too. And when you connect with it, even esoterically, it starts to balance you and it returns you to the knowledge of your shamanic lessons. But what filters do you carry into this meeting today, which might get in the way of that? The filters we speak of are the same ones we gave you earlier tonight in channel when we spoke specifically about what the Akash carries.

You had one specific lifetime under the tutelage of a pure Lemurian – a Pleiadian. Only a few Humans on the Earth right now received this. That's what the Sisterhood celebrates – a remembrance of that.

What came later fills your Akash with other things. It clouds the issue completely. Can you sit here, women all, and clear yourself to such an extent that you can sense that first voice so you can hear it yet again? What does it tell you? Metaphysically, the instructions remind you that you're special. They remind you that you will carry a lineage on the planet that will someday awaken to something larger. You will reawaken in a new energy someday, and the things that were taught in Lemuria will be needed.

This voice will tell you that there will be the potential of a new Earth, Old Soul, and when you realize you're in it, here are the attributes to remember in the shamanic way: Then there will be the list of how to balance and care for the planet, and more. However, your Akash is very deep with many things that have happened since Lemuria. Only a few of you will remember the teachings clearly right now. It's because you had to slog through the rest of history. What's happened since Lemuria? The answer is: Just about everything.

Again, the negativity and the darkness are there. The horrible things that happened, lifetime after lifetime, are there, and things to deal with, even in this lifetime. I know who is here. Dear ones, you're all still getting over what happened in this lifetime! It's all in your memory, in your consciousness, and etched into the Akash. How does one get through all that? The answer used to be – "with difficul-ty." Not anymore.

There is an energy now which is supporting all of you. It's sup-porting women in particular because these are the ones who are awakening first to the truth. These are the ones who are awakening to what happened back then, remembering who you are and what's next. You are asking the questions if you are really "one of those."

Dear ladies, you wouldn't be interested in any of this if you were not one of "those." You are in a Sisterhood meeting! You are partici-pating in these ceremonies, in the songs, and in the meditations. You're not just singing and meditating for a good time, for this is the work!

The idea of all this is that, through intent, you're going to clear everything that does not suit your magnificence, Shaman. Everything that is not pure and not compassionate, including the things that have happened this time around, can be identified and voided. What do you bring to the party tonight? How about the biases that you've seen and felt and experienced that are no longer suitable for you? This Sisterhood is a clearing-hood!

It's time to drop that which used to be associated with women in recent times and, instead, go right to the beginning when it was pure, known, respected, and celebrated. All of the civilization in Lemuria knew it. That's who you are today, and anything else is periphery, but there's a lot of periphery. Ladies, you can clean this and it needs to be cleaned.

Let this be a time in this next few moments after I depart [leave the room] where you work on digging it out and throwing it away. Everything you brought with you today, which is not commensurate with your magnificence, gets thrown away. It's not for you. If you've experienced things in this lifetime that were less than pure, they go, too. Do this in earnest, so that when you step away, you feel clean; you don't carry the baggage and you don't have the disappoint-ments. The *anger buttons* will not be pushed anymore.

It's the beginning of a new woman, who is a new Human on this planet. So the purpose of the Sisterhood becomes clearer and clearer. It is a return to the purity of the original time. It's a return to a remembrance of who you were, what you did, and the instructions that you received. What a beautiful message this is, to be able to depart from that which does not suit you and never have it in your dreams or in your consciousness again. That's your potential, every single one, and it's beautiful.

Women, you are needed as Old Souls on this planet, returning to the original source of what you did and who you were. It doesn't fly in the face of men, dear ones. Rather, it enhances the family, and it's what they expected from a wise Shaman. They'll love you more for it, for you become balanced, beautiful in thought, and helpful beyond belief. That's who you are.

Kryon live channelling given during a Lemurian Sisterhood Meeting
in Boston, Massachusetts – March 11, 2016

Pleiadian Teachers

The female Pleiadians came to Earth for two reasons: (1) to give us divinity; and (2) to impart their wisdom and knowledge through their teachings. The role of the Pleiadian Mother was also that of the teacher. This is an instinctive attribute of motherhood. The primary concern for mothers, all over the world, is to give their children love, food, shelter, care, and protection. As their children grow, mothers are also teaching them how to speak, how to act and behave, and imparting their values and beliefs. It, therefore, makes sense that the female Pleiadians in Lemuria were both mothers and teachers. However, they were not just teaching children, they were teaching all humanity about the God inside.

Lemuria was, therefore, the launching pad for both humanity and for the individuals who lived there (see Chapter One: Ancient Lemuria: Lemuria and Atlantis). Whatever portion of time a soul was in Lemuria, it was only there for one lifetime; the next lifetime, that soul went somewhere else. When the experienced Lemurian soul reincarnated at a different place on Earth, there was still a potent Akashic remembrance that carried forward as a blueprint of divinity. This created the beginning of an enlightened humanity (worldwide), and the beginning of what took place after the creation story. Why would this "one lifetime experience" in Lemuria remain so profoundly within the Akash? The answer is because that "one Lemurian lifetime" was filled with the shamanic energy direct from the Pleiadian teachers. These were the same teachers throughout the existence of Lemuria.

If you take a look at the Akashic launching pad that Lemuria was, it's a profound idea. Dear ones, whatever portion of time you might have been there, you played a part that was only *one lifetime*. The next lifetime, you were not in Lemuria; you were somewhere else. But when you arrived "somewhere else," you had the pure Lemurian remembrance in your Akash. This was the beginning of an enlightened humanity. This was the beginning of what happened after the creation story – the Adam and Eve story.

It's not necessarily true that you came in [to your next lifetime] with other Sisters remembering, just like you remembered. You might have been alone on the second lifetime, or the third. What you carried with you was a remembrance of the Sisterhood and what you learned there. Even if you came in without other Lemurians, you still had the training with you. And what was the training? The women were the Shamans!

Now, in Lemuria, you were a group literally in training for the lifetimes that would follow. Now it is time, during the shift, for you to remember certain parts of the training. We've told you who your trainer was and why. For a long time, Mele'ha was there, but let me tell you something I haven't said before: Who was her trainer? She had a Pleiadian, in love, training her, and every so often, you would be exposed to her trainer. What do you suppose the training was? To be a Shaman!

Number One: Being a female was primary for this. It is the way of it. It's still the way of it. I'll say it again: The women carry the equipment of the intuition. They are the ones who raise and train the children. They know things. They have that which is *enhanced* intuition. Who better than the life-givers of the planet to carry this, and be the ones who would advise the rest of the planet, on a regular basis, in love and compassion, on how to live?

Ladies, you were seen this way by all of the men. This was their training, too. Have you ever considered a remembrance from men of that time? There were no issues with your shamanship. Do you think this can happen again? You think that's going to be tough? However, what if the men are remembering, too? You see, there were Lemurian men as well, and they are awakening again as men. Are you getting this?

I return to this: What do you think your primary training was as a Shaman? We've told you what the exercises were, and we've given you information about what you did when you were there. But, literally, you were in groups of women in shamanic training for your next lives.

So, let's pretend you are standing in front of a master teacher, a Pleiadian, who is going to give you information about you as a woman. What's expected? How do you work this energy? What do you think she would say about intuition? Turn a page for me. Pretend you are in your second or third life now, and you find yourself literally as the leader of a group of people, not women, who are turning to you for intuitive leadership for the tribe. What to do?

You would start giving them information about what you learned in Lemuria. You'd remember it. Someone may come to you and say, *"Dear leader,"* maybe they even kneel in front of you, and they would say, *"I need guidance. What do I do?"* What would be your answer? Would you say, *"I don't know, what do you think?"* No, you wouldn't! You'd call upon your trainings, and the intuition that you were taught to draw from, from your beautiful teacher. Are you hearing me?

Dear ladies, it's time to remember those lessons! What's the next step in your life? Can I make a suggestion? Don't ask, *feel*. Because the next step of what you're supposed to do here is to think: What is the most intuitive and glorious thing that will amplify my magnificence on this planet? The answer? Don't go to an outside source! Instead, pull upon the training that you had in Lemuria, Shaman. Start remembering!

That's the first thing to be taught here. That's the first thing to do: remember. You are in control and will have intuition for your task. If you start asking everyone else instead, you have given away your magic. Ladies, do you want to make this practical, or do you want to just get together and sing songs? That's the question, isn't it? This channelling I'm giving you here is for a reason: Dear ones, I want you to remember things! It's in there [in your past]. It doesn't matter how long ago it happened, since time is irrelevant to the Akash.

You put the energy of your past lives in a linear fashion, don't you? You say, *"How could I possibly remember 40,000 years ago? It's too long ago!"* You have no idea of the multidimensionality of the Akashic record. It's not stored according to years. Instead, it's stored according to energetic experiences and profundities, and it's not linear. That's what you're here for – to start remembering a beautiful, beautiful power you have: intuitiveness, remembrance of shamanic teaching, and knowing how to draw from the Source.

This remembrance will not only give yourself guidance, but also those around you. All will see it as accurate, true, loving, and having integrity. That's what you're here for, dear ones. Start remembering everything ... but not just the songs, or what Mele'ha has said, or the experience of togetherness. Remember the lessons you had, above all else.

Kryon live channelling given during a Lemurian Sisterhood Meeting in Asheville, North Carolina – June 17, 2017

The Pleiadian teachers imparted their wisdom and knowledge to the Lemurians. They also gave special training to the women of the Sisterhood. Not every woman in Lemuria was part of this extra training (see Chapter Two: The Women of Lemuria). What, exactly, did the Pleiadian teachers teach? Kryon has said it was "shamanship" and describes this Shaman School in the following channel:

Ladies, you might think that the Sisterhood is all about ceremony. It isn't. Ceremony was actually done sparingly. We've talked about the shamanic principles that were shared from the women to the men [see Valentine's Day Ceremony] but how can you have all of the women be Shamans? The answer: You can't.

So what it was, dear ladies, was a shamanic school. Mele'ha was the teacher and she had her teacher, too. Throughout the generations of women that she taught, the main teaching was of shamanship. We have said this before but now it becomes refined. The women helped to guide the men and the tribes, but not all the women were doing it. Most of them were in "learning" because that was the purpose of Lemuria.

If the Pleiadians had a main principle to teach humanity, it was this: that the female gender is very specialized, and magnificent. It contains that which is soft, compassionate, and wise. The female gender can teach other Humans much easier than the male gender can. Their minds are built for this, since they are the ones who teach children. That is why you are who you are. Even today, you know that. If you look at modern schooling, so many of your teachers in the lower grades are female. It is absolutely natural.

So what about this school of Shamans? The women who were learning and excelling would go on to be the elders, and they would eventually teach other women. Mele'ha? She could only teach the core group of excelled elders [this specific group was determined by society]. Some of you were there.

So, what were the lessons? What is it you teach to become a Shaman? Dear ones, I'll tell you: It is not information; it's processes of the mind. Last week we sat in front of you, giving you one of them and we said one of the processes that must be learned quickly, is to trust your intuition. Develop your intuition to a point where you will know you are correct, and move on it. This, instead of a position of suspecting or questioning if you are right, then asking everyone around you what they think. Does that sound like a Shaman? No. That's not what a Shaman does. People go to you, as a Shaman, for advice. You have to know. You stand in your own knowing and you *know*.

So let's go to the next lesson. By the way, Mele'ha has been given many things in her Lemurian remembrance here in this time. I asked her, "Where was the Sisterhood?" Now we have one. I asked her, "Where were the songs?" Now you have some. She was asked, "Where are the codes and some of the secrets of healing and learning?" And now she has those as well. Now I say, "Where are the lessons?" And she is developing them. There was a school and there was a syllabus. There had to be lessons. What do you teach to beginning Shamans? You don't teach them to sing. You don't teach them how to do ceremony. Instead, you give them the core of the shamanic nature, and number one is to trust and develop intuition.

Ladies, as you sit here learning, what do you do with your intuitive thought besides trust it? Well, the alternative is to not trust it, and perhaps even to shelve it. Perhaps you will think to yourself: *"I'll think about it later."* Or, *"Oh, it's true. Yes, it's accurate, but not for me right now."* Let me ask you something in this new energy: When you are given an intuitive thought, do you really think you're supposed to put it in the drawer? Of course not. This is the lesson. The second part is this: Don't just trust your intuition, act on it now! This is important, especially for this new energy.

In an older energy, all of you sitting in these chairs would get an idea, perhaps mull it over, perhaps share it with others, then you would review it and present it again. Then, perhaps, you might even put it in a drawer for later. Do you see the resistance? There was a resistance because it required action and change, and might even disturb the norm. That was then, this is now.

I'm here to tell you that intuitions that are being given to you and any women who are listening to this, are ripe for the time. They wouldn't be given to you, otherwise. Some of you, right now, are sitting on projects. Let me ask you, why are you delaying? What is the reasoning? Do you think, perhaps, it's not time? It is time! This is why you had the idea. There are books to be written in this room, and from those listening and reading. There are projects to be launched. There is teaching to be done.

We speak specifically of action items that many of you are feeling now. Perhaps some of you had this feeling before, and acted on them before the 2012 shift – and they didn't work? We've said this before: Things that did not work in the old energy will work today. So I'm stirring the pot, am I not, in the room ... of those listening ... of those reading? Perhaps you have had these ideas for some time? It's time to proceed to look at them carefully and act on them with appropriate timing. Don't put them in the drawer.

Some will say, *"I'm too busy."* Dear ones, that is up to you. What is busy? Is it something that you invent so you won't have to move forward on the idea? That makes you busy. Perhaps it's some things that you enjoy doing? And that makes you busy? This is up to you. Know who you are, and if you are, indeed, part of the Sisterhood that was Lemurian, you have a purpose today. There are wonderful things you are thinking of that you might do.

Can you bring other women together and expand their thinking of who they might be? Is it time to expand your thinking beyond what you did in the past? If that is your intuitive thought, dear women, then it's time. So this particular lesson comes down to this: Besides trusting your intuition, learn to act on it quickly, not like in the past where you put it aside. I'm speaking to several of you here, and many who are listening and reading.

It's different today than it was before. It's especially different for those who may find it in their Akash to say, *"I am part of the core group that started it all."* It's not about taking your power, dear women, it's about taking your wisdom and passing it on.

Kryon live channelling given during a Lemurian Sisterhood Meeting
in Buffalo, New York – June 24, 2017

Earlier, you read about the Nodes and Nulls of the planet. They represent the original landing places of the Pleiadians. Think of these places as the birthplaces of humanity (with a spiritual core). The Pleiadians not only gave Humans divinity, but they remained to teach the generations to follow. Slowly, over a long period of time, the Pleiadian teachers transferred their energy from their corporeal bodies into the grids of Gaia. This is what Kryon is referring to when saying, "The Pleiadians never left, they are still here."

The Aboriginal Anangu in Australia absolutely understand this concept. In fact, it is forbidden to go to certain places at Uluru, their sacred rock, because those sites are the home of "where the ones whose names you can't pronounce" still live. For the Anangu, the land is still inhabited by ancestral beings. Perhaps, this explains what the Anangu mean when they say, *"Kulilaya, ngura milmilpatjara; Tjukurpa alatjitu!"* (Listen, this land is sacred; Alive with the Dreaming!).

Many have also felt the profound Pleiadian and Lemurian energies within the node known as Mt. Shasta. Kryon has told us that many Pleiadians and Lemurians went there and put themselves in a quantum state within the mountain. A channeller, by the name of Aurelia Louise Jones, moved to Mt. Shasta in 1997, after receiving guidance from Adama. Adama is a High Priest and spiritual leader in the sacred Lemurian City of Light, called Telos, beneath Mt. Shasta. The description of this Lemurian City within the mountain is a linear interpretation of a multidimensional energy that we have yet to fully understand. This is due to our Human bias of singularity, and our Human filters when receiving channelled messages. Instead of a Lemurian City, think of Mt. Shasta as a quantum portal. This portal, in connection with all the other pairs of Nodes and Nulls, is now broadcasting high consciousness information to the grids of Gaia and the Akash of the Old Souls.

What about the node at Hawaii? How does this compare with Uluru and Mt. Shasta, or any of the other nodes? The answer is that this node was remarkably different. The reason is because Lemuria was the one place on Earth where the Pleiadian teachers stayed throughout the entire civilization and society. Each soul that experienced Lemuria was taught directly by the Pleiadians. The information was, therefore, always pure. It did not have any distortion or dilution that occurs when handing down original information from one generation to the next. This teaching lasted until the island began to sink, which was not just the signal for the Lemurians to leave, but also a signal for the Pleiadians to become entangled with the planet in a multidimensional way.

The Pleiadians were always present corporeally in Lemuria. Imagine what that must have been like. Imagine learning core spiritual truths from those who had already reached ascension status within their own planetary civilization for over a thousand years! What would those core truths be and how would the Pleiadians have taught them? How would an advanced race teach about the God inside, or how consciousness changes physics, for an emerging humanity? Kryon gave the answer of how this was done during the "Return to Lemuria" conference in 2017.

I wish to give a message that has never been given before. I wish to speak of attributes which have never been heard before. I sit in this place [referring to Hawaii], and wish to give a specific message that can only be given here. It's time to give this message, for there are those here who will take this, understand it, and work with it.

The message is beautiful, for it talks specifically about the teaching of the Pleiadian Mothers. It speaks of how the teaching was done, what was taught, why it was taught, and who learned it.

I could not give this message unless I was in this place on this mountain where it happened. It did not happen on the top, but rather, it happened on or near the shores. However, this is the mountain and you're here and I'm here.

I could not give this message unless I was surrounded right now on both sides by Lemurian teachers [referring to Dr. Amber Wolf –

Mele'ha, and Kahuna Kalei'iliahi, who are sitting on stage next to Lee]. I use their cumulative Akash, as well, to bring this to you in a way you'll understand. Dear ones, what I present at this moment will be studied for what it is, and some of it is cryptic. Some of it will only be understood by the teachers of the teachers of today. Some of it will only be understood by physicists, believe it or not.

Where do I begin? This mountain was used as an *Akashic launching pad* for truth. What would the first lessons be like from a Star Mother to a Human Being? This Star Mother and her group are responsible for the 23 – the number of modified chromosome pairs that humanity has right now. What would the information be like from this source? What would the purity and the simplicity of it be?

Whatever was learned would be carried to the next lifetime as Humans reincarnated. This pure, beginning information would then last and last, through the next time, and the next time. This teaching would follow, through their Akash, into the world, no matter where they were. They would know it, and would remember it, and, with free choice, they'd use it or not. However, it would be the first and original information, representing the first teachings from the stars.

With Human evolvement, some of it would grow, and some would be thrown away. That's free choice. But I'm going to give you the raw truth that was taught right at the beginning, right from the children to the adults. I'm going to tell you what it was and why.

The information and teaching were different than what you might imagine, and there was high wisdom in all that I'm going to give you, given from an evolved race from the stars. Perhaps you can envision Human Beings gathered together, like what is happening in this place – where they sit and watch a teacher. But it wasn't that way at all. The teaching started early; everything they learned was taught from a specific shape. From children to adults, the shape remained the same.

The teaching was complex because what was within the shape actually evolved. Let me explain from the start. First and most complex, the shape was a wheel. It was a circle with spokes to the center.

The spokes to the center numbered five. Five spokes to the center of the wheel. My partner, go slow. I'm going to give these things to you, and you've never heard them before. I'm going to give you visualizations that you will then enhance, using the Akash of the two who sit next to you – how this looked – what happened, and what it felt like.

Education on this wheel started with the children. The Lemurian teacher, who was always a Pleiadian Mother, would not be at the center when she taught. She would walk around the circle when teaching, so there never was an exalted place. This meant that there was no bias, regarding a place on the wheel, which might have been more important than any other.

The circle had a name, but let me explain first why there were five spokes on the wheel: The name and the number go together and it's not just numerology. This was long before numerology, and long before the Human Being saw the energy of the numbers and the systems. This was raw. You can apply it now as you study it, and the numbers will supply you with enhanced meanings. But back then, it was very simple.

There were five spokes to the center of the wheel. The wheel had a name: It was called *"Seeking Balance."* It was the name of the wheel, and it was then put on the ground before the students for them to study. So picture it as a circle on the ground with five spokes. Why five? This is a good question, for five is not that which you would expect, since everything in nature is balanced with pairs. The pairs are the push-pull energy of the galaxy, the yin and the yang of all energy, the light and the dark, and the laws of your own physics, both strong and weak forces. Everything is paired up – but not with a five.

Seeking Balance was the subject of this sacred wheel and the spokes all had names, too. These names would be explained to the children and to the adults. Why five? Now we get into what the Pleiadians wanted humanity to understand and to know in these beginning teachings: *Magnetic fields*.

Dear ones, this won't take long, so don't *check out* [disengage your attention] if you don't like science. The basics of magnetics are at the very prime of all information, and are super simple to explain in this context. Physicists, forgive me for this [Kryon smile]. An atom that has too many electrons versus an atom that doesn't have enough, create a plus and a minus push and pull as they try to connect with one another and to balance themselves. This process creates a magnetic field, and the polarities of plus and minus within that field.

Magnetism is one of the things in standard physics that allows constant change as a norm. It always begs to be changed and balanced. Magnetics are created within the relationship between the parts of atomic mechanics. Atoms with too many electrons are always trying to connect with those with too few. So you might say that atomic structure itself is always "seeking balance."

This wheel represents *five*, for it begs for balance, even within the shape of the teaching wheel – five spokes with five truths. The five spokes create a shape with six spaces. You will see this when you construct the wheel, with more information that is coming. Even before numerology, the six was known as a high-balance number.

Again, the teacher was always a Star Mother – beautiful, and lovely to behold. The teachings were always given in benevolence and compassion, and the children loved these very special and amazing creatures. Every adult session featured those who had started as children with the wheel. Children before the age of seven had pretend wheels. It was only after seven that they got to learn from a Pleiadian Mother and got to see, touch, and play around a real wheel.

Children were taught from the age of seven to thirteen. At thirteen, there was ceremony, and then a gender split for further teaching. From thirteen on, the wheel information was taught to the men separately and differently than to the women. Thirteen was the average representation of menses for the female. The former children females were starting to be mothers and that changed everything. For then, they were available for the sacredness of shamanic teaching that the men didn't necessarily want or need to know. The men understood and honored the natural common sense cultural split between them and the now "women of Lemuria."

There was a big difference in the tasking of what the women and men did well. There was no separation due to class. The separation was from what they did well. You didn't ask men to have babies. You didn't ask women to fish. Let me tell you how this worked: The women stayed and they studied, and they had their children and they continued their very special education. They were the ones who were the most intuitive, and they learned to guide and teach using intuition, and that even meant that they could tell the men where to fish. Men expected this. It was a cultural norm, and they sat and listened to the elder women, because it worked.

The women didn't want any part of fishing. They were good at what they did: They birthed, taught, and learned to become Shamans [spiritual energy specialists]. The women got the advanced information from the wheel.

I want to give you some other information about the men and the women: The men would never, ever think of going to sea, catching fish, and then giving it to a woman to cook. It was *their* fish. Cooking your own fish made total sense!

There are some jokes that Lemurian men told about the women, and that the Lemurian women told about the men. Are they appropriate? I'm going to ask this question to the Lemurian ancestors, which are represented to my left [Kahuna Kalei'iliahi is sitting to Lee's left]. *"Ancestors, is it appropriate to tell these jokes?"* [pause] The ancestors said no. [pause] I am Kryon, and I do not answer to the ancestors! Here are the jokes – they are short:

The men would get together and they would joke: *"Don't ever give a woman a fish. She won't know what to do with it, and it will end up just being blessed and it will be put into ceremony."* The men knew that.

The women would get together and say, *"Don't ever let the men discover the elements of the sacred circles. Because they will try to cook them."* The women knew that. Those were the jokes.

Back to the children – back to the circle – back to the teaching. *Seeking Balance* was the name of the wheel with five spokes. The children would sit around the wheel receiving basic information at the beginning. That's what I'm going to discuss with you, because the wheel evolved and changed. How can you teach one wheel for a lifetime? I'll show it to you eventually, and I'll tell you about it, and then you'll begin to understand the complexity. However, it starts extremely simple.

The children sit in a circle, and a Pleiadian teacher walks around the wheel. What is next is important, and fun for the children: There is no position of importance within the wheel that is more important than anything else on the wheel. So the teacher is always moving so that the Human Being does not then linearize the process and assign some kind of bias to any specific teaching of any specific part.

The biological mothers of the children are always present – always. From seven years old to thirteen. This was done for a very good reason, and one that has been almost forgotten in your modern society today. Children do not learn in a vacuum. With the mothers there, it always allowed them to intelligently discuss and review what had been taught. This also means that the mothers had their teaching times in addition to this [as adult women in shamanic training], so the women had busy lives. This is the other reason why the men did the cooking and almost all the physical things in the Lemurian society.

This was the way of it, dear ones. Look at this and the reasons for it, because, again, the women had the intuition that was needed for the children's care, and the guidance for the men. The men had the intuition and skill sets to build the villages, to put together the things for survival, and to make certain their families were cared for. They also were required to find the food source in an ever-changing ocean. So they listened to the women elders each day so that they knew where they could go to have a good harvest of fish.

The Center

Now I will reveal something about the center of the wheel. This wheel represented the full extent of the total teaching of all of the Pleiadians for the Lemurians. It was one wheel laid on the ground, quite large, with the students sitting around the circumference. All the spokes went to the center.

The center was not small, and seemed to be actually over-sized. It came to be known as the *Great Center*. In this center, the Human Being could put whatever they wanted to visualize or represent. It was not lost upon any of them that the sun might be that which they could imagine, since the sun was at the center of the solar system. You see, part of the teaching wheel was simple astronomy, given by the Star Mothers. So even the children understood that the center could metaphorically be represented as the sun.

At night, when special teachings were given, they would light a flame, using fish oil, representing the sun itself. Shortly, the center of the wheel got a nickname: *The Great Central Sun*. If you have followed my teachings for 28 years, you will now know where that expression came from. However, the center of the wheel doesn't represent something in your galaxy or your universe. It isn't something that you move around at all. Instead, it represents the center of all learning. It is the center of all truth, and all the spokes come and go from this, the center. That is *The Great Central Sun*.

The Beginning of Teaching

The spokes had names, and each one had specific teachings. I'm going to give you all the names before you leave this island. The children memorized the names because the names didn't really make sense. It's like you memorize some things in school at first that later will make sense. Before you ever really understood the times-tables and their place in mathematics, you were memorizing them. Before you ever understood grammar, sometimes you were memorizing the rules. Children are good at this. They memorized the five names of the spokes because they were going to need them later.

These names mean something to a seven-year-old, and they mean something else to a fourteen-year-old. Then ... they mean so much more to a thirty-year-old and a forty-year-old. By the time you are done with the teaching, you expect the wheel itself to ascend, filled with such grand truth that it represents. As the spokes begin to *evolve* in their simplest of meanings and their names, the teaching becomes far more profound. From the beginning, the children have an idea what the spokes mean, but most of those perceptions are wrong. The spokes actually have energy in both directions, from the center to the circumference and the circumference to the center. However, that's not how they are seen at first. They are simply spokes with names.

Let me give you the names, but first let me tell you how they were presented every single time, which was especially fun for the children. When the Pleiadian teacher began, she would say, *"Let the numbers game begin."* You see, there was a short game of numbers, where each person would participate, that would end abruptly due to the rules. Whether the students were young people, children, or adults, the game was always the same. Wherever the numbers game stopped, the closest spoke to that person that had not been studied in the series, would then be studied and reviewed. In the wisdom of the teacher, this meant that there was no hierarchy of spokes. You see, there was no importance assigned to one above the other. There was no ceremony to a part of the wheel where they started or ended. There was no hierarchy at all. So it was the numbers game that would then choose where the teaching would begin for the day. Do you see the wisdom in this? Nothing was more important than anything else because the teaching all centered around a circle with no beginning and no end.

The Spokes

So let's pretend that the numbers have been done [the game has been played] and we are now going to identify the spokes. There will be no hierarchical order to them at all. I'll give you their names, and

I'll tell you what the children thought they meant. Then I'll tell you what they really meant. Perhaps you would then be able to see how a student might study one spoke for a lifetime, and never really learn the full truth of it.

Simple Spoke Names

I paraphrase the names because I do not give you the language of the day [Lemurian]. I give you the best I can and what the language meant to the children. This is where I will start. I'll call it spoke one, but that's only for today's teaching.

The first spoke we tell you about is called *Center Return*. The children felt they knew right away. They said, *"Well, this is the home of our Pleiadian Mothers from the stars. There has to be a place where we go when we're finished here."* You see, the idea of the essence of a soul was right there with them from the beginning and they all said, *"When we are done here, we return to the center, The Great Central Sun, where all things emanate from. The center, the beautiful center. They memorized Center Return."* The children didn't know.

I'm going to give you the names of the remaining spokes and then we are going to back up and give you the meaning, the real meanings.

The second spoke is called *Star Steering*. The children were very excited about this because they knew the Pleiadians came from the stars. In order to get here, they had to steer their way somehow. They said, *"This is going to be a spoke, eventually, where we are going to be taught how to steer among the stars. We will do what the Star Mothers have done."* Were they right? We will get to that.

The next one is difficult, difficult. *Child Life*. What could that mean, Child Life? The children said, *"This is the name given to the spoke today, and it will change tomorrow when we're older."* They said, *"This is for us. We're children, and it's about the life we have as a child. We're going to be taught how that works – Child Life."*

The next spoke is *Human God*. The children had already memorized these names and, during their first discussion, they postulated that there might be a prophet, or a mother, a Human who becomes God. *"This is going to be for the future,"* they said, *"We don't understand it now."*

The last one is not so simple. It was called *The Mirror*. The children had no idea.

So there are five spokes, having odd names, memorized by the children. Then, over time, it started: Slowly, methodically, simply, and with elegance, the Star Mothers would start teaching what the spokes were, at the child level, the adolescent level, and then the adult level. The child-like ideas were enhanced slowly for children, and then every session and every year got a little harder and more complete.

The children got the idea, only in the third year, that the spokes worked both ways! The energy of the teaching traveled from the center to the outside, and outside to the center. But rather than giving you the lessons and all the permutations of the lessons, let me just give you the truth and the purity of the spokes, and what the Pleiadians wanted Humans to know:

The Meanings

The five basic truths, as represented by the spokes, are these:

Center Return

This spoke was all about reincarnation. The whole idea that you go both ways was the teaching. You come and go from The Great Central Sun – The Hub. Did you study this today [in the seminar]? Did you see the beauty, the elegance, the complexity, the honor, and the love that went into a system that allows you to come and go from that which you call the Creative Source? You see, the Pleiadians knew all about what you call God.

Soon, the children, who were getting older, understood that The Great Central Sun, that Hub that sometimes had a fire burning in it, was God or Spirit. This is where everything that was anything, was. This became the Creative Source. It's very difficult to tell a child about the Creative Source unless, year after year, they are exposed to an elegant teaching with layers of understanding. That spoke was the beauty of the return to the center, then from the center to the outside [beyond the veil] and back. It gave the wonderful truth that your soul never, ever dies. This was what was taught: Death is a transition, and it is not to be feared. The essence of *you* comes back. The body wears out, but the soul does not.

Star Steering

Oh, you're going to love this! That is how your life can be steered by the stars. It's astrology. It was called Star Steering. Right from the beginning, we've explained why astrology works, and we're not going to do it again. Let's just say that it works because it has to do with physics, not esoterics. It has to do with your sun's magnetic field and the Earth's, and how they are related. It has to do with the imprint on your sun of the gravitational pull of the planets, which the children see as stars. To them, these planets are simply lights in the sky.

However, as I've told you before, that gravitational pattern of the planets around the sun is then "pushed" to this planet by the solar wind, and intercepted by your magnetic field. Have you ever seen the Aurora Borealis? These are the *sparks* where the solar wind and your magnetic field combine, and information is put onto the planet regarding astrological energy.

Star Steering was the name given to the idea that what you see in the heavens may affect who you are on Earth, and what you might do, all depending upon your date of birth [arrival on the planet in this incarnation]. The children and the adults were also given basic navigational hints. Although they didn't stray far from the island, the teachers knew that there would come a time when they needed to. So, they were taught navigation in BOTH hemispheres, using stars they couldn't even see.

Child Life

The third one was called Child Life. Oh, you won't understand this, and some of you will scratch your heads with this information. This is one of the basic spokes of life that is so important! Here it is, dear ones: The longer you can maintain that which is the attitude of natural humor and joy of the child, the longer you will live.

Child Life. Don't lose it. The children are taught from birth that what you have as "child-like" wonder may go away if you're not careful. Don't lose this, because you'll start dying as soon as you do! This was the teaching. Disease can attach to you far more easily if you have dropped the "inner-child," but as long as you have the joy and excitement of the little child, you will live a very long life. It changes your chemistry and your immune system.

Don't drop it, remember how it feels. No matter what occurs, no matter what sorrow there is, no matter what you have to wade through later as an adult, don't forget it. Child Life. It will affect the length of your life and you will start dying as soon as it's gone.

How important do you think that spoke is, dear ones? It talks about the health of the Human Being, and it speaks about your consciousness being able to affect your biology. Can you imagine how long that spoke could be studied? Don't lose the kid inside. That's what the Pleiadian Mother says. Don't forget it, it's primal to existence. Laugh through your life!

Human God

This is the training that teaches that The Great Central Sun, the Hub, is connected in more ways than Center Return. Center Return was teaching about your soul journey. This spoke is about the fact that God is in the Human Being. You are God. God is You. You are Sacred.

From the beginning, these spoke names were memorized by the children. But the elegance wasn't understood. Later, the advanced lessons were given of what it is like to know that you are part of that Hub, and that's the reason why you reincarnate. The Hub and spokes then start to relate to the each other and that's part of the advanced training for the adults.

There aren't really five or six. Instead, there is one, as the layers of information of the five talk to each other. Four talks to one, and two talks to three. That is the elegance and the complexity of the wheel of the five. The God in you never goes away and the child is taught that there is a relationship to the Hub. It's a beautiful one, they are taught, and one that you will learn more about when you're older – but get used to it. They are taught, "I am the Hub," which later becomes "I am Sacred"; "I am God." Beautiful.

The Mirror

Spoke number five, the most mysterious – The Mirror. The children didn't understand The Mirror until they got a little older. Then, they would say, *"Yes, we think we know. We think we know. You've got to take a good look at yourself, clean up your act, behave better for your parents. Look in the mirror at yourself. Be reflective."* They got it wrong.

Let me tell you what The Mirror is, if I can. The Mirror – how can I tell you this? You get to see yourself and God together in The Mirror. But you don't see yourself as you think. What you see is God. Then you are taught that each Human Being is a mirror for you, and when you look at another Human Being, The Mirror is in them. Therefore, you look for yourself and God in others. That's just the first layer of training and teaching: Looking for God and looking for you in others.

It's the beginning of the teaching of oneness. It's about a commonality of all things, where there is a oneness in everything. Then, The Mirror starts to reflect that which is Gaia, nature. It starts to mirror the Human and the Human mirrors it in the compassion, the systems, and the way they work. You might say that The Mirror is an elevated study, and you would be correct, but it is equal to all of the others – not above it.

The Mirror, to this day, is misunderstood. It is the oneness of all things together. It is the study of the "one." It is the derivative of – get ready – it is the derivative of "I am that I am." That's the five.

Can you see why, at a certain point, the teaching would move into what you call the Sisterhood? The women were separated later from the men's teaching of the wheel. More advanced information was given to the women, since they were going to become the spiritual guidance counselors for the group, or the Shamans. The men were elegant enough in their understanding to know they were not necessarily equipped with the intuition that would be required for shamanship, and they were fine with all of it. They knew that advanced spiritual teaching belonged to women, and were happy it wasn't them! Dear ones, all of society understood this – all of them.

This is the story, dear ones, of the beginning teaching that occurred on this mountain, given by those from the Stars. This is what happened here, and it continued for thousands of years. The basic truths of love and creation were taught here, the truths that would create Humans whose Akash would then carry this forever in incarnation after incarnation. All would get a chance to awaken someday and continue the study of the wheel.

Welcome, then, to the continuation of the Lemurian Teaching Wheel! Call it what you want. Everything you've learned today and seen is part of it. Everything. I want you to take a moment and congratulate yourselves for coming through a time frame that many did not come through [speaking of cultures and societies that didn't make it this far]. You are awakening with the Nodes and the Nulls, and the Pleiadian Mothers' return. You are awakening to feelings and things that you didn't think you would feel. You are awakening to understandings that you didn't think you'd understand. There's much to know and to remember, dear Lemurian. That's enough for now.

Kryon live channelling "The Teaching Circle"
given in the Big Island, Hawaii – December 20, 2017

Within the same event, a few days later, Kryon continued discussing the Lemurian Teaching Wheel:

I want to continue with you just for a moment, the teaching from the Pleiadian Star Mothers, which I spoke of earlier. It was two days ago when we presented the circle with the five spokes called The Lemurian Teaching Wheel. At that time, I gave you basic elementary information that the children would be given. We told you that the children often decorated the center and that, as children, they had no real idea what the center was. Sometimes, they'd even put a light in it – a candle burning either from the oil of a fish or from the leaves of a tree. They called that the sun and, at night, it looked like it, especially in a circle that represented the solar system – something else they were taught about. When they got to the age of thirteen, all that went away and they'd begin to discover so much more.

So now we're going to give you information that we did not give you before. It's not that important for the teaching, but it's an enhancement: We want you to visualize this for yourself and, perhaps, even remember what the wheel might have looked like on the ground. It's two-dimensional on the ground [nothing sticks up from it]. Slowly, we're going to count the spaces and examine the shape.

The wheel part was thick and substantial. The shape and dimensions of the spokes and rim were also wider than you might think. It didn't represent a wheel like you would see on your vehicles. Here are the dimensions: You are measuring from the edge of the wheel to the exact middle: From the outside of the wheel, the width of the rim represented one-third of the distance to the center. From the inner edge of the rim, the spoke length, five of them, represented another one-third of that distance, bringing you to the Hub's outer ring. The Hub's space was the remaining third.

So, if you draw this, you will see that the Hub space really is quite large, so anything that would have been put in the middle of it would have been quite small compared to the space in the Hub. For those of you who took the time to draw a circle and put five spokes on it since the last channel, it may have seemed puzzling. You see, there are only five spaces between the spokes. Let's talk about the sixth space in a moment, but not before we remind you of the sacred geometry. Those of you who understand this will see it.

You're used to geometry being in straight lines. Most sacred geometry is. However, the five spaces between the spokes are not. They represent a very, very strange triangle. For you see, the bottom of the triangle is curved [the rim of the wheel]. You have five triangles, which are unusual because the bottom of them is not a straight line. Now, the definition often used of any curve is an "infinite number of straight lines," so there is a message even within the space's shape, five of them. But where is the sixth space?

The answer is the Hub. That's number six. Now, to a child learning, they would never see that, and they're not taught that. The women are taught that. When the gender teaching had split, the girls begin to study the spaces and they began to be identified. That which is invisible, as I've said before, is more difficult to understand. A study of the six spaces is very advanced. The reason the women get it is because they are going to need it to teach the sacredness of advancement of a profound relationship to the center Hub, which is God and Love.

Even the children are taught that the center is God. The Great Central Sun is God, and around it is life. The spokes tell about the relationship to the center. All the spokes touch the middle and, therefore, all the spokes touch each other. They also see that there is no beginning or ending of life; therefore, no matter how long they study it, it never ends.

Eventually, they will understand the concept of "no beginning no end," and the relationship to the essence of the Human.

I want to talk, yet again, about the sixth space, the Hub. The Hub is beginning to show itself. Those spokes, they go both ways and, again, you have the teaching that there is no directionality on any of the spokes. There is no hierarchy or priority within the spokes. They all connect to the center in the same way, and the center connects to the outside. In addition, if you remove a spoke, the system is weak. Advanced teaching says that the entire wheel is connected in such a way that there really are no parts at all. The spokes, the outside rim, and the center Hub space, all vibrate at the same level. Therefore, all things relate to the center, and are one.

Here is an advanced teaching that I don't need my partner to develop, since it was specific to the kind of duality of the Lemurian. However, there was also a teaching that, in the middle of each spoke, there was a kind of separation. Those who would make the wheel out of wood would create different kinds of wood for the spokes so that they would change color in the middle. The advanced teaching would begin to color the wheel and the reason why there was a separation for each spoke, a name for it, was about this beginning duality and free choice. Remember, duality was new.

This is what would separate, instead of bring together, the outside and the inside of a spoke that was designed to work in both directions. Basic teaching began that the Human Beings, even with the circle of life, would have to cross the colors of wood – the separation between the spokes – something not given to them by God. It was the concept of complete free choice – belief and free choice. There was even an exercise where they would start coloring the spokes fully with one color instead of two colors. Later, in graduation, they would have the spokes all one color all the time.

Some of you will understand this, and some of you will not. It was a lesson in creating the energy of cognizing full free choice, meaning that they could create a full connection in both directions with any spoke to and from the Hub. Today, this is automatic with you since you have been with this free choice since the beginning.

There were even some Old Testament prophets who saw the wheel in the sky. Ezekiel saw many wheels, some within the others. I asked my partner to go find this. This teaching, given in Lemuria, went to all cultures eventually, since the Akash carried it there. It went to some of the most basic belief systems on the planet.

Where are you in all this? Can you envision something as simple as this kind of teaching, and yet, as complex as how you might now apply this to guidance for your life?

Every once in a while, we give spontaneous readings for a few in the audience. Three of you, sitting in front of me, are in a certain state of depression. I know your spiritual names, not the ones you were born with.

Dear ones, I know you and I want to tell you something: You are waiting for something to clear – to get out of that hole that you have dug for yourself, which is black and so dark. I want to give you something. I want to give you some information right now from the other side of the veil: I know your name and we need your light! You are a Lightworker and that's the reason you're here! After three days in Hawaii, you thought perhaps it would clear? But it didn't, so let's clear everything right now.

I want to take your hand and pull you out of the hole. I want you to see light and feel joy. I want you to feel the chills of confirmation you haven't felt in perhaps weeks, as you've been in this ugly black hole of depression. I know you. I know your name and it's time for you to come out of it. We need your light. Do you hear this? We need your light and we need you to slowly climb out of this darkness. Right now, you have free choice to reveal who you are in all this. You may even start to remember the childhood where you giggled a lot, or you ran just for fun, even with the parents who didn't care.

I know who's here, and you still have that childlike attitude inside. You understand play, so let's return to that. It is your choice. You can break the color in one of the spokes right now and fill in that color to be complete, a two-way communication from Spirit to you and you to Spirit. One of the reasons you are in depression is because you won't let yourself see the majesty of your real name and who you are.

Fourteen of you came here with health issues. There is a beautiful thing in physics and chemistry that winds itself around your DNA, something that has been taught this very day. The Star Mothers gave you this in birthing. Your DNA does not have an odd number of chromosomes at all. You have 24, even though you see 23. The number 24 pair is invisible to you because it is in a quantum state.

DNA has been proven to be multidimensional. DNA, when present in a specific experiment, can change the spin of an electron in a quantum field. Dear ones, only another quantum element can do that. Therefore, your DNA is not three-dimensional like in other mammals. Instead, it is hooked to the Creative Source and it is ready to work to its fullest. It doesn't have to be activated. Only your belief has to be activated.

I don't want to step on any healing process that is currently activating DNA, but that language is actually a misnomer. DNA is activated in a Human Being and it is ready. It lays there literally ready for you to awaken to it, attune to it. Reframe your ideas about this and become aware that you are part of this! A healer who "activates" your DNA is helping you to become ONE with an already activated attribute.

Fourteen of you are ready for this. Did you know that everything that you may be experiencing right now, that you are concerned about, that you feel may be shortening your life, can be reframed and, therefore, be cured and restored? This can be done within the consciousness of compassion and oneness in your minds. You must understand who you are for this.

Without a physician, without exotic substances that you call drugs, you can do the healing yourself. The pattern for this is activated and ready to go. The template is always there for spontaneous remission. You've seen it! Why do you doubt it? Why do you assign it as a miracle of God when you could claim it is your own doing? When it happens in a hospital, there should be a party! You can sing songs of victory around the bed, congratulating the Human for doing something advanced and beautiful. Then everyone can look at it and say, *"There goes me too, if I want it. There goes me!"* You deserve it! I know your names, I know who you are as you sit here.

There are others who are continuing to wonder, *"What am I supposed to do?"* My partner had an inkling, based upon a question that was asked him during the seminar break, and so he looked up something. It was something that I was going to channel, but he got it in advance. He often does that so that he will be more prepared.

Two years ago, in January, we gave an informative channelling with a very interesting name, based upon everything I've been telling you. The channel was called "Five in a Circle." The information is about how Human Beings task themselves, or specialize themselves. It speaks of a kind of *specialization grouping* that many have, and what they choose to do that's different from each other.

Some are introverts in Spirit. Some are extroverts in Spirit. Some are profound meditators, and some are tree-huggers. The information speaks about the incredible variety of what Humans do with the piece of God inside them. Some are all of the above! They work together.

The entire reason they are *five in a circle* is the same teaching from the Pleiadian Mothers: Anything you are doing that is sacred, using your *piece of God*, is appropriate for you. You don't have to compartmentalize it. That's for a linear Human school. Early in life, parents address you and say, *"Well, what are you going to do in life? You've got to choose something, you know? Choose a thing that you're going to be and do for the rest of your life."* This is how you grew up, dear ones. These were the questions of your culture.

If you replied, *"Everything,"* they would say, *"Okay, little one ... we'll see."* Then they would chuckle among themselves at how naïve you were. Well, some of you are doing everything! I want you to know that that is perhaps one of the most advanced things you could be doing. You want to compartmentalize yourself and say, *"Well, I race around and I do a lot of things, but I'm no good to anybody because I'm fragmented."* No, you're not! You're not fragmented. You're multitasking the God energy within you and that is advanced, dear ones.

I hope you can reframe some of the ideas that you might have as a Human in an old energy, which are starting to come out and be seen in a whole different way. New paradigms are here. All of you, every single one on stage, listening and reading, and on the seats in here, are still filled with a residual that needs to be examined. It is the residual of *poor self-worth*.

You're crawling out of this hole of the past, and we've said it before. There are some listening [and reading] who still fully expect termination of the planet soon. Why? It's all you have ever known! It's also what you have been told. That's the information you received when you were born. *"Yes, Earth is going to end soon. It has to end since all of the prophecies and the wars told about it in history."*

In addition, some of you have been part of other unrealized civilizations on this planet who have terminated themselves. You were there, too! How does it feel to have gone through *the end* three or four times, then to find yourself in the same paradigm here? Of course, you are going to expect this! *"The end is coming, just as it did before. I feel it."* This is a *residual Akashic energy* that hangs there with most of you. It touches you every once in a while and says, *"I wonder if we're going to make it. I really wonder if we're going to make it."*

Negative and scary things will be reported on your news and you'll say, *"See? We're not going to make it!"* This is without you understanding that the new paradigm is starting to show itself. Massive change is upon you in ways you didn't think could be, including the catalyst that is here which we have called a Wild Card [Trump]. He is putting a stick into everything you cherished and stirring it vigorously! That's the only way things can change. The status quo must be stirred up. Some of it must even be broken apart.

I've said this to you before: If you want to know what the future is bringing for your country [United States], the old paradigm says you are on the cusp of failure. A system like yours doesn't usually last much longer than two hundred years. Look at the elegance of [Ancient] Rome, or the majesty of the elegance of [Ancient] Egypt. It only lasts so long before Human nature takes over and it fails. What you have going on right now is a rewrite, a reframe. A big stick is sweeping in all directions. Like it or not, that is the only thing that will let you start again in an elegant way without a stock market crash or total failure.

A wildcard that sweeps through will allow you to build something different, and restructure whatever shows up that doesn't work or that couldn't be changed before. These are all things, dear ones, that have been carefully given to you. The love of God, which allows for this, has come from the Hub, the middle, space number six. This is not political. It is the shift.

There is a wall, a barrier that is starting to become thinner. This has been called "the veil." Now it starts to become less than it was, and what it gets is "an invasion of light." Light is more powerful than dark, the yin and the yang are no longer equal [push and pull of light], and light starts to come forward in a way it never has before, and many are frightened of it.

Many say, *"It's not the same as before. Things are not working as smoothly as before."* Fourteen of you are worried about your health because of an old energy paradigm and the things you've been told. You have received a prognosis that does not suit your magnificence. It does not understand that light is here and is starting to work with you in a way that is going to help you understand what's next, and heal yourselves.

Self-worth is the last thing we speak of here. It would be a great time for you to start accepting that what you see and feel in your old reality is a paper tiger. It's false. It is no longer accurate. It is a residual that is very strong, and one that hangs with you because of what you have been through, Old Soul. Think how long you might have been here on this planet. If you were on this mountain [Lemuria], think how many civilizations you have seen, and how many inappropriate deaths you have had. Think of how much sorrow you have endured, or how many times you have been a Shaman and it didn't work out?

How many people do you know that are still *closet Lightworkers?* They are good people who won't come forward because the last time they did, it was a death sentence. You are in a new paradigm in a new time, where light is going to be seen, understood, and accepted. It is going to change your society and also Human nature itself.

It will eventually spread across this planet, healing societies and continents that have always been sick. There will be the building of new consciousness, new governments, new ways of thinking, and will create new inventions that deal with energy and water. Human population growth will not be an issue! You'll be smart enough to figure it out, instead of thinking that reproduction simply runs rampant because Humans have no idea why children are born. That is low energy thinking! You will achieve a "zero growth" potential for the planet. That's coming.

Feeding the planet? No problem. That's at hand all with wonderful technology coming from Lightworkers and those who start to awaken. Three of you! We need your light. Fourteen of you, we need your light! That's the reason we want you to stay. There's no reason not to. It's inappropriate and not in your magnificence to feel the way you're feeling today in this place.

This is a new age. It is part of the shift that was prophesied by so many Ancients, and here it is. This is not a Kryon *thing*, dear ones. This is a *world thing* and it is happening right now. Leave here differently. Leave this island differently than you came, then look back on it and remember this homeland, the original homeland, this island, the mountain of Mu.

Kryon live channelling "The Teaching Circle, Continued"
given in the Big Island, Hawaii – December 22, 2017

The information about the Lemurian Teaching Wheel demonstrates that the Pleiadians came to give us divinity as part of a loving, benevolent plan. Their origins came from the Arcturians and someday, we Humans on Earth will reach ascension status and give divinity to another planet somewhere in our galaxy. The Lemurian Teaching Wheel is a simple, yet practical way to convey esoteric concepts to a beginning society. Figure 1 assists us in getting a visual perspective of what this five-spoke wheel would have looked like.

Surprisingly, very few organized belief systems on the planet are using the original teaching wheel given by the Pleiadians. The closest resemblance is the dharma wheel, *dharmachakra* in Sanskrit. It is one of the oldest symbols of Buddhism, and similar symbols

Figure 1: Illustration of the Lemurian Teaching Wheel.

are found in Jainism and Hinduism. A traditional dharma wheel has varying numbers of spokes. It can be any color, although it is mostly gold, and at the center there are three shapes swirling together, a yin-yang symbol, another wheel, or an empty circle.

Just like the Lemurian Teaching Wheel, the dharma wheel has three basic parts – the hub, the rim, and the spokes, but that's where the similarity ends. Over the centuries, various teachers and traditions have given diverse meanings for these parts, while the number of spokes signifies different aspects of teaching. For example, four spokes represent the Four Noble Truths, eight spokes (the most common) represent the Eightfold Path, ten spokes represent the ten directions, twelve spokes represent the Twelve Links of Dependent Origination, and twenty-four spokes represent the Twelve Links of Dependent Origination plus the reversing of those Twelve Links, and liberation from *samsara* (the condition of suffering and endless rebirth).

As you can see, the Dharma Wheel has evolved greatly from the original five-spoke wheel in Lemuria. The reason is because information will distort over time, and in this case, the original information was given over 30,000 years ago to an Ancient society. So why is the information re-emerging now?

The consciousness shift on the planet changed everything. Through free choice, consciousness is evolving, and there is the gradual awareness of a multidimensional Human. The new consciousness on the planet means that Humans are more caring, compassionate, gentle, empathic, and loving than ever before. Humanity is displaying greater wisdom and the collective consciousness is "remembering" what works, directly from our Pleiadian ancestors, with an understanding that war is not the solution. Every new child born on the planet comes in with innate wisdom to honor life, not destroy it. Humanity is poised to rekindle the original core spiritual truths, first given by the Pleiadians as the Lemurian Teaching Wheel.

Note from the Author: Since the writing of this book, Kryon has revealed further information about the Lemurian Teaching Wheel. For instance, it was double-sided because the front of the wheel was used to teach children while the back of the wheel had more advanced concepts for the adults. There were also more than one type of wheel and they had symbols [light language] on them. Unfortunately, it is beyond the scope of this book to document the profound teachings of the Lemurian Teaching Wheel. Perhaps, there will be a future book that will be written exclusively about this subject (smile).

Questions for Kryon:

Given the similarity between the teachings of Buddha and Kryon, and the development of the Dharma Wheel in Buddhism, was Buddha (Siddhartha Gautama) a Lemurian?

Answer:

Yes, very much so. The core teaching of the Pleiadians in Lemuria sticks tremendously into the Akash of the Old Soul who experienced it. Hence, it makes sense that, in the early days of the spiritual evolvement of belief systems, the concepts would reflect the Teaching Wheel in Lemuria. The masters who started these systems were those selected to "remember the Akash" in acutely evolved ways. Those at the heart of what is today called Hinduism and Buddhism were Old Souls selected for this.

Let's expand on this just a bit. First, remember that, in these early historic times of your current civilization, approximately 6,000 years ago, things were linear, simple, and had to be understood by those not used to any systems. The development of "Gods" within these systems were not Gods at all. They were energy helpers. Some took away negativity, and some were for good futures. Others helped with fertility and others with health. The statues and multiple energy helpers allowed Humans to see and feel the unseen. However, take a look at the principles or doctrines of these early systems: (1) No prophet – remember that Buddha himself did not claim to be a God or a prophet, but just an enlightened man; (2) Reincarnation – the original intuitive idea of the journey of the soul; (3) Karmic energy – the idea of energy of a past life being part of the current one; (4) Nirvana – the ability to raise yourself up into ascension; and (5) God inside – seeing the God in you and in others.

Therefore, if you truly understand what I'm teaching here, you will begin to realize that the entire New Age movement is a return to the beginning. The study of esoteric information on the Earth is a return to the core information given by the Pleiadian Star Mothers, and is beautiful, benevolent information for a magnificent Human.

In a previous channel, there was mention of several solar discs still in existence. Were these solar discs part of the Lemurian Teaching Wheel? Can you tell us more about them, such as how were they made, and did they have any inscriptions?

Answer:

Artifacts of the original wheel do not exist. The basic reason is that they were all made from organic material. There were none in stone (as we have spoken of before).

However, the Akash is a magnificent storage of truth and conceptual core information, and it often comes through to Humans as their "intuition." It's far more than that, and is the revelation of things that were precious in past lives. Therefore, many wheels and disks continued to be made thousands of years after Lemuria ceased to exist.

You have referred to "solar discs," which is just one example of many that *mirrors* the Lemurian teaching from the past. Solar discs were the name of certain sacred discs that were in South American indigenous history. When the invaders came, many were tossed into the lakes of that continent, since the invaders eventually were all through the land. So there are legends that there are golden solar discs at the bottom of some of these bodies of water.

Indeed, they remain there, and yes, some are gold. The reason for the gold is that it was actually abundant in certain areas, and soft enough to hold inscriptions and symbols. Some are still there, buried deep into the silt, and only available on lakes that have survived as lakes for at least 20,000 years.

If found, they will be valuable for many reasons, but the greatest of these is the revelation of truth. For the inscriptions and codes will tell a story of the core truth of Lemuria, as altered for their culture.

Lemurian Ceremonies

Depending upon your culture, ceremonies and traditions will mean different things. In Ancient Lemuria, the Pleiadian Mothers were the teachers of the ceremonies that were handed down and became tradition over thousands of years. Due to the long lifespan of the Pleiadians and the Lemurians who visited the Temple of Rejuvenation, the ceremonies and traditions remained pure and unchanged for the duration of Lemuria. Our knowledge of these ceremonies comes from the Akashic remembrance of Mele'ha, and the channelled messages from Kryon.

Whatever your perception is of Lemuria, it's probably wrong. Lemuria and other areas like it were the beginning of the society of humanity and were simple. The language was simple in Lemuria. There were few letters and few vowels. It was simple, yet arranged in a certain way that everything you wanted to say could be said.

The society itself was not elegant, but, truly, it was a high caliber of thinking and spirituality. It's difficult to really relay to you what you did in Lemuria, since it's a completely different paradigm than anything you have now. As long as we've been channelling messages to you, we have given you many of the ceremonies and activities that were there, but I don't necessarily want to review anything for you because you can research from previous channels. Instead, I wish to continue the information.

You can ask Mele'ha, for she knows many things that I channel and can feel them as I tell you. The Human Akash is different than what you may think. Many of you are here because you remember some things or you would like to remember some things. Not all of you are aware of Lemuria, yet there is something even in the name that seems to *ring a bell*, as they say. Something at the cellular level seems to remind you that you may have had a part in the history of humanity as a woman.

The feminine energy, which is here in this room, is what we are really discussing tonight. It is a gentle, beautiful energy, and this is the energy in Lemuria that was truly revered. It was an energy balanced very well with the men, and we have told you this before.

You might have wondered what you actually did in Lemuria. Let me tell you what you did: You did ceremony, and then, when you were done, you did ceremony again. This is very common for simplistic cultures. There was ceremony with everything. If you want to see proof in this, go back to the indigenous, even today's indigenous, and sit with them for a day. What do they do? You will see them doing ceremony around everything that they perceive has energy.

The only thing that really separates today's indigenous ceremony from Lemurian ceremony is an honoring ceremony for their ancestors. You see, they didn't have any! Even after many, many years of

Lemurian civilization, the idea of honoring the ancestors was still not there. Believe it or not, this is an advanced and mature idea.

So the ceremonies performed included the weather and the fishing. It would be in thanks and appreciation to Gaia. It would be for longer life, and it would be for health. However, it was very, very common that you would have ceremony about something we have never discussed. The reason why I discuss this now is that it's time to revive it. Mele'ha, perhaps you might do this, and it's not just for women.

There was a word that was used in Lemurian tradition. It was a fairly long word that translated into what you would now call *transfer*. What that really truly meant was the ability to move energy from one person to another. But in the case of the ceremony involved, you did it with the men. It was transference of both male and female energies in an honoring ceremony for "gender wisdom." The tradition was that if you did this ceremony long enough and often enough, you would then transfer wisdom and knowledge from person to person.

Many ceremonies in Lemuria were not done in a full circle, but this one was. Many of the women, not all, who were the older elders, would get into a circle. They would face outward. For each woman, there was a man who would face her. It was tradition that the oldest men in the village would be the ones who would be most privileged to then stand outside of the circle, facing the women. These elders, of both genders, were now facing each other.

Eventually, you would have a circle of women looking out and a circle of men looking in to the center, face to face. All would be standing very close to one another. The ceremony would go on for a while and there would be a female leader who had no appropriate partner, facilitating the *transference*. The woman who was the leader had no partner for transference. In the age of Lemuria we speak of now, the elder facilitator was often Mele'ha, who, by the way, had no partner.

Being without a partner is also very common for the shamanic energies anywhere on the planet today. But it was especially true at that time. Partners were a distraction. Mele'ha would lead this circle in a way that would be a bit different than you think.

There would be what you now call a meditation, but it wasn't really a meditation at all. Instead, it was a *remembrance focus* based upon a specific teaching that was given by the Pleiadians. It was a remembrance of the teaching of the land and the culture.

The women would then take the hands of the men in front of them, who they were facing. Of course, they knew each other because all were a part of the village. Be there with me for a moment, ladies: The men would take your hands and you would take theirs. You would look into each other's eyes for transference.

Now the tradition and the idea of this ceremony was that the advanced wisdom that you would have from the Pleiadian teachers could be transferred to the men in some form. The wisdom of the men, being a slightly different kind of wisdom, would be transferred to you. Why do this? This was a recognition that men had practical things that women needed and never received from the Pleiadian Mothers. The men needed certain kinds of knowledge that they never received from the Pleiadian Mothers. So, it became a meld of wise information for both genders. Almost like an open-eyed meditation, you would literally stare into each other's eyes.

Now, there was a specific kind of plant that was in Lemuria called a *fast-burner*. You called it the fast-burner because it consumed itself very quickly with fire. In the ceremony, you would take sticks of a specific size, wrapped in this fast-burning plant, and light them. There would be a central mound with one stick and it would burn down until it extinguished itself. Then, at a signal from Mele'ha, all of the men would drop your hands and move over one woman to the right. Another prepared stick would be lighted, you would take the hand of the new partner, and the process would be repeated. Depending upon how many women and men there were, this would determine how long the ceremony lasted. Look at the rules. The men did the moving. The lighting of the stick prompted the women to take the hands of the men. The extinguishing of the stick caused the men to drop the hands of the women. All this meant something.

Look at what you were doing. It was an honoring – a full honoring of the wisdom of both genders, shared with everybody. This was an "elder ceremony," as was the tradition. It was a circle of wisdom that involved both men and women. Let me tell you something: Everybody felt it. Everybody felt it! The men enjoyed it because it was a spiritual connection they never were taught. The women enjoyed it because they got to experience a male connection of a practical nature that was refreshing.

It was special. It wasn't done that often, but when it was performed, the rest of the village watched. At the end, when all the women had shared with the men, the men would finally drop hands and would turn around and look at the village. Now both elder men and women were all looking outward. Those who were watching would then stand and applaud!

This is just one of many things that you did so differently than today. It was a gender-honoring – there is absolutely nothing like it today on the planet.

Kryon live channelling given during a Lemurian Sisterhood Meeting
in Ottawa, Canada – April 16, 2016

How do you feel about what you just read? Is it possible to apply this kind of ceremony in our everyday life? If you could honor the divine feminine and the divine masculine within you, what would that change? Can you also honor these attributes with the members of your family? How about others that you meet? Can you fully love and embrace the gender that you are and, simultaneously, love the other gender? If you did all of these things, how would that change your life? Kryon's teaching about honoring the gender is all about balance. Kryon has told us that, "the new balance on the planet is the paradigm of *balanced survival*. The balanced ones are the ones who are going to be seen as strong. These are the ones who will bring peace to the planet."

Birth Day Ceremony

Regardless of what culture you are from, there is a ceremony common to all, which is your birthday. Generally, when a baby is born, there is so much excitement from the entire family and the friends. Upon the anniversary of this joyous occasion, the family will celebrate the birthday. In western society, there is often a gathering of family and friends, gifts are given, and a birthday cake is presented. The ceremony of the birthday cake is accompanied with songs of wishing a happy birthday, and a certain number of candles will be lit on the cake, signifying the number of years since birth.

The Lemurians were no different and had their own way of celebrating a birth. They also regarded death as a kind of celebration, as they knew they were reconnecting with the Creator, due to the teachings from the Pleiadians. They understood that time was in a circle, and that death was not the end.

Life and death were both honored and, just like modern society today, birthdays were regarded as a special occasion. So what did they do to celebrate? The answer relates to the fact that Lemurians were essentially an island nation in the middle of the Pacific Ocean. The society, therefore, had a close association with the water that surrounded them. It gave them their food and nourishment, and was the location for many ceremonies. Lemurian births took place in the water and so it should be no surprise that birthdays were celebrated as a water event and a return to the ocean was part of the celebration. Often, the exact birth day was not known, but it didn't matter because an approximation of the birth date was based upon the sun and stars. Here is what we have learned from Kryon:

Dear ladies, I feel the warmth of your personalities and of your expectations. I feel the beautiful thoughts that you are currently having. I know of the countenance and the gentleness that is here.

As many times as I do this, I again tell you what is happening: I take you back to a specific time you call Lemuria. I remind you that

Lemuria spans a large duration of time, and so, we focus on a gentle time in Lemuria, a time before it started to submerge. The submergence of Lemuria was very slow and distressing for all. The time we speak of is a time of stability, maturity, and learning within Lemurian society. It was a time when the Sisterhood was active, without outside worry or drama.

The Sisterhood was not called a *Sisterhood*. In fact, it didn't even have a gender-specific kind of name. Eventually, I will give you that name, but not yet. For I don't want you to be consumed with some kind of a name that would be different than what you might imagine. For now, I want you to have the togetherness of the Sisterhood, and to feel the camaraderie of this, the purpose of the moment.

Is it possible that your group could have been part of this kind of thing from so long ago? Again, I know who is here. The distance of time we speak of spans eons and thousands of years. Is it possible that you sat together before? Perhaps with other faces or perhaps even with what you would call other souls? The answer is yes. It's not an accident that brings you here and the synchronicity is complete. Once again, you feel that which is the Sisterhood of togetherness. This is not an organization, but rather, it is an honoring of family.

The subject that I wish to speak of in these few moments this evening will center around Mele'ha [Dr. Amber Wolf]. She has had the meaning of her name given as close as it can be, using the language of a current Hawaii. There are actually similarities in language from then to now, based on some of the original words that are very much like the ones today.

Basically, her name means "The celebration of life – the breath of life itself." This was actually something celebrated by saying her Lemurian name out loud. Mele'ha, your name is not unique and we have not said this before: There were a very few priestesses, leaders of certain groups, who, like kings and queens throughout the ages, all took the same names. So, Mele'ha wasn't a personal name as much as a status. The status was that of the leader of a profound spiritual group of women in Lemuria. There were always a few.

The Sisterhood was not a social gathering. It was a spiritual gathering for certain women who would gather together. Their "business" was the spirituality of the continent of Lemuria. So there were many Sisterhoods on the small continent, and she had one. There were many priestesses who all had the same kind of name, but slightly different. This is actually a tradition that you still have today with Hinduism, and some of the indigenous of the planet. So you might call this the "Mele'ha Sisterhood" and that would be accurate.

After the life that she lived in Lemuria, which spanned several normal lifetimes, her name was then passed to her family. In the tradition of the day, she would select who would then replace her.

Now, what I want to tell you today is that this [today – the date of the channelling] is her birthday in this lifetime [as Dr. Wolf]. This is well known by you tonight, so I wanted to review with you what happens to a Lemurian woman on her birthday.

Based upon the past channellings that I have done, what do you think might happen on the birthday of a Lemurian woman, especially one in the Sisterhood? The last time I talked to you, we spoke of how birth was treated in Lemuria. We talked about the gathering and the singing of the women during the birth process. It was done to ease the pain while they all held hands, and the birth was accomplished under water.

We spoke of the beauty of this and the gentleness and the peacefulness of the child's first experience. Can you imagine the child's first sound when it emerged above the water and the cord was cut? It was the singing of women. Even the strongest of all men of the ages of Lemuria speak of these first sounds – the singing of women. This was soothing to them, and so it was, and still is, appropriate that the Sisterhood would return to the ocean to celebrate the birthday of a Sister, and it would be a water ceremony, a beautiful one.

Ladies, you would simulate the coming out of the water with singing. Of course, the birthday woman looked forward to this, and there were specific songs that would be sung, and food that would be there. I guarantee you, ladies, that if you were to hear those songs today, you would weep, and your Akash would remember.

This became the same for men, but slightly different. They also had a water immersion ceremony, but not necessarily with the women singing. However, the women were there, helping with the ceremony, since it was a celebration of birth. The simulation for both genders was done by the mother, if she was living, or by the next woman of kin as a surrogate. If there were no relatives, others were appointed. Of course, there was a separation of energies for the men, and eventually, the women would leave the party and let the men sing alone. However, all birthdays in Lemuria were seen as a water event. Only women celebrated women's birthdays. Men's birthdays were celebrated by both genders. However, returning to the ocean was always part of the celebration.

Many times, the actual days of birth were not known, so it was fine just to have an approximation, based upon that which was known by the stars and the sun. It didn't matter if it was accurate. Only the honoring mattered.

Now, Mele'ha, what you should know is this: All of the collective Mele'has, and all the priestesses that were involved in the Sisterhoods, often had another kind of ceremony for themselves. A priestess's birthday was one where the other priestesses from the other villages were invited as well. After the standard ceremony from the women in the village, the collective priestesses all remained. Some of the priestesses were related, since they were all direct descendants of a specific Pleiadian Mother. They rested for a while, and then started a three-day journey to the top of the mountain.

The top of the mountain is where the rejuvenation process took place for the specific birthday priestess, and also for the certain ones of Royalty who were also given extended lifetimes. We have spoken of this place before, where the Temple of Rejuvenation was in a very cold place. So, this was as important as the birthday because an extended life is seen as another birth day.

There were not a lot of priestesses in Lemuria, but all of them were invited on their biological birthdays to the mountaintop to be involved in the rejuvenation of the one who was being honored. What this also meant was that this trip to the mountaintop was actually done fairly often.

Here's what you should know: I will not give away how many times the rejuvenation process was done at the Temple, but it was always done on your birthday. So you might say, you were *born again* with each birthday due to this rejuvenation process. Your birthday in this life, this day, has a numerological equivalent of a one, which represents *new beginning*.

Let this day be a new beginning for you, Mele'ha. Let it be also for those who wish to join you in remembrance of what it was like for each one of theirs. May this also be an Akashic remembrance of longer life, and rejuvenation of your structure. Perhaps you would consider redeveloping, through the memory of Mele'ha, a ceremony just for birthdays? Maybe, just maybe, the songs will come back to you as well?

Kryon live channelling given during a Lemurian Sisterhood Meeting
in Salem, Massachusetts – May 16, 2015

Winter Solstice Ceremony

For thousands of years, the winter solstice has been celebrated by different cultures and civilizations throughout the world. The winter solstice is an important part of the yearly cycle, as it marks the shortest day and longest night. From that point on, there is an increase of daylight hours until the summer solstice; hence, many festivals celebrate the rebirth of the Sun. What follows is a brief review of how a few cultures celebrated the winter solstice, demonstrating an intrinsic connection that links humanity across time and space.

In ancient Rome, the festival of Saturnalia was held on the winter solstice to honor Saturn, the God of agricultural bounty. The festival lasted for seven days and celebrated the end of the planting season. Boughs of evergreen trees and bushes would decorate the house and banquets were held. Grudges and quarrels were forgotten; normal business was suspended; wars were interrupted or postponed; and slaves did not work (briefly, they were treated as equals). It was traditional to offer and exchange gifts, such as imitations [wax models] of fruit, dolls, and candles. Eventually, the Saturnalia festival degenerated into a week-long spree of debauchery and crime. With Emperor Constantine's conversion to Christianity, many of these customs became adopted by celebrations of the birth of Jesus, eventually called Christmas.

The Feast of Juul, or Yule, was celebrated in pre-Christian Scandinavia to celebrate the rebirth of the sun. The festival lasted for 12 days and was marked by burning fires, symbolizing the heat, light, and life-giving properties of the returning sun. Homes would be decorated with holly and ivy in the hope that Nature Sprites would join in the celebration. A sprig of holly was kept at the front door year round as good luck and mistletoe was also hung as decoration (representing the seed of the Divine). Children would be escorted to each house carrying gifts of clove-spiked apples and oranges (to represent the sun), which were laid in baskets made from evergreen boughs (to represent the eternal aspect of the Divine), and wheat stalks dusted with flour (to represent the harvest).

The highlight of the winter solstice festival was the ceremonial Yule log. Once it was brought into the home and placed in the hearth, it was decorated in seasonal greenery, doused in cider or ale, dusted with flour, and then set ablaze in honor of the Scandinavian God, Thor. A piece of the log was kept as a token of good fortune and to use as kindling for the following year's log. In some countries, the Yule log was burned until nothing but ash remained, so it could be used as fertilizer on the fields. Many of the customs associated with the Feast of Yule are now part of today's Christmas celebrations.

In Peru, the winter solstice is celebrated as *"Fiesta del Sol"* (The Festival of the Sun), also known as Inti Raymi by the indigenous people. This also marks the first day of the New Year in the Inca calendar. The celebrations took place in the main plaza in the city of Cusco, and lasted for nine days. Three days before the celebration, each participant had to go through a purification period. Those who could participate were the Sapa Inca, the nobility, and the Inca army. On the main day, the Sapa Inca would drink *chicha de jora* (a maize-based drink) in front of the pilgrims, in honor of "Apu Inti" (the Sun God). Inside the Temple of the Sun, the priest would light up a flame.

The Inti Raymi winter solstice ceremony was prohibited by the Spanish conquistadors and later banned, along with many other Inca traditions. However, since the mid-1940s the winter solstice is once again celebrated in Cusco, Peru, as a modern-day re-enactment of Inti Raymi. Every year, thousands of spectators gather to watch the ceremony. A short promotional video featuring the re-enactment of Inti Raymi can be viewed on YouTube:

https://www.youtube.com/watch?v=4OShU3lQaGs

Another famous celebration of the winter solstice takes place in the ancient ruins of Stonehenge, England. Every year, thousands of visitors from around the world gather in the early morning to see the sunrise above the stones. This is accompanied by a re-enactment of Druidic ceremony and celebrations.

Other cultures to celebrate the winter solstice include the North American Native Indians. Each tribe would have its own traditions and ceremonies linked to this astronomic event that signaled a time of change and renewal. It marked the New Year and represented new life.

Celebrating the winter solstice is an honoring of the alignment with Gaia. This is why our Ancient Ancestors did this ceremony, which continues within indigenous tribes and is performed by those who feel an affinity with Gaia. They recognize and under-

stand that Mother Earth is a part of them. In the following channelled message, Kryon reveals the Winter Solstice Ceremony that
Lemurians participated in every year:

Dear ladies, I wish to tell you about a ceremony that I haven't
told you about yet. Once a year, on the winter solstice in Lemuria,
something happened.

Now, Mele'ha, you already emulated it in your current history,
and now we're going to give you a little wink. You had no idea what
you were doing on December 21, but you emulated something that
your Akash was telling you was appropriate. In Hawaii, December 21,
2012, you had a gathering of men and women and you called it a
Sisterhood.

You could have put the men anywhere you wanted to, but you
chose to have them on the outside of the group. If there had been
enough, or if you had framed it differently, perhaps you would have
created a circle with the women in the inside and the men surrounding you? This is what you did in Lemuria at every winter solstice! Does
it also sound like another multi-gendered ceremony that I have previously described to you? This winter solstice event was "a celebration of
life." However, it was also a celebration that the men had for you.

Here's what the men would do. First of all, the circle had to be
complete and the women had to be inside like the center of the flower.
The men surrounded you completely, there was no break, and then
they sang to you. Have you ever heard the beauty of a men's chorus? It
was a full male chorus singing together, not strongly, not bravado, but
sweetly, in what today is sometimes called Hawaiian chants.

These were the songs they had learned from you as mothers. All
of the songs had harmonies that they all knew, in celebration of you.
Do you think that, perhaps, this was about men and women, like
some of the other ceremonies I told you about? It was not. It was all
about balance.

Today you are meeting as women, without men. It's the beginning of a return of something that was beautiful, and that you need

to rekindle and appreciate, and understand and know. Back then, they knew that women carry the life-force, and that the celebration of life should be for them. So the men sang to you. The songs that they sang to you were beautiful, and there was weeping. More than a "mother's day," this was an appreciation for the guidance that you gave them all year long. You told them the places to fish on the shoals of the island. The fish would move from place to place, but you had the intuition of where they would be. The men realized the power that you had to communicate so fast and so easily with the Creative Source. They didn't have it, and they knew that, too.

A man's connection was firmly in Gaia. Men took care of Gaia for you. They caught and cooked the food, but they knew who you were, and this is what the celebration was about. Mele'ha actually emulated this in 2012.

The potential is on the planet for some of this respect to return. It won't be for fishing reasons, but, instead, to honor and acknowledge what you [women] really are here for, and how good you are at it.

Women are soft, gentle, compassionate givers of life. They teach the children and care for the masculine and feminine future leaders of the planet. They are the current wise Shamans of the future. That's who you are, that's who you are as women, and they knew it. The men of Lemuria knew it.

You loved hearing their voices raised in song as many male voices around you in a chorus. You waited all year for it. It was beautiful and you didn't even sleep at night when it was over. That's balance. It's part of the history of Lemuria.

Kryon live channelling given during a Lemurian Sisterhood Meeting in Phoenix, Arizona – January 16, 2016

Valentine's Day Ceremony

St. Valentine's Day, as we know it today, contains traces of both Christian and ancient Roman traditions. While the exact origin is still disputed and yet to reach consensus, the ceremony has become tradition and February 14 is a day to celebrate love and romance. People from around the world mark Valentine's Day by showing appreciation for the people they love or adore. In many countries, this day is big business for florists, restaurants, and greeting card manufacturers. But what has this relatively modern ceremony have to do with Ancient Lemuria? Kryon reveals the remote connection:

It's very close to Valentine's Day, so perhaps it is time to reveal a little bit about the relationships between men and women in Lemuria. These things may be of interest to you, for they are very different than the way they are today. You would think that the relationships between the sexes would be similar due to the very biology of your race, but that's not so.

I speak to a group of women here who are life-givers, not all, but most [speaking of those in this life who have given birth]. I'll say it again: You have come here to this place, this room today, almost as an appointment. Through all of these thousands of years, in many incarnations, as both genders, you arrive here. Again we ask, *"What are the odds that you were a woman back then, and you are a woman now?"* I will tell you: One hundred percent!

There is no accident that this time around, dear Old Soul, in this new energy, dear Old Soul, that you came in again as a female. Your Akash will serve you well to remember that which was Lemuria, for you were the life-givers as well as the Spirit-givers. You were the Shamans of the village, the ones who held the torch, and here you are again.

It serves you to know this, and it helps you to feel the self-worth of who you are, and who you've been throughout history. Through this Sisterhood, you remember some of the pieces and the parts that you were, especially aligning to a time in Lemuria. What are the odds that you were in Lemuria at some point in time through the thousands of years of its existence? What are the odds? One hundred percent. Synchronicity brings you to this place. The shift brings you to this place. Before you were born, the Old Soul that you are knew of the potentials that you would pass this marker. Now, here you are.

There are men who wish they could sit here, because they remember it differently. They were there, too. I want to talk to you about that. I want to talk to you about relationships that perhaps we have never spoken of before between the men and women of Lemuria.

What was life like back then, beyond what we've talked about in multiple channellings? If you've listened to the channels, you know your history. You know who you were. You know that the men counted on your guidance as shamanic intuitives. The men wanted and needed this guidance from you. This was natural. It is natural for the giver of life on this planet to be the one who is connected first to the Creative Source ... and you were.

So what about men and women? Would you like to know about marriage? There wasn't any! Instead, there was just a simple intent ceremony. It's different than you might imagine and everyone was involved.

Lemuria was very simple. It was different, a beginning, a very beginning. There was immature consciousness about society and protocol. Later on, it became more sophisticated, but at first, it was more communal. What I mean by that is that you lived in times and places together instead of in couples. You only took one husband at a time, but you lived together with many others.

At appropriate times it was private, as it is today, where you go to a place and shut the door. But without doors, the others simply left you alone – respect. There were also seasons and times set aside for this, unlike today.

Marriage was sacred. It was not arranged since there was no reason for that. Arranged marriages today are often due to caste and birthdays [astrological chart], but you were a fresh, beginning society with no social lines yet. Women, you had choice of mate. All women had choice.

The interesting thing about it was that the woman got first choice. The rules for men were that they could only "get married" after fifty! More on this in a moment, for it's not what it seems. Many mated while younger, but the first "women's choice" was given only to a man over fifty.

The life span of all those in Lemuria was far greater than in your society now. In addition, due to the shamanic teaching of the women, they consistently outlived the men. Having constant energy with Spirit creates a very long life. This attribute is still seen today with some of your cultures on Earth.

Why did Lemurians live so long? It is only common sense that when you have an isolated society, on a mini-continent, and you do not have the diseases of the mainland, it becomes an encapsulated society with different attributes, where you could live a very long life. You lived very healthy lives as well.

One of the reasons for long life is non-exposure to disease. The other is because everything you ate was super-fresh. Most of the things that you ate, over ninety percent, came from the ocean. Your husbands and the men of all families – fished. This is what they did. We've told you before that part of your jobs, dear women, besides birthing almost every month to someone in your circle, was to "bless the catch." You met with the men very early in the morning, in another ceremony, and told them where to find the fish that day. Do you see how they counted on you?

How did you know these things about the fish? It's the ability to sense things that others cannot. It's about wisdom, and it's about a connection to the other side of the veil. Can you see the value of why you were so valuable to society with these gifts?

There were ceremonies, and times of mating one with another in a system. I told you the women had choice. But it wasn't an Earth calendar system at all. It had to do more with the stars, and it had to do with the weather, a lot about the weather. It was about the winds – how they shifted, and when you did certain kinds of things, and when not to fish.

Let's return to the odd idea that men could only get married after fifty. Women could get married as soon as they were able to conceive. Now, this "over fifty" rule may seem odd to you, but there was reasoning there, and it had to do with fertility and life span.

When the women came to childbearing age, they chose a man over fifty. Don't get ahead of me. With extended Lemurian life span, a fifty-year-old male was only twenty-five percent through his life, and very fertile. But the woman did the choosing, not the men. The men liked this system, by the way, for what is to come in a moment. A man over fifty received a young wife, and this was an honor for his age and ability to care for that women. There were plenty of men over fifty.

However, now comes the interesting part: When the woman outlived this man, and she always did, she would then get the choice of which brother to go to next. If no brother was over fifty, she selected the oldest one. So almost all women eventually had at least two husbands in the family lineage because one would eventually pass on.

If that brother died, then the woman was designated as a special kind of widow and she could choose again, another fifty-year-old if she wished, from another family. They all had society rules, just like you do now. Men and women also had some of the same compatibility problems, just like now. Humans are Humans, but I want to tell you about something. I want to tell you about a special "time of year" between couples. This didn't last more than three days, but once a year, when the wind blew a certain way, there was another kind of honoring. It's the closest thing you'll ever get to today's Valentine's Day.

You might be interested to know that the work was shared in an interesting way in this place, a way that you might not realize. Because of your own society, you just assume the women stayed home and did domestic things. They cooked the meals and cared for the children. In this particular society, however, they were also the Shamans.

Ladies, you were busy, but what was just described is not necessarily what you did. First of all, it would have been unconscionable for a woman to cook the fish that the men caught! That was prohibited. Men cooked the fish. Doesn't that make sense? They go out, they fish, they catch them, they say hello to the fish [as part of honoring Gaia], the fish dies in their hands, and they cook it! All of the men cooked their own fish, and by the way, it was men's communal cooking. Not everybody caught the fish they wanted, so they mixed it up a bit, and the fishermen often traded with each other. Does that make sense? Women did not cook, but the women did harvest crops on the island.

The tropics were wonderful for growing many kinds of things, so instead of cooking, the women were out harvesting and caring for the children. So in Lemuria, women didn't cook. Do you like it so far?

Now, the special time of year: It's hard to describe a society without a clock. Instead, you ladies felt it. You knew what to do. The cycles were the cycles. The cycles of birth are the cycles, and that seldom changed. But when it came to certain kinds of celebrations, it really was Gaia who dictated when it was time.

There was a three-day celebration, a celebration of women. The men loved it, for they got to dress up in special colors. Don't laugh, the colors were the women's colors. They dressed as women! It was to honor the women ... a kind of role-reversal-honoring. What the men did was to swap roles for three days, and they cared for the children. So "Valentine's Day," for them, was a time when they said "thank you" to the women for all they did, and the men took the burden of the children, and they still cooked – imagine! [laughter]. It was an honor.

A senior woman was always revered. This is the one who usually had the most grandchildren. They sat in front. Anytime there was ceremony, they sat in front. The senior women were seen almost as Gods because they had been in the Lemurian Sisterhood the longest. It was also because they had communicated with Spirit and guided the men for so long to the fish. So, everyone recognized this. These women were the ones to thank for the actual survival of this civilization for so long, and they got to sit in front.

You might say, *"Well, where did the tribal elders sit?"* Indeed! These WERE the tribal elders, did I tell you that? The women had this aspect as well since, again, they were the shamanic leaders. The men loved it. For three days they dressed as you did, in your family colors. They cared for the children as a way of saying, "We love our women." That's who you are. That's Valentine's Day, Lemurian style.

Kryon live channelling given during a Lemurian Sisterhood Meeting in Toronto, Canada – February 13, 2016

New Year Ceremony

Those of us living in a western culture celebrate New Year's Day on January 1, the first official day of the Gregorian calendar. However, there are many different dates of the New Year from other cultures around the world. For example, the Chinese New Year celebrates when the new moon of the first lunar month occurs between January 21 and February 21. The Jewish New Year is celebrated in the Fall (autumn) on the first two days of the seventh month of the Hebrew calendar, while the Thai New Year is celebrated on April 13. Regardless of the date of celebration, it is evident that each culture has their own unique way of celebrating the New Year. The Lemurians also celebrated the New Year and Kryon tells us how:

There is a great history represented by the idea of this which you call *The Lemurian Sisterhood*. Through time and many channellings, we have slowly presented the concepts of the society of Lemuria. We speak now to all who listen who are female, and we say to you this: In this current shift, in this magic time, the end of this precession of the equinoxes, your gender is not random. That is to say, it was on purpose for this time.

The plan was always this: Although it was free choice for humanity to go through this shift or not, in case you did, all female participants of the original Sisterhood, over the many years it existed, would be alive again today as women in these years.

Let ancient history remember that there was a time on the planet when the women carried this needed banner: the torch of shamanship. It was natural and the men needed and expected it. They turned to the women for this kind of advice and help. This has been the premise all along.

Indeed, as we have discussed before, you ladies today were not necessarily together [participating in] a Sisterhood [at the same time]. It was scattered over many years and many lifetimes, but that doesn't matter because the *seeds of your Akash* all experienced it. The seeds of your Akash are what you're discussing in this meeting right now. It brings you together. It doesn't matter how many lifetimes [ago] it was, or whether you lived them together or not. There is a togetherness now, which is the Sisterhood – something that all of you have experienced at one time [or another].

The questions here have always been similar to this: *"How do you apply all this to now? What does it mean?"* We have discussed some of those things already. We have even said the last time we were together, "Look for a *void* of things that are not being done today. These are an absence of things you knew worked back then, and a potential where you might rekindle them. However, you don't have to rewrite anything that's happening now, to do it.

I want to present something right now, and it's for Mele'ha [Dr. Wolf]. It's also for those women who are here. If I could take you back to the small continent that you call Lemuria, the 30,000-foot-high mountain of Hawaii when it was out of the water, where was the Sisterhood?

The answer is that there were Sisterhoods everywhere. This Lemuria of yours was a fairly large place, and you all lived next to the ocean. Inland living was almost always up the mountain, and wasn't desirable. So you all lived close to the coast. This is also where the fishing was, and this was where the teaching took place. The weather was almost always nice, and it wasn't cold. There were the equivalent of Sisterhoods, everywhere.

Did you ever think that it was a collective, that is to say, there may have been forty or fifty Sisterhoods going at the same time all over this mini-continent? Indeed, this happened, and it's the same now in cultures that have very similar spiritual experiences. They end up being much the same, but isolated to smaller groups.

Now, there was only one central mountain with many peaks, and one main volcano. There were no islands as there are today. That came later as the sinking began. So you must think of it differently from today's chain of islands. However, there were many Sisterhood-like gatherings because there were so many villages.

Part of the tasks of the Mele'has was to do some traveling from Sisterhood to Sisterhood almost all the time. Although there were many Mele'ha-like priestesses, there were not enough to have one in every village. They all traveled to service other women's gatherings. However, there is something that took place that I would like you to emulate, Mele'ha. I want to give you some instructions and you have a year to put this together.

On the beginning of the Lemurian yearly calendar [equivalent to New Years for you], they all did something together. The calendar was different then, but as the seasons progressed, there was indeed the "beginning of the new cycle," as they called it. They didn't call it a new year, really. Instead, it was a new energy and it was a new beginning. Each and every time the cycle was renewed, the women's gatherings did something together.

Some might ask, *"Well, how did they do something together when there was no clock – no time reference – and no real fast communication between villages?"* In the case of Lemuria, the most consistent thing they had together was the tides. So each woman's gathering had a tide marker to use after the sun went down. When a rising or falling tide was at a certain place, and the marker was slightly covered or uncovered (depending on the situation), they all got the same message at the same time.

The women would begin the service, and it was a grand celebration. It was more than normal since men attended, but did not participate in speaking much. Each woman in the circle would tell about what happened that year that was beautiful. They talked about the birth of their children; they reviewed those who passed away, and would celebrate those souls, one by one. Even if some of the women had health issues, they would talk about the help they received throughout the past year, and name the women or men who had cared for them, bathed them, and touched their heads. There were no complaining times for the teachers who were Lemurians. This consciousness came from the original teachers within Lemuria.

Dear ladies, they didn't do affirmations, for that was a bit too progressive for them. However, the idea was that positive things created more positive things. Negative talk created more negative things. The ocean itself was listening to them that night, and they knew about how the mountains and air were part of their lives as well. They spoke only positive things about themselves and others that evening, and the celebration really was a New Year celebration.

It was done as close as they could on the evening before the new season began, the new cycle began. They called it something completely different from what you call it now and it was at a different time of year. All of them coordinated it over this place you called Lemuria, and they all knew they were doing it at the same time.

Mele'ha would supervise over a central or regional one, which was her home, but she also knew that most of them were doing it at the same time. Again, they were singing the same songs, and were giving the same messages. It was a celebration with new-cycle protocol ... the same celebration was known to all.

So, once a year they were allied together as one. I want you to do that, Mele'ha. It might be tough right now, because nothing has been planned for this year. However, within a year, it is possible. You have the technology to come together all over the planet as one giant Sisterhood, if you wish. Design it so you're doing the same thing as in the past: Nothing negative is spoken, no matter what. [This is] where you can reflect on the year and celebrate the things that need celebration. Look at the challenges as something you got through. Look at the times you struggled as a victory over struggle. This will strengthen you for the next time it takes place. The togetherness of this one ceremony sets the stage and the attitude for all the villages for the whole next season cycle and, again, the men were there.

The men sat in the back and they got to hear, once a year, what the women had to say. They felt the beauty, gentleness, and spirituality of the rejoicing, of the sacredness. They sat there in silence, with the torches burning, respecting that which they understood fully. They knew what the women did for them. The women knew how to touch the face of Spirit – to communicate with the Creator – the ones who told the village men where to fish. Many times, the women told the men to stay home, and then a storm would quickly sweep over the mountain. The woman's intuition and shamanship had saved countless lives.

Once a year, something special happened – all together and everyone attended. You have a year, Mele'ha, if you wish this to be. The Sisterhood is getting bigger, and it truly represents the love of women in communication with women and also women in touch with the Creative Source. It is beautiful.

I want you to conjure up a vision right now – of what it was like. The sun went down; the torches would be lit; the breezes were blowing and you began in a loud voice. The women around the circle could all hear you starting the celebration and discussing what had happened that year. Then the others would review the year and speak about those who had passed, in such a positive and rewarding way.

Everyone looked forward to this, and it was the highlight of the year! I bring it up right now because this is the last Sisterhood of the year and, perhaps, this will be the last year that there is no collective ceremony. Think about these things, what they meant then, and what they might mean now as the Sisterhood starts to graduate into something larger. Thank you, Mele'ha, for what you're doing for the planet.

Kryon live channelling given during a Lemurian Sisterhood Meeting in Las Vegas, Nevada – December 10, 2016

Ceremonies, by definition, are ritual observations and procedures, often set by tradition, marking a special occasion. Ceremonies can celebrate a particular event or anniversary. Many organized belief systems (religions) have ceremonies or a series of rites. The original ceremonies came from the Pleiadian Mothers and teachers. Kryon mentioned that ceremonies were done sparingly and this suggests that, when ceremonies occurred, they were extraordinarily special. The Lemurian ceremonies described above essentially involved women, and occasionally children and men, coming together with purpose. What about ceremonies that are completely and totally private and personal, done alone? Did such a ceremony happen in Lemuria? The answer is yes. Here is one that you should know about:

Greetings, dear ladies, I am Kryon of Magnetic Service. My partner steps away. These channels are slightly different. They're different because they are for you, the Sisterhood. Indeed, they will be listened to by others, but they are mostly for the ones in the room and that changes from channel to channel.

The cumulative lifetimes represented here are absolutely unique. Some were part of an early Sisterhood in Lemuria and some represent later ones as well, and they all feature very different energies.

I want to change the name that I call you today. I'm tired of *dear ladies*. There is no gender here except the feminine. Don't be fooled by the masculine voice. The meeting is in great honor for the gender that we speak of now. Kryon has no gender. The voice you listen to, who gives the channelled message, is genderless as he speaks because he is in a genderless space, so it's just "us ladies who are here."

Listen. I'm not going to call you *ladies* anymore tonight. You have a new name that I'll use. Perhaps Mele'ha will use it, too? It's up to her. I want to call you *Star Sisters*. That's who you are. You received the original teaching from the stars in Lemuria. That's who you are, and you carry the origination of the knowledge first given to the planet. You received the knowledge directly, which would start a lineage of shamanic females on the planet.

Today, my partner talked about the system of reincarnation that would involve gender [how gender works is different from the reincarnation system]. The system was a bit different at its beginning. I'll tell you this: The Star Sisters remained female for a very long time. Time after time it had to be this way, for you carried the lineage of the shamanic energy that was female: The star information as Star Sisters. So, whereas the rest of the planet might come and go with genders in a system, you were female longer than most, and that is *etched* into you.

Old Souls that are part of the original Lemurian experience have a far grander idea of who they are than most Humans. Sometimes, it's confusing and sometimes, it's frustrating. What if I told you that you walk this planet basically frustrated and in trouble because, deep down, you recognize you're a Star Sister? You recognize the shamanic lineage that is in there, in the DNA, yet you are surrounded by issues.

Some of you are bold enough to think and say, *"This frustration shouldn't be happening. I'm better than this!"* Not better, perhaps, in an egotistical way, but in a historical, factual way. Women are now saying, *"My lineage is grander than my current experience."* If you said this, you'd be right.

I want to paint a picture, and this is something I want you to think about because of what's coming next. As you know and we have told you before, Lemuria, the small continent of Mu, was a precursor to what is today the Hawaiian Islands. When Lemuria existed, it was all one huge island, pushed up by a bubble of magma at this hot spot on Earth, which is still Hawaii today. It's so high that there were even remnants of glaciers being formed at that time. It was higher than any other mountain on the planet in its day. Today, you think of Hawaii as vacation islands with active volcanoes. For the life of humanity, that volcano has always been active, dear ones.

Hot spots are often that way and Lemuria, in particular, was hot and volcanic. However, it wasn't the same back then because the island-mountain was pushed way up, and the rim of the volcano [caldera] was always in the ice and snow. Add the winds at altitude, and it was treacherous and you didn't go there. Today, you are able to walk to the rim and throw things in and do ceremony in the tropics, but back then it was not possible. It was too high, it was too difficult, it was too cold, and there was way too much ice.

The Lemurian mountain volcano [Hawaii] is not the kind that builds up and explodes in a massive event. These volcanoes [in Hawaii] often will carry an attribute where an eruption will spill lava out of the sides of the mountain and flow to the water. Indeed, this was the case then, so there was always lava flowing to the water, and you could find it easily without going up too high. In addition, the topography of the land created a "known" lava potential flow area, where most of the cracks occurred. Villagers knew better than to build in those areas. But they built paths that would allow them to easily visit the flows.

I want to introduce you to someone who is nameless. She's a Star Sister and, maybe, she's one of you. She could be. She has made her way into one of those lower altitude places where the lava has exposed itself. Many times, the lava was carried in tubes underground and you couldn't see it flow. But eventually, it would show itself as a kind of small river. She had to be in a place where it flowed where she could see it.

This Star Sister couldn't get too close since it was way too hot, but she could get close enough to where, if the flow was entering or exiting a lava tube, it would be far enough away that she could do her task. She made her way to this place usually by herself and, when she got to that place where she was poised on the rim of the lava canal, where the lava was flowing into or out of a lava tube, it was far enough away not to hurt her. Then you see her take something from her skirt and unroll it. It was a giant leaf, and on that leaf there were inscriptions. It wasn't writing as you would know it, but it looked like line drawings that she had inscribed into it with the edge of a twig. She was going to do something with that leaf and the lava.

She looked at it for a moment and she held it upside down. Then, she let it go into the lava. It had to go into the lava. If it got stuck on the way down, she'd go home, make another one, until into the lava it went. It had to be completely and totally consumed instantly by the fire, and if she did it right, it would be. You would see her raise her hands in thanks and she would have a big smile. Then, she turned around and went back to the village, victorious. I want you to remember this because of what's coming. What was she doing?

Star Sisters, you started out with some precious information back then. It's still in there, somewhere [meaning in your Akashic memory]. How far back it was in time doesn't matter. Listen: I'll tell you, again, that Humans count years in linear fashion, but in your Akash, it's about energy, and not linear at all. You don't use more energy to go further back in Akashic reading [smile]. It's all together and some of it can feel very current, even if it's absolutely ancient.

Can you imagine what has happened to you, with you, for you, or against you, since you might have been in Lemuria? Eons of time have gone by and so much happened. Lifetime after lifetime has occurred as the planet itself has gone through its own cycles. Can you imagine the children you've had? Ladies, Star Sisters, can you imagine the children you've lost? It's in modern day, by the way, that you expect children to live! You knew that, back then. Mothers, you knew that. There was a good fifty percent chance children wouldn't make it, and sometimes you didn't name them until they were at least a few months old. It was a different time, dear Star Sisters.

In Lemurian times, you expected them all to live, but after that, you didn't. Moving off of Lemuria created a far greater life experience, and you all participated. Who are you? What have you been through? There is an entire area of horror and disappointment you all have had, and I'm going to call it *junk*. It's junk that you carry around with you today that obfuscates, or covers up the precious information from the stars that you also carry. Here you are, in a Sisterhood meeting, trying your best to have good, positive Akashic remembrance of pure things from the stars. How can you get through the junk?

What do you do? How can you take that which is the junk and decipher it and separate it? Like the wheat from the chaff, it's the pure positive things from what you don't need, the darkness from the light. Today's energy makes that a tough task.

In today's seminar lesson, I told you about your Innate, the great sorter of Akashic information. If you never recognize your Innate, all you get are difficult Akashic remembrances coming forward, and sometimes they can affect your entire life. However, all you have to do is acknowledge your smart body (Innate) and the Akash will begin to sort itself. This is part of some of the new hidden tools of this new and beautiful age of the shift. In the sorting, you'll start to remember parts of who you were. Remember, not episodes or flashbacks, but energy.

Now, you haven't gotten there yet completely. Some are better at it than others, but it's doable. Dear ones, the Lemurian that you were, wasn't there either. You were simply a student. You did not have an elevated consciousness to the point where your Innate was even part of your biology. This came later. Instead, what you had was precious information that actually manifested energy. It was fresh teaching from the Star Mothers, and this is what Shamans have. But this spectacular information was covered up, year after year, lifetime after lifetime, with junk. Wouldn't it be great to be able to separate the junk? So let's talk about it.

First of all, as I said, it is doable. However, in this energy, it still requires a process. Mele'ha may not have thought about this, but her entire training in this lifetime has been in processes. She stands at the right time at the right place, being able to lead the processes of ceremonies that you would have today and in the past years. It is part of who she is this lifetime, married to her own life processes. Did you know that, in Lemuria, there were processes as well?

Lemuria was incredibly pure, and this lasted a very long time in that place. It's the reason it was in the middle of the Pacific Ocean and you only had ONE lifetime there. Only those in the first wave [Lemuria] stayed pure and then Human nature and duality developed over time all over the planet with free choice, and it would create junk. It's the old energy you call Human nature: you would have disappointments and work the puzzle of dark and light. Even as a Shaman, or because of it, there would be the creation of the *junk*.

Let me give you the process and it may sound familiar to some of the things you might be doing today. Here's the definition of *junk*: Akashic junk is anything that keeps you from seeing your magnificence – anything. Frustration, fears, inappropriate thoughts, lack of faith, lack of trust, unworthiness – it's all junk. Layer on layer are things that you have actually experienced, and it's huge – enormous. However, I want to tell you that it doesn't hold a candle to the pure information that you were given by the Star Mothers and, to this day, all that purity wants to come forward and allow you to understand who you are.

Today you've got wonderful language and the elegance of communicating it on paper. So I want you to start writing down, in private, the nitty-gritty junk, and the stuff that hurts your heart to write. Don't write your wishes for tomorrow. Write your frustrations from the past, and the sorrow of losing your children, the anger you've had at others around you. Include both genders and write about the anger you've had at your parents, the inappropriate things you see now, and the frustration to the max over the difficult things you see. Write the frustrations that you don't even want to think about, that you've gone through in this lifetime. If you have been betrayed, write it down.

Put all of this on paper, and when you think you're done, keep going. *"Have I written down anything that separates me from the magnificence of God?"* Did you write down your own frustrations? Think again and continue writing. What else frustrates you? Make sure you put all of it on paper.

When you think you're complete, don't review it. You felt it as you wrote it. That was enough of a review. I want you to fold the document quickly so you don't have to look at it ever again, ever. Then I want you to do a ceremony around the energy on the paper. That's the process. The best thing you could ever do is burn it and watch it burn. You'll remember that, because that's exactly what the shamanic woman was doing, dear Star Sisters. She was looking for the lava, the hottest thing she could find, to dispose of that which she had inscribed on a leaf with a twig in her basic light language that she had learned.

Back then, there wasn't the junk you have now, but still, she may have had inappropriate anger for others, or for herself, where she knew there was something she had to purge within. This was always based upon the beautiful Star Mother information she had been taught from birth. See, duality is something that belongs to all of you. She knew she was working with her duality as all Humans do, and when she watched the leaf burn, she knew she was free!

This carries over, even today, into certain spiritual systems and what they do in order to cleanse energy. This really has nothing to do with sin and everything to do with duality. All of you have it, and it's about time to get rid of the junk. That's the message. I want you to remember this because you all did it. Each of you. It worked back then, and it works today. When you do this, your *Innate* feels it. It's ceremonial, purposeful, and represents conscious intent, and your body knows what you're doing. Your Akash knows what you're doing and, in the process, the spiritual eraser comes out and the frustrations diminish and diminish. Then, over time, they're gone.

"Kryon, is it really possible to erase things from the memory of your Akash?" I'll tell you this: What has happened in the past has happened. It cannot be changed, but your perception of it is what is carried in your Akash. The Akashic record is about energy, not events. If you bury something dark and you dig a hole and put dirt on it, does it still exist? Yes, but it's six feet under and that's where it belongs and stays and it's out of sight. It's the same with negative energy within the Akash. The energy can be reframed, and put into a space where it will never be "part of you" again. Star Sisters, I invite you, one way or another, to burn the junk.

Kryon live channelling given during a Lemurian Sisterhood Meeting in Minneapolis, Minnesota – July 22, 2017

Is there any junk in your life that you would like to permanently release? The invitation is there for you to "burn the junk" in your own personal ceremony, or a ceremony with others. There is a shift on the planet (see Chapter Three: The Great Shift), which has created a new energy that supports Lightworkers and Old Souls in a way that it never has before. Kryon says, *"the wind is at your back,"* and the benevolent energy of the universe wants to harmonize with those who seek benevolence.

This shift is why affirmations are more powerful today than they were in the past. When you speak affirmations out loud with a conscious intent, you hear it with your ears, and your body understands what you are doing. Statements of intent carry energy, and words in the air have frequencies that your intelligent body consciousness (Innate), will understand. Combining affirmations with ceremonies of release is a powerful way to change your life. Spend some time thinking about who you wish to be, and what you wish to co-create. Trust your inner wisdom to guide you to the tools, techniques, and solutions to manifest the life you choose to live.

Questions for Kryon:

At first glance, there appears to be conflicting information regarding birthing, in which births happened every month, but also seasonally. Can you give further clarification?

Answer:

The subject is procreation and birth in Lemuria. First, there is the birthing from a Pleiadian Star Mother, and secondly, there is the birthing from a Lemurian mother. There are two separate scenarios.

First, for the Lemurians: There is a selected time for just about everything in older civilizations. Even today, you can interview the indigenous and see that almost everything they do is for a reason, and often is a reflection of the seasons of Gaia. So almost everything, from the times and ways to hunt and fish, to the ways to procreate, are tied to the wisdom of the planet. This is the exact thing that is totally missing in your current modern experience, and also the reason for runaway population growth.

The Lemurians had a season for coming together, resulting in the birth of their offspring falling into its own season. If you look at the intuition of the animal kingdom, you will see this exact thing. There is a mating season and a birthing season. The reason in Lemurian culture was to take advantage of weather and resources for the newborns. Even in Lemuria, there were Gaia seasons, and the idea was to not give birth in the rainy season on the mountain. It also was critical to allow birth to be on the "dry side" of the mountain, since the "wet side" was always wet, no matter what. Hence, there was travel and planning involved.

Thus, there was a non-rainy "season" on the dry side, where births for Lemurians were happening and popular. Each time a woman was ready during this season, she and the other women would travel to the dry side, and go to the pools to help her give birth and celebrate the new life. It was often exhausting, with the pools in operation continuously for up to 60 days. But it was the "season" for birth. Also notable was the fact that most of the

Lemurian population was on the dry side of the mountain for easier living.

Second, for the Pleiadian Star Mothers: They controlled their pregnancy, and had a completely different system that was NOT seasonal, but a rotational monthly event. What I'm saying is that, among the Star Mothers, they created a monthly birth rotation from which the timing of conception occurred. This allowed them to keep teaching and rotate the duties they had, as well as their trips up the mountain to the "Compassion House." Consequently, once a month there was a Star Child born on the mountain, and it was known and scheduled.

The birthing from a Pleiadian Star Mother was only helped, in the pools, from other female Star Children (direct children of a Star Mother). Since the births were fairly well scheduled by the Star Mothers (almost to the day), these "Star Children" were then ready.

So ... you ask, how many Star Mothers were there in Lemuria? The answer is yes.

There was mention of what happened when women became initiated, and when they passed away, but what about the men? Did they have similar ceremonies to the women, during which the men were initiated into manhood?

Answer:

Yes, very much so. The core teaching of the Pleiadians in Lemuria honors Human Beings, with a later emphasis on spiritual teaching for the women. The women "came of age" with their first menses. The men were gauged for ceremony by a certain age. At the age of 13, there was a "coming out" ceremony for the males. The name implied a *"coming out of childhood"* and it really didn't matter if the male thirteen-year-old was sexually mature yet or not. It was simply an acknowledgment that soon the seeds would be ready within them to help the women create another "soul journey" for a child of the Earth.

Both genders had this kind of celebration, and that's what it was – a celebration. Both genders did it with only their gender present (with one exception), and both kinds of ceremony were gentle and filled with singing and dialogue. Also, for both genders, there often were multi-celebrants, meaning that it was for all those children who were qualified, instead of doing it one-at-a-time. The celebrations were staggered in time, depending on how many were *coming of age*.

One of the most interesting parts for both genders was how the honoring was done. The honorees would take the "chairs of the elders" for that day, and be in the front row of seats. This wouldn't happen again for at least 30 years! The number of honorees in the ceremony created the amount of time it took. This is due to one of the biggest parameters of the event: The oldest elder from each family (gender-specific to the ceremony) would come forward to deliver a "message of life" for the honoree. This would be a discourse of advice, which could last as long as the elder wished to speak.

Hearing the elder's "message of life" was a bit boring since it was often the same one each time, from the same elder. It was also the source of humor among most of the village. One joke went like this: How long will this year's rainy season last? The answer: Slightly less time than the "message of life" from a certain elder. The elongated messages from the older men and women were because this was their moment to finally have permission to speak, and they just loved to have the attention of that day. Therefore, they wanted that moment to last and last and last! After all of the elders had spoken from each family group, there was a brief, small, customary meal. Then there was one last part, and it was for both genders. It was also the reason why it was worth suffering the hours of "elders' talk!"

A Star Mother would appear and give a song and a dance. The dance, however, was not a dance, at all, but an "energy motion" for the day. It was always connected to motions that the children had learned from the Teaching Wheel, so they knew it and loved seeing it from the Star Mother. The Star Mother's singing was spectacular, and that's the reason most of the village wanted to attend. She had a split vocal cord that meant she could sing harmony with herself! No other creature on the planet could do that. Listening to her was truly an otherworldly experience.

The personal ceremony of the Star Sister releasing the inappropriate anger provided a simple, yet profound technique that is just as relevant today as it was in Lemuria. Were there any other ceremonies like this, and if so, can you describe them?

Answer:

Humans all have duality. This is defined as the balance between light and dark consciousness, and the process of managing it. Even without a past Akash, each Human is unique and different, and deals with life in different ways. One might think that, without an Akashic Record, Humans might not have anything to work on, or to be influenced by. However, each mind is different, reflecting a sacred soul hooked to a linear mind. So logic is different, feelings are different, and life still has variety of decision and emotion.

When the DNA of humanity was changed from 24 pairs of chromosomes to 23, there were vast changes in Human consciousness. The addition of the intuition of the master Creator was just one of those changes. There was also "Creative energy within" (painting, music, sculpture, etc.) and "free will of consciousness" (ability to decide your own path). Then, you had the addition of soul awareness (the Higher-Self). The hidden 24th multidimensional chromosome was still another, and it deals with an evolving spirit. So there was plenty of variety from Human Being to Human Being.

We have described a private ceremony of a Sister releasing her anger, and what was involved metaphorically for her. But there were other ceremonies and activities, too, and almost all of them featured the release of something. The teaching of all the society from the Star Mothers told Lemurians about free choice, and about the ability of any person to change energy within them. Lemurians actually learned that feelings were energy, not subconscious hidden emotions or acting-out from past trauma. Instead, the teaching was that anything that didn't work for a person was an energy that could be released or changed. Self-introspection was the solution, or guidance from a Sister (counseling) to facilitate the individual's release protocol.

Love and jealousy were exactly the same as today, with all the attributes that go with them. There were love triangles, disappointments, and self-worth issues because of it. Issues between men and women were also the same in partnerships as today, especially the way they were often arranged after the death of a partner. Marriage, as you know it today, didn't exist in Lemuria, but other kinds of rules were involved (as we have discussed before). Within that system, there were disappointments, as well. Imagine your husband dying, and you being passed to his younger brother! Imagine being in love with a childhood friend, only to see them going with another for political reasons. Feelings are feelings, and these were things that created constant issues that had to be resolved.

So there were processes involved in the dissolving of energies that got in the way of joy. This is what was taught. You could change the way your heart felt, if you wanted to. You could "rebirth" your attitude (what Lemurians called it), and joy could return. This allowed for a ceremony that could either be individual or collective. Matters of the heart almost always dealt with water, so that they could be dissolved. Anger, however, was listed and burned, as we have described.

The water had to be the powerful waves of the open sea for the ceremony, as opposed to an alcove or pond. The waves washed away the sorrow, and brought new life or love into the heart. So you could expect many Lemurians at the beach, dealing with that. The irony is that this is also where many met their partners for life. Synchronicity also happened in the land of MU. Broken hearts found others and mended accordingly.

CHAPTER THREE

The Great Shift

Why are we discussing the Great Shift in a book titled "The Women of Lemuria?" What has this topic to do with any of the information given in the previous two chapters? The answer is that the Great Shift has *everything* to do with what humanity is remembering regarding ancient wisdom and knowledge. The shift is also the reason why Lee Carroll is channelling an entity called Kryon.

The Great Shift refers to the passing of the 2012 marker, known as the galactic alignment, heralding the birth of a new energy and consciousness on the planet. What does that even mean? In order to answer this question, we need to understand a premise. The premise is this: the 2012 galactic alignment is not an esoteric prediction. It's pure astronomy! Perhaps, you thought it was a new age philosophy? Throughout history, there has been an endless list of predicted dates for events that would result in the destruction of humanity, the planet, or the entire universe. Many of these predictions have been based on sacred scriptures describing these events as the *Rapture, Last Judgment,* or the *Second Coming of Christ.* Then there are the predictions of Nostradamus, a pseudo-astrologer who wrote mysterious quatrains, warning of the coming Apocalypse. Such predictions have remained within the field of Human consciousness throughout history, with almost all of them coming from spiritual sources. These predictions, combined with humanity's fascination for drama, created many blockbuster Hollywood movies cashing in on the fear factor. Some of these movies include *War of the Worlds*, *The Day After Tomorrow*, *I am Legend*, *Armageddon*, *Independence Day*, and *2012*, to name just a few.

In the lead-up to 2012, the media had a field day regarding the end of the Mayan Calendar. What the mainstream media failed to mention was that the end of the Mayan calendar cycle was NOT the end of the world. In fact, the Mayans had calendars projecting out to the year 4000! When we come to the end of a calendar year, we don't panic and say it's the end! We simply remove the calendar off the wall and put up the new one.

Regardless of what prophecy you heard, you should know that the 2012 event is completely based in astronomy. Let's discuss the 2012 galactic alignment. The galactic alignment is a precise astronomical term that occurs as a result of the precession of the equinoxes. This alignment is caused by a 26,000-year wobble of the planet that starts and ends when our sun perfectly lines up (as we look at it from Earth) with the center of our galaxy. All over the planet, a few days on or after December 21, 2012, was the alignment of the solstice point with the Galactic equator – this was the 2012 galactic alignment!

I want you to visualize the true shape of the Earth – an oblate spheroid with an "equatorial bulge." The Earth is also tilted and it rotates (wobbles) around an axis that is inclined with respect to the orbital plane (the flat space in which Earth orbits the sun). The tilt creates the four seasons on Earth, while the axis wobble is responsible for the precession of the equinoxes. This wobble (rotation) of the Earth's axis is extremely slow and takes a period of 26,000 years. The start and stop point of the 26,000 year cycle is known as the center of the galactic alignment.

Now let's take a look at the precession of the equinoxes. The precession refers to the apparent motion of the equinoxes along the plane of Earth's orbit caused by the Earth wobbling very slowly on its axis. The position of the equinoxes and solstices shifts one degree every 71.5 years. Because the sun is one-half of a degree wide, it will take the December solstice sun 36 years to precess through the galactic equator. This means that the 2012 experience wasn't something that happened on December 21, but was a part of a 36-year event. It began in 1994 and will finish in 2030.

Modern astronomers are all aware of the galactic alignment, but how is it that ancient cultures knew about this? Civilizations such as the ancient Egyptians, Chinese, Mayans, Toltecs, Aztecs, Druids, and Incas studied the stars. They knew about the movement of the sun, the moon, the equinoxes, and they noticed that the Earth wobbled. They didn't need telescopes as they used observatories, and in some instances, they used this knowledge to create calendars. The most well-studied and known calendar was from the Mayans.

Ancient Prophecy

The Mayan civilization was complex and they had both the Mayan Prophecies and the Mayan Calendar. The prophecies came from an intricate system and hierarchy of priests that had subjective opinions, while the calendar was a direct astronomical observation. However, within the Mayan calendar work there is evidence of esoteric information and knowledge of fractal time. What is fractal time? According to scientist Gregg Braden, ancient traditions viewed "time" as the great ripples of a galactic wave that ebb and flow as they travel throughout the Universe. Late 20th century discoveries revealed that even the most complex things in nature are really simple patterns – fractals – that repeat themselves in predictable ways. Kryon has told us that, "Fractals are the way of all physics, of all biology. If you ask a physicist about fractals, they will give you all of the mathematics – big to little, bigger, smaller – and all of it represents fractals of sameness. Biologists have known that everything goes from small to large in fractals. It's simply the way of things."

The glyphs found in Xochicalco, Mexico, reveal the time fractal predictions of the Mayan calendar. According to Jorge Baez,* who has extensively studied these glyphs, they give the prediction of the potentials of Human consciousness from year to year. The Mayan calendar glyphs' message about 2012 is that it represents a period on Earth that will experience the highest potential consciousness that humanity has ever seen.

One of the things Jorge Baez was able to do was duplicate the work of the Mayans within the ancient Maya observatories. Jorge tracked the movement of the Earth via the directed sunlight entering the observatory chamber. When Jorge superimposed known history onto the Mayan calendar, he discovered the accuracy of the calendar in relation to predictions of low and high consciousness on the planet.

Are there any other ancient prophecies that relate to 2012? Absolutely! Indigenous cultures from all over the world, including the Amazon, Andes, North, Central, and South America, have a similar prophecy that is thousands of years old – the prophecy of the Eagle and the Condor. It was predicted that Human society would divide and take different paths. The path of the eagle represents the brain, a rational and material world. The path of the condor represents the heart, an intuitive and compassionate world. The prophecy indicated that, during the 1500s, the two paths would diverge, and the eagle would drive the condor to the verge of extinction. But, the prophecy then states that, in the next 500 years, the eagle and the condor would have the opportunity to reunite and fly together along the same path. If the eagle and the condor accept this opportunity, the world will come into balance and create peace on Earth.

In Peru, there is another prophecy, known as the "Awakening of the Puma." It represents the awakening of the wisdom of the Andean masters, allowing the secrets of nature, intuition, dexterity,

---

* *Jorge Baez has written a book (Spanish only) called El Secreto del 2012: Energía vital en movimiento (The Secret of 2012: Vital energy in movement).*

and vision, to be revealed, in order to create and transform energy for the purpose of peace in humanity. The prophecy stems from Inca society, when Pachacuti Inca Yupanqui, the 9th Inca ruler, founded the Inca empire in the Cusco Valley and beyond. Andean Shaman Mallku Aribalo, has been recognized as an intuitive expert in the understanding and translation of esoteric knowledge within the Andean Archaeo-astronomy.

Within the Inca culture, the Andean city of Cusco is in the physical shape of a puma, as viewed from above. The design of the city was created through the visionary master, Inca Pachacuti, as a way of bringing the celestial animal of the puma to Earth in order to illuminate and strengthen all the inhabitants and pilgrims. This Puma, at the center of Inca society, is progressively illuminated by each sunrise, symbolizing the gradual awakening of awareness and evolution of Human Beings. Shaman Mallku describes the new era we are entering as one where spiritual and psychic doors are opening, allowing us to create new heights of responsibility, higher consciousness, and a reconnection with our planet.

Another ancient prophecy, from Mexico and Central America, refers to "The Journey of the Feathered Serpent." This prophecy is about the movement of the Kundalini of Earth. The prophecy speaks about a potential of a magnificent change for the planet, represented as a shift in consciousness. The journey of the Feathered Serpent is the movement of the Earth's Kundalini from the northern hemisphere to the southern hemisphere. The two hemispheres represent the planet's polarity, where north is masculine energy and south is feminine energy. Therefore, the movement of the Kundalini of Earth is a rebalance in consciousness. Mayan Elders have spoken about the Feathered Serpent moving to the southern hemisphere in 2012.

Many Native Indian Tribes from North America also have ancient prophecies, with the most well-known coming from the Hopi Prophecy Rock, located near Oraibi, Arizona. Gregg Braden, has studied the petroglyphs that have been etched into the sandstone rock. Gregg explains that the petroglyphs show humanity following a path until the path splits into two. The split in the path is where humanity must choose one of two worlds. On one path, the petroglyphs show Humans living in a world where crops are growing, and Humans are connected with each other and the planet. On the other path, the petroglyphs show that Humans still exist, but they are not in touch with themselves or connected with the planet. Food is scarce and life is tough. The prophecy also relates to a future decision point where there will be three great shakings of the Earth. The Hopi interpret the first shaking as World War I, the second shaking as World War II, while the third shaking cannot be predicted because Humans are determining how that shaking will occur by the way we live our lives right now.

All of these prophecies share a common message: if humanity makes it past the 2012 galactic alignment (decision point), a rebalancing of the planet would begin. This rebalance is a recalibration back to wisdom, love, and compassion. Against all odds, humanity has passed the marker. Passing the marker signals a rebirth for humanity, with new energies and new consciousness emerging. Slowly, Human nature is changing and the very fabric of our society is changing as the new consciousness creates new attitudes.

Is there any evidence of these changes? Yes, but don't watch the media that is invested in only portraying drama and horror. Instead, take a look at the global events that have occurred since 1989, when Kryon arrived. The predicted World War III between the Soviet Union and the United States of America didn't happen, due to the fall of the Soviet Union. Later came the fall of the Berlin Wall, ending the division of the capitalist west and the communist east.

Countries that have had stability for decades are suddenly having revolutions, demanding a change from their governments. Governments and institutions that lack integrity are being questioned. Take a look at institutions such as the tobacco industry and financial banks. They have had to change the way they operated due to the exposure of greed and inappropriate practices. Humanity is starting to demand change, due to a change in consciousness.

The Lemurian Sisterhood and the Shift

If the Great Shift had not occurred, the modern-day Lemurian Sisterhood would not exist, because there would be no purpose or reason for its existence. The creation of the Lemurian Sisterhood by Dr. Amber (Mele'ha) Wolf is further evidence of passing the marker. Passing 2012 heralds humanity entering a new dispensation of time. However, when moving from one consciousness to another, a period of recalibration needs to occur. Such a transition isn't automatic. In Kryon Book 13, *The Recalibration of Humanity: 2013 and Beyond*, Lee Carroll provides profound information and direct instructions on what is happening on the planet.

Kryon has described the year 2013 as the year of recalibration. When Lee Carroll presented lectures that year, he went even further, stating that it was a year of full moons. Kryon even told Lee it would be a good year to stay in the closet and be fed under the door! For many Lightworkers and Old Souls, 2013 was a challenging year. What about you? Notice anything different in your life during that year? Perhaps it wasn't until a year or two later. Why would 2013 be so challenging if we passed the marker in 2012? Kryon says it is because of the recalibration of moving from an old energy into a new. An adjustment period is required. 2013 was the year of recalibration, which meant that 2014 was the first year we experienced within the new energy. This makes 2014 Year One of the newly-evolved Human Being. As of the writing of this book we are in 2018 – Year Five of the New Era. What do we know about five-year-old children? They are still growing up and figuring things out. This explains why the evolution of humanity and the change in Human nature is happening so slowly; but rest assured, it is happening.

The following channel from Kryon was given in 2015 and, therefore, gives a perspective of what it means to be in Year Two of the shift. Although we have passed this timeline, the messages are still relevant.

On the other side of the veil, there is no gender. Therefore, we come to you completely and totally gender neutral, without bias, and with the wisdom of the ages. There are those who are listening to this who may not appreciate or fully understand the information that I'm going to give. It's only because they have not heard the rest of the story that was given earlier in the day [Kryon seminar]. Let me just say that we were speaking of the numerological implications of what we call *Year Two*. This is referring to the fact that the year 2012 was the end of a dispensation, the end of a very long age. And 2013 was a recalibration year that we did not even count in the new energy. Year One was the year 2014, and now you are in 2015. We then call this *Year Two*.

There is a lot for you to read into [understand about] Year Two, which I want to review with you in just a moment. Some of the things that I have said in past meetings regarding the Sisterhood should be reviewed. What are the chances that you would be your gender this time around and also have been the same gender when you were in Lemuria? The chances are remarkably against it. It would be what you would call *chance* or *luck*. So the first review is to tell you that there is no chance or luck. Old Soul, you carefully planned this!

When you came into this planet originally as Lemurian, you had no idea that you would pass this final marker. In fact, it was against all odds. You had failed three other times and the predictions this time, at your birth, told of the same. Yet, there was always the potential and the chance and, indeed, now here you sit in 2015. You passed the marker and you are a woman. Within this, there begins a special kind of change.

As you sit here, you have (1) the society that you live in, (2) the expectations and biases you carry, and (3) all of the things that you deal with that your gender specifically carries with it. Some of you are comfortable with this and some of you are not. It really doesn't matter, for what I'm going to tell you concerns things you don't expect. It's the *Year of the Two.*

Two, in numerological terms, means duality. So for you, duality includes that which is real world for a woman in your society combined with the sacred world. It includes the things that you bring in with your gender, specific to you. When you speak of *survival,* it often refers to your role and responsibility for bearing children, raising families, and being with partners. These things are all part of your duality and you balance them against a sacred energy that doesn't really have any gender to it at all.

So regarding this meeting, and a Sisterhood, what is it we ask you to do in these days? This is the beginning of Year Two and the true beginning of a new age. The answer comes with explanation: Heightened duality awareness is going to start creating a recognition within you of the differences between who you think you are and the sacred one that you really are.

There would be those who would say you're in a major *women's movement.* This would be where women are starting to be seen more equal. Many would tell you that it's time to take your power, or it's time to do this and that. Dear ladies, no, it isn't. Instead, it is time to lead the way in compassion!

This is what we would expect of the soft gender. This is what we would expect of the wiser gender, the ones who would bear the children of the Earth, which would become all of humanity. So the duality that is sharpening for you is going to make you more aware of the differences and also of the similarities. What you especially can do now is to meld them, so you can become more compassionate.

You're going to lead the way in this area. Now, can I say that this information is really not that new? Women were always the softer gender. But in this new energy, you're going to have a far greater influence – far greater. There will be more listening to you because others will see that your life reflects greater wisdom than theirs does.

Some of your gender on this planet are victims. History and their Akash make it so. But you are not. Even if you were, you are not now. I want to tell you that every single one of you here is powerful in your compassion. You have *compassionate action.* You are the ones who will make a difference, because what you do as an Old Soul is something that is going to spread to those who don't necessarily have what you have. You have greater knowledge and wisdom than many in this culture. It's due to your Akashic age. You have a more powerful light.

Dear ones, the more awareness and light you carry, the more benevolent and noticed you become in your actions to your families and those around you. You will have higher respect than ever before. I tell you that there is a reason why. In Lemuria, the women ran the spiritual show. Oh, the men were important for survival, but the women were seen as life-givers. This made all the difference to those who were there with you as partners and family. The life-givers were shamanic.

There will come a time again when this is the case, and there is no role that you play that is one thing or another. You all have the role of masters. So this is what we are asking: Recognize who you are in your society. Recognize it gently, lovingly, and wisely.

Kryon live channelling given during a Lemurian Sisterhood Meeting
in Sun Valley, Idaho – January 10, 2015

The planetary shift in consciousness is real and the balance between the masculine and feminine energy represents mastery. What would our planet look like if it were inhabited with balanced Human Beings? This is what peace on Earth is, and is the potential we are moving toward. This is why you are here. You are part of the shift and helping to birth these new energies.

The Re-emergence of Ancient Wisdom

Humanity is beginning to recognize the knowledge held by the wisdom-keepers of indigenous peoples from around the world.

There is recognition of the Shamans that carry ancient information. There is something else that is going on that explains the slow re-emergence of Ancient Wisdom, and it has to do with the Old Soul.

The Old Souls, who have incarnated for thousands of lifetimes on this planet, have an Akash rich in experiences. The Human Akash represents all the energy of your past, present, and future expressions of life on Earth. Your personal Akash is stored in several places, the most profound being your own DNA. Each time you are born and die on this planet your essence (soul) comes and goes from the Cave of Creation. This cave is a real place that Kryon says will never be found. The Cave of Creation connects and unites the physical with the spiritual and the multidimensional with the dimensional. Within the multidimensional part of the cave, it holds an esoteric crystalline object for every soul that has ever been on the planet and every soul to come. Each crystal holds the Akashic Record of each specific soul.

The Cave of Creation interfaces with Gaia through the Crystalline Grid. When you affect the Crystalline Grid with your consciousness and actions, it then alters the Cave of Creation. The Crystalline Grid is a multidimensional spiritual grid that lays over the planet's surface and remembers everything that Humans do and where they do it. The energy of humanity affects the vibrational level of the planet in actual time. The Crystalline Grid *responds* to Human consciousness, but it goes both ways: it receives and gives. As humanity passed the marker of 2012, both the Crystalline Grid and Cave of Creation have been recalibrating to a new vibrational level.

The biggest change of this recalibration is that the Crystalline Grid is no longer going to remember in a linear way. This changes the *importance* of certain energies, so that the energy of war, hatred, and drama from the past are *reduced* in importance. This recalibration means that the Crystalline Grid is now responding to light and dark differently. The old energy of the past, no matter how dark, will not have the effect it did before. This is why light is winning over dark.

For many of us, there is a tendency to be frustrated by how slowly things are changing. This gives us the opportunity to practice patience and understand that things are not always as they seem. This is a phrase that is often used by Kryon and it refers to a perception of life. Let's look at a new perception of our lineage of the planet, as given by Kryon:

Looking at the lineage of the planet, we have information. It wasn't until the year 1900 that the actual new enlightenment process started on the planet. Indeed, there was not much before then. It then took 87 more years to bring the vibration of the planet up to a point of decisions – decisions about vibration and the future. Whereas all the prophets said that you would have a termination at approximately the millennium shift, instead, you changed the vibration of this planet to a rate where that did not have to happen. Make no mistake, there was no plan of God's to terminate this planet. It was the vibration of the test that you had created over the eons. Humans create their own futures. You create your own prophecy. It is the consciousness of the planet that does it. You, therefore, created a different future than any of the prophets had seen, and now, almost all of the prophesy from before 1987 is moot. You are on a completely different track.

Now let me tell you something that you may love to hear. Between 1987 and 2007, something amazing happened. Due to the new energy, the crystals awakened in the Cave of Creation that had Lemurian names. They whispered, *"Time to come back!"* Three hundred fifty million of them. Listen to this, listen – all of the Lemurians who ever lived on this planet are alive again in Human bodies right now and are back! They are spread all over the globe. Listen, I've got a roomful of them right here. I'm looking at them. And that's why you're here, dear one. That's why you're reading this. And you wonder why you resound with these things? You wonder why you're vibrating higher? You wonder why there's an alliance with your cellular structure and the Kryon? It's because you're Lemurian, an Old Soul in a new energy.

"Kryon, does that mean my soul hasn't been here before 1900?" Now, that answer is complicated. Pieces and parts were here, but not the full Lemurian core energy. You think of yourself as one entity, one soul, one name, and one face. But you're not. You're a combination of many energies. It's difficult to explain, if not impossible. Each time you arrive, you're like the soup that gets made and comes to the planet. There is a Higher-Self, which is the same core energy every time. But what surrounds it has great spiritual variety. But now, some of you are back with the Lemurians' core energy surrounding you, something that hasn't happened for 50,000 years. Those pieces of DNA are being re-activated.

Listen to what I've been telling you for years: Less than one-half of one percent of this planet has to awaken to make a difference in the vibration for all. You will move into 2012 with a new vibration. Less than one-half of one percent of seven billion people have to awaken. It's not that many. In fact, it's only 10% of the 350 million Lemurians who are alive today – a very reasonable percentage.

Where are you in this puzzle? How long is civilization supposed to last? I will tell you. The answer is your future, and you will decide that. You are totally in control of it, so it can go as long as you wish. But I will tell you how long the test was designed for. Some of you will laugh. There are many kinds of popular numbers that float around a culture that have become doctrine and mythology. But quite often, there is core truth to their importance. One of them, which appears many times as many things, is 144,000. It's intuitive and you all know it. It represents the length of the test in years – 144,000 years.

You sit at the 200,000 mark (measured from when the Pleiadians came). You see, there's plenty of time left if you don't destroy yourselves, and Lemurians can change that. They already have. You have a time coming up that is going to be what we call cooperative or

213

commensurate with this entire growth. And the Mayans prophesied it. The energy of Gaia itself will start beginning to shift in 2012. A cycle that will last longer than 1,000 years will occur, one that is more friendly to your spiritual growth than the energy that you were born in.

The question has been asked, *"So, when are we going to meet your brothers? When will the Pleiadians return to the planet?"* Oh, I don't think it's a mystery to any of you. They visit regularly. Some see them, some don't. There's no sinister plan, dear ones. When they watch you, they watch in love to see how the garden is growing. Should you last through the 144,000 years, at the end of the test you will be just like them – a planet that is enlightened, one with the attributes of the Great Central Sun. [Kryon smile]

And I'll tell you something that many of you don't want to hear. If you're a Lemurian in the room, you're going to be there! That's how many lifetimes you've got left. That's how much you love the Earth. We've told you many times before, as a Human, you look in the mirror and spiritually you say, *"I'm tired. I'm not going to come back."* You say, *"I've done my job. This is a lot of work. I don't want to go through this again."* Then you make up your Human mind and you have a one-sided conversation with God about coming back ... and that's funny. [Kryon laughter]

You're all coming back! It's what you do. You can hardly wait. "Tired" is Human talk. There is no tired on the other side of the veil, only compassion. This test you're in, it's all about compassion. 1987 brought the Harmonic Convergence. 2002, the completion of the magnetic grid and the beginning of the crystalline experience. 2004, the tsunami and the Venus Transit. 2012, another Venus Transit. These are the delivery events of compassionate feminine energy to this world, to be picked up and used slowly so you can move into the next energy with integrity. It provides a compassionate balance to a planet that has not been balanced for eons.

"Kryon, if you could give a marker of where we are now, how are we doing?" You wouldn't be here right now with this channelling going

on unless it were right where it belongs. There'll come a time when you look back on this history and you will call this time *the dark ages of enlightenment*. And some of you know it. This is the time where the door is simply being opened slowly for the light of spiritual understanding. Here's a term that may not translate correctly in all languages, but the time you are in now will come to be known as the age of *conflicting monotheism*. Everyone agrees there is one God. But no one agrees which one. That's what you're going to have to figure out next, and just as you look back on some of your history and see how that was solved, this one will be solved as well.

I close now. What is the energy of the day? I'll give it to you. Compassion and synchronicity. How much light can you send to those around you? Can you send light to a Human Being on this vessel who needs it without them necessarily participating in the meeting, or even knowing about this energy, or having any idea about God? Can you temper someone's sorrow? Do you have the ability to hold their hand with light? Let me tell you something. The system brought them here so you could do exactly that. Do you accept that? Then do it, Lemurian. Do it.

Welcome to a new age.

Kryon live channelling "The History of Humanity"
given in western Mediterranean Sea 8th Annual Kryon Cruise –
August/September 2007

Is there any evidence that light is winning and humanity is choosing love and compassion over hatred and war? Not only is there evidence, there is a growing movement of people all over the world participating in compassionate action in everyday life. There are many examples; the following paragraphs describe two non-profit movements that anyone can become involved with.

The first is "The Abundant Love Project" created by visionary artist, Deborah DeLisi. Following the tragic loss of her daughter, Kate, Deborah spent many months crying while walking the beach, looking down at the thousands of stones beneath her feet.

In her grief, these stones became comforting. She began picking up stones, taking them home, and bringing them to life by painting faces on them.

As the clan of stone people grew, Deborah began to sell them to make room for more stones. At the same time, she began drawing hearts on the smaller stones and writing "You are Loved" on the back of each one. She gave these love stones away. As she did, she realized that her daughter Kate would have loved them. That thought sparked an idea that maybe a random act of kindness could make a difference in someone's life, especially those who are experiencing depression, fatigue, the loss of their job or relationship, or simply having a tough day. The thought of Kate's approval propelled Deborah to continue making these love stones and hiding them in public places for strangers to find.

As interest grew in Deborah's actions of compassion, she created "The Abundant Love Project" page on Facebook, giving instructions on how to make the love stones, complete with a note that people can print out and place with the hidden stone. From all over the world, people have been decorating love stones and hiding them, while others are finding them and posting their stories of how they were touched by such kindness. A community of compassion and kindness was born, with love as the guiding force.

With thousands of Facebook followers, the love stones are being hidden all around the planet. "The Abundant Love Project" continues to spread, reaching out to others in a fun, creative, and contagious way. This project demonstrates that everyone has the power to make a difference. Even the smallest of stones can create a ripple of love that reaches beyond what we can imagine. To find out more, or to become involved, visit:

www.abundantloveproject.com
www.facebook.com/abundantloveproject

The second example is "The Compassion Games International." The origin of the games has its roots in Seattle, Washington. In 2008, Seattle hosted a free public event called the "Seeds of Compassion" with His Holiness the Dalai Lama, Archbishop Desmond Tutu, and other luminaries. It proved to be the largest event ever held in Washington State. Two years later, Seattle became the first city in the world to affirm the Charter for Compassion and began a ten-year campaign to become a compassionate city. In response to this campaign, the Mayor of Louisville, Kentucky, announced that his city was the most compassionate city in the world until proven otherwise. Following this challenge the response from Seattle was the creation of the Compassion Games: Survival of the Kindest!

Unlike other games, absolutely nobody can lose in the Compassion Games. In fact, the more people who play, the more people win! Any individual, organization, or community can sign up and play the Compassion Games. It offers fun and creative ways for compassionate action to become an integral part of a community. Since 2012, over 700 teams, from over 40 countries, have signed up to play the Compassion Games. The impact and benefits of those who participate is enormous and, in many instances, lives have been inspired, transformed, and healed. The numerous stories found on the Compassion Games website validate Kryon's message of planetary change and the evolution of Human consciousness. For more information visit:

www.compassiongames.org

You may also wish to view a video on YouTube that shows how the Compassion Games have been played in prison and high schools resulting in a dramatic change of the culture:

https://www.youtube.com/watch?v=vu7SQlm_IjQ

Question for Kryon:

While there is evidence of The Great Shift, there are still a few cultures and countries that are governed by dictators and rulers who are addicted to the old energy. There are even some countries how appear to be going backward in their policies and leadership. How will future generations be different if they are still surrounded by old energy consciousness?

Answer:

Humans all react certain ways to certain things. It will be impossible in a new energy future to have holdout governments when they can no longer trade with the rest of the planet. No country is completely self-sufficient for all of its resources, and they must be allowed to trade.

When these leaders start to be closed to interaction with the rest of the world, due to low consciousness, they will be forced to change. If you have slavery of children in a country next to you, your government will shut the border, all trade will cease, and that country will be cut off from everything, as though it did not exist. If it tries to use force to threaten or correct the issue, the rest of the world will also get involved. Eventually, the low consciousness of the old guard will die away.

Sometimes, the old energy leaders will see it and move accordingly, and other times, the people themselves will begin to starve, and replace the leader. Either way, time will begin to correct the dysfunction of the old energy, allowing the planet to slowly be able to communicate with integrity and honesty.

This is no different than the physics of the flow of water into an area. You can dam it up for a while, but, eventually, it will overwhelm all efforts to stop it, and it will go where it wants to go. Light is that way. It is active, and dark is passive. So, light will flow to areas that are dark, no matter what kind of barriers the darkness tries to put up. Light peeks through all the old broken doors of dysfunction, and, eventually, illuminates even the darkest corners of all that is.

CHAPTER FOUR

The Lemurian Sisterhood

The Lemurian Sisterhood was birthed directly from the Akashic remembrance of Dr. Amber (Mele'ha) Wolf. Dr. Wolf has been practicing holistic health care and education since 1982. Her interest in women's health and women's empowerment has been a primary focus throughout her career. Her spiritual experiences, and seminar partnership with Lee Carroll and the Kryon work supported the initiations, information, and remembrances she received about her life in Lemuria as Mele'ha – the last Lemurian Priestess.

However, her Akashic remembrance (as Mele'ha) was just the beginning. The physical creation of the Lemuria Sisterhood meetings required action on behalf of Dr. Wolf. When we receive intuition, it's important to put action behind the intuitive message, paying attention to synchronicities with regard to the timing. The Lemurian Sisterhood gained momentum, one meeting at a time. As the Lemurian Sisterhood grew, so did the remembrances of Mele'ha. This is the power of the collective consciousness.

Interestingly, the first meeting took place in Argentina, South America, on November 11, 2011. This represents another piece of the fulfillment of the prophecy of the Eagle and the Condor. Amber's first meeting involved traveling from the northern hemisphere to the southern hemisphere for the specific purpose of reawakening the Divine Feminine Essence of Lemuria. Since then, the community of Star Sisters within the Lemurian Sisterhood has become a global movement. The following section describes how the Lemurian Sisterhood began.

The Akashic Awakening of Mele'ha

Many of us feel we have experienced a spiritual awakening, but what does an Akashic awakening mean? Is it the same as a spiritual awakening? Yes, and no! A spiritual awakening represents a Human awakening to spiritual truths. Further, these spiritual truths are different for each person. Someone can awaken to the Spiritual teachings of the Buddha and never seek beyond these teachings. Another person can awaken to the spiritual teachings of a different organized belief system, only to continue exploring other systems of spirituality on their path to seek out truth.

While an Akashic awakening can bring spiritual truths and information, this particular type of awakening is specific to the Akashic remembrances that are held within the Akash. Your Akashic Record is an archive of everything you have ever done or experienced throughout all your lifetimes. However, the way the Akash is felt and experienced relates to profound energies, rather than accurate details.

Kryon tells us that your Akashic Record does not push linear things to your brain, such as who you were, your name, or where you lived. Instead, your Akash gives you experiential and emotional concepts. For example, past experience that created fear, drama, and unfinished emotional resolutions, are delivered to your consciousness not as a remembrance of what happened, but as emotional triggers from experiences. This explains why someone won't go to a certain place, or do a certain thing, because of what they *feel*. Sometimes, it makes no logical sense and, often, this manifests itself as fears and phobias that seem to be with you all your life, but without a trigger from this life.

The good news is that your Akash also contains hidden talents and latent abilities. Kryon calls those who have experienced thousands of lifetimes on the planet "Old Souls." The Old Souls are the ones who have the most experience and often have deep knowledge and spiritual wisdom. Within their Akash is a spiritual jar ready to be opened when they give pure intent. Since the Great Shift, Kryon tells us that our Akashic Remembrance is increasing. The re-establishment of the Lemurian Sisterhood is a direct result of Dr. Amber (Mele'ha) Wolf's Akashic awakening, and the following is her description of how it unfolded:

The Last Lemurian Priestess

In 1989, the City of Boulder, Colorado, welcomed me for my own life "do-over." It was there that I met Kryon through books – this was pre-internet, remember. Living in Boulder gave me access to a plethora of spiritual teachers, classes, books, readings, and groups. I admit I dabbled ... a lot. However, I was also a single mom, working full-time, so mostly, it was books for me.

One summer afternoon, I was browsing through the metaphysical section of a used book store, with my three-year-old son in tow, when a shiny white book fell off the shelf and landed on my sandaled foot with a thud. Ouch! That got my attention! When I bent down and picked it up and saw the glistening holographic logo of the Earth with the word "Kryon" written over it, I was immediately entranced! I opened the book at random to see if it spoke to me – and boy, did it! That was the fateful day when Kryon Book One, *The End Times*, came home with me, and I hungrily dove into it. This was the first time that I'd read anything about the "honoring the Human" and I was thrilled with that concept. Raised as a Catholic, being a sinner and born dirty were ingrained in me from birth, along with a large helping of guilt, sin, and shame. This "Kryon" had a whole new take on us Humans and I wanted a full helping! I devoured each Kryon book, written by Lee Carroll, as soon as it was published, as well as every Kryon channel, featured in the Sedona Journal.

By 1993, I moved to the small town of Lyons, about 30 minutes from Boulder, to a quiet neighborhood on a dirt road. That was where my life went in an unforeseen and remarkable direction.

My First Lemurian Teacher

In the spring of 1997, I met Sid Wolf at a health fair in Longmont, Colorado. Sid and I both did healing work for a living that has a spiritual overlay and, when we met, we both experienced an immediate strong energetic connection. Little did we know the plan that was awakening that day!

Meeting and talking with Sid was the first I had heard of Lemuria. He had moved his family from the east coast of the US (Maryland) to the west coast (California) to be a part of a spiritual community called the Lemurian Fellowship. Fourteen years later they moved to Colorado. Growing up on the east coast of the US (Connecticut) I had only heard of Atlantis and the Bermuda Triangle – maybe they were one and the same? Sid, on the other hand, had not only heard about Lemuria, he had been a member of the Lemurian Fellowship for 14 years and knew their teachings inside and out. He was more than happy to tell me all that he knew. That summer sped by, filled with life changes and, by the fall, he was reading to me nightly from the book, *The Sun Rises*, the Lemurian Fellowship's introductory story to the building of the spiritual civilization of Lemuria. It was a fascinating read, channelled by Dr. Robert Stelle, the founder of the Fellowship (which he inaugurated in 1936 in Ramona, California). *The Sun Rises* takes the reader to the "beginning of time" in Lemuria, or Mu, where Mu is short for Mulkulian Empire, which later became known as Lemuria.

What resonated with me in the Lemurian Fellowship philosophy was the way that women were esteemed – elevated and recognized as a necessary part of the balance of all things. Women were the center of the spiritual civilization – the hub around which the rest of life revolved. I loved it! As a feminist, this was the best news

I'd heard since the '60's. Apparently, the married women stayed home and educated the children and kept the home in good vibrations. The women were both the teachers and healers. I was intrigued by the idea that the women were honored and revered for their spiritual wisdom and connection with the greater Universe, the one true source. I'd never heard anything like that before – certainly not in my Catholic upbringing, or anything since.

The Lemurian Fellowship called themselves one of the original mystery schools of this Human *life wave* (or incarnating as a Human), and they say on their website that their teachings come from the Master Christ; not the most recent Christ of 2,000 years ago, but the one that was in the Mulkulian Empire 50,000 years ago. I didn't know about that, but what I did know was their Master Christ certainly thought that women had an exalted place in the world, and that was good enough for me.

Whenever I describe my first exposure to a place called Lemuria, I'm often asked if I knew right away that I had been Lemurian. Specifically, I'm asked if I ever felt like I had been there. My answer was always, no. Whenever Sid spoke about their society and teachings, I did not have any *déjà vu* sensation or resonance with my possible past in Lemuria. I wasn't drawn to study the Lemurian Fellowship further, but the first seeds of awakening had been planted. Whether or not I remembered a Lemurian life at that time was not the issue, but those first teachings opened my Akash, just enough of a crack for the light of future to begin to seep in.

My First Kryon Meeting

The next "interesting" connection was that Sid knew Lee Carroll – yep, the Kryon guy. The following summer, Sid and I drove to Santa Fe, New Mexico, to the Kryon Summer Light Conference, where I was introduced to Lee. He was warm, funny, charming, and kind ... and then he channelled! Wow – that was an experience! My first channelling is still memorable – *"Greetings, dear ones, I am Kryon of Magnetic Service."* I had been around channellers, psychics, yogi's, and spiritual teachers for years, but when that voice came through Lee, something totally unexpected happened; I started crying ... not just crying, but body-shaking sobs – I was completely startled! I was feeling the love of God in a way that I had never experienced in this life – I was overwhelmed! I felt as though my soul was being recognized and touched by sincere love; it was almost painful, after waiting for so long! Like an old wound that was being opened, cleansed, held up to the light, and healed; it was painful, but in a good way. Sid gently put his arm around me and told me to breathe – that helped. I spent the rest of the channel in a daze of what Kryon calls the "love wash" – simply feeling the love of God continually washing over me in a wave of love and honoring.

That was my first meeting with Kryon. What happened between then and now was the journey of getting to know Lee and Kryon more. Sid and I often traveled to his seminars to present our work, becoming Lee's seminar host in Colorado, then a facilitator and producer of the "Journey Home" and "Discovery" Workshops. Since 2011, I've been traveling throughout the US, Canada, and internationally with Lee to share Kryon's teachings, my practical applications of them, and the Lemurian Sisterhood.

There are those words again – Lemurian Sisterhood; that's how this story began.

The Akashic Awakening Experience

The first time I had a conscious awakening of my Akash, was September 9, 2011. Take a look at the numerology, 9/9/11, because it will have an interesting synchronistic relevance later. At the time, I thought I was just having a past life regression, something that my healer-person had muscle-tested me for and said, "You are wanting." After our therapeutic relationship of 17 years, I trusted the response she was receiving from my Innate and I would go with it. From the beginning of the session, my senses were relaxed but alert. She began a simple hypnotic regression that took me slowly down some stairs to a door. When I opened the door I didn't recognize anything. I could tell I was in some kind of cave, but not a rocky, musty, dark cave. This cave had smooth, shiny black walls and a floor that felt cool under my bare feet, with a domed roof above me. It was lighted from the bottom up by a large, round pool of water; the light pouring up into the dark from the white sandy bottom below. I was aware of being outside myself, watching the scene unfold. I took off the unusual robe I was wearing because I was drawn immediately into the water – aahhh, a perfect warm and delicious temperature as I slipped in and submersed myself. Floating effortlessly in the pool, the water enfolded me with unfamiliar buoyancy. I began feeling restored, subtly nurtured from the outside in, as the water seemed to penetrate my skin, filtering its healing power deeply into every one of my cells. As time stood still, a profound tranquility washed over me, as though I was being gently infused by a therapeutic elixir. With a feeling of detached awareness, I sensed when this process was complete and almost levitated out of the pool! The rock floor was cool and smooth under my feet as I crossed the chamber to climb up slowly onto a large slab of the dark rock, wrapped in my cozy robe. I was conscious of drifting in serenity, suffused with gratitude.

In a sense of suspended timelessness, I became aware of several colorful and gently glimmering Light Beings surrounding the table. One by one they began infusing me with their individual rays, each particular ray bringing a specific healing into me. Some of the rays were physical aspects, like flexibility and strength, others were the emotion of joy and humor, and others were deep connection with the Beings themselves – all of them brought healing. Not only was I being restored and recalibrated, there was something very familiar in what was taking place. I was having an energetic *déjà vu* – I had done this before, with these Beings, though I didn't know who or what they were. I didn't question it, but received the delicious and loving energy, soaking it up without question.

Just before this "treatment" came to a close, a towering, golden-white Being appeared behind my head and gently connected its radiance to my third eye, the point between my eyebrows. My body slowly lifted up horizontally, hovering as this light-beam streamed through me, transfusing me with more cellular restoration, spiritual connection and, again, the feeling of "Yes, I have done this before." I was utterly relaxed and trusting, and surrendered to something beyond. Gradually and tenderly, I was lowered back to the stone slab. The Being slowly drifted back from my awareness until the light was just a vaporous trace. I was in the cave, alone again, but certainly not the same person as when I had come in!

When I felt I could move, I sat up slowly, my feet coming into contact with the smooth rock floor once again. Touching my hands together at my heart, I said a prayer of earnest gratitude. I had just experienced a profound healing, but more than that, I knew I had been here in this cave before, many times. My mind was too serene for asking any questions of when and why; I was content to just be in profound peace. I turned to leave the cave, pulling the heavy door closed behind me. It was in that moment that I had a "knowing" of where I had been. The answers to my unasked questions came flooding in! "Yes, you have been here before. This cave is a lava tube, in Hawaii, and you came here with your Lemurian Sisters many, many times for healing ceremonies such as this. The benevolent energies you experienced are with you now, just as your Sisters are. You are drawn to each other in this life to love and support each other. The great Being of Light is your Pleiadian Parent." Yes! The tears of joy and recognition flowed! I had to focus strongly to stay in my body with this news, breathing fully and deeply into my belly and feeling my feet on the stairs as I gradually climbed back into the present.

Once I was back in "now time" in the treatment room, I opened my eyes and was overwhelmed by a sweet and familiar love wash. The Divine was blessing me again, and my grateful tears softly flowed. I floated out of the room, and I'm sure my car floated home. The question niggling at the back of my mind was, "What does all this mean, and what do I do with it?" The answer was, "Just enjoy." Okay, I thought, easy enough for now.

A Lemurian Akash

When the words "Akashic Records" first came into my life, I was living in a Sikh ashram in Espanola, New Mexico. I was wearing white from head (literally, a turban) to toe. I had changed my name to a spiritual "ashram" name. This was another one of those life do-overs that happened before I moved to Colorado.

At first, I understood that the Akashic Records were like a multidimensional storehouse of past life experiences; the good, bad, and everything in between. The concept was that I kept adding learning experiences in with each life, but for what purpose? I wasn't to find out until 20 years later when I was listening to Kryon's first teachings about the Akash. I felt the purpose in a practical way to know about my past and use that information now. That resonated with me! This information became so practical that I was inspired (and guided and coached by Kryon and Lee) to create a CD called, *Mining Your Akashic Record*." This was five years before my Lemurian Akashic awakening in the healing cave experience, but, as we say in metaphysical circles, "It's all Divine timing." This means that our world of linear time, calendars, clocks, even the moon's phases, and seasons, have nothing to do with the timing of Spirit, which is non-linear and quantum. Even with the creation of my Akashic Record CD, I didn't know what was waiting for me in the "Cave of Creation" where our Akashic Record crystals reside.

Investigating the Akash

After my Lemurian cave experience, I began wondering why it had happened, what was the reason that this was revealed to me, and how was it relevant? My life was already fulfilling, active, and busy with patients, traveling for work, and a family. If anything were to be added to my very full plate, I would be overwhelmed. But I knew something was bubbling up from deep within me; I was curious and wanted to know more. In a month, I would be seeing Lee and have an opportunity to share my cave experience with him.

A month later, in Jacksonville, Florida, during our Discovery Workshop, Spirit created the perfect opening for me to have a few private moments with Lee to tell him my complete cave encounter. From my first word, he listened attentively and without questioning. As glad as I was to get the story out, I finished up by saying, "I don't need to do anything with this; I don't need to be responsible for creating anything. I just feel blessed having had the experience, and would like to know what you think." He looked up at me and smiled, sensing my anxiety; he gently touched my arm and said, "It's okay." I was so relieved! YES! I'm not responsible! But, my relief only lasted a brief moment when he followed up with, "You're in charge. And I want you to have a women's meeting when we're in Argentina next month at the 11:11 conference." What? What did he just say? This meant I would be presenting a completely new meeting in ONE MONTH in Argentina in SPANISH – a language I don't speak! I was flabbergasted and scared. This was not at all what I expected – no way! I wasn't breathing! His suggestion was beyond anything I imagined, but I returned a stunned reply of, "Okay," and we parted ways. I was still in shock when I told Sid, but, as usual, Sid was very supportive and said, "You can do it. You have a month to prepare and I'll help you if you need it." That was some relief, but still, I couldn't stop thinking that this would be next to impossible.

Later that night, as I wrote in my journal about Lee's instructions that day, I realized that the date was October 10, 2011 (10/10/11). "Hmm," I thought, "my first experience in the Lemurian cave was on 9/9/11, today is 10/10/11, and I'll be presenting this on November 11, 2011 (11/11/11)!" Spirit was probably having a good laugh, because I don't believe that was a coincidence, but a big wink of acknowledgement!

So it was that only two months (of Earth time) after my first Lemurian cave experience, or, as I have come to understand it, my Akashic awakening, where I was creating my very first "women's meeting" (that became the first Lemurian Sisterhood) event in Argentina. Despite the number of years that have passed since then, I am just as passionate about these meetings! I am honored and blessed to help facilitate the awakening of many more Old Soul Lemurian Sisters. Each Sacred Circle meeting presents women with the opportunity for them to glimpse into their own awakening of their ancient Akash. Once the door to the Cave of Creation begins to open, they can experience a balance of their power and grace – the female energies from lifetimes ago. When women integrate their Divine power into daily life, they influence the minds and hearts of the world from a point of balance and compassion. This has been my sacred assignment with the Lemurian Sisterhood since my Akashic awakening.

The Journey of Our Soul

It has taken me a lifetime to transform the ingrained beliefs and patterns of being raised as a "casual Catholic." The more deeply I see the beauty and the depth of my Akashic Record, the more powerful living this life becomes. My Akash shows true Divinity – the piece of God that I am – the eternal, limitless nature of my soul. Here, I say *God* as the genderless form of the Divine Source, or the All-That-Is. It is empowering to think and feel yourself as a piece of God, and there is a responsibility that goes along with that ... a responsibility to live as God, or as a God would live and behave (or Goddess, as the case may be), a tall order!

This piece of God (that we are) is always with us when we are in Human form, and always with us when we are not. We don't give up being Divine when we have a Human life – this is a new concept. In Human form, we are not separate from God, we are different. We have this Human life, that is time-limited, and we have this body or physical vessel to carry around the Human life and Divine soul in. But we forget that we are a living piece of God and we let our connection to the Human part become the important and more meaningful part. Big mistake! But, here we are waking up and learning our way through this misunderstanding.

Where Do We Go From Here?

After 11/11/11, I continued receiving visions, messages, and healings. When subsequent Lemurian Akashic Awakenings (also called Initiations or Activations) have followed, they come in visions, sometimes one picture followed by words, or often, like a movie with narration. In the first visual downloads the priestess/leader role that I had in Lemuria hadn't come to the surface yet. My understanding now is that my energetic body was being recalibrated to hold my new mission and place in the world, but I had not received any real direction.

That all changed in January 2014 at a Kryon event in Boulder, Colorado, when I was hosting Lee Carroll. I organized a Lemurian Sisterhood meeting for that Saturday evening. Lee asked me if I would like Kryon to channel before the meeting. I was thrilled of course, and I said, "Yes!" It had been exactly one year since my beloved husband (and first Lemurian teacher), Sid, had made his transition. 2013 had been difficult for me. I had held Lemurian Sisterhood Sacred Circle meetings for more than two years, but this was the first time Lee offered a Kryon channel. That night, in January 2014, Kryon gave me my Lemurian name of Mele'ha. When Kryon said my name was Mele'ha, a rush of tingles and heat washed over me, and I felt like I lifted out of my chair! What did that name mean? I understood from Lee that the original spoken Lemurian language was similar to today's Hawaiian language, so I asked my dear "sister" Kahuna Kalei'iliahi if she could translate my new name. She was happy to and told me that the basic translation is "celebration or gift of the sacred breath or sacred life." What a blessing and another nod to my ancient Lemurian Akash. In this life, I've been a competitive swimmer as an adolescent and young teen, and have been teaching breathing and yogic breathing since the 1960's. Breathing had always been a big part of my life, so the translated meaning of Mele'ha was another affirmation that Spirit has a plan (big wink!).

Of the two audio recorders on that night, neither recorded that channel! What are the odds? What was Spirit's plan with that? Obviously, since then, the Lemurian Sisterhood Kryon channels are all recorded and available on my website (www.amberwolf-phd.com), but that night in Boulder, the energy signature was recorded in my cells. I can go back to that room in my consciousness, and to those moments and feel the love wash humming through me. That night I understood that the path was unfolding right before me – in that moment – and I was saying a big, slightly scared but dedicated "Yes!"

When I thought of myself as a Lemurian priestess, it was a big stretch for this (formerly) small-thinking woman, programmed since childhood with low/no self-esteem. Besides, it's not like toiling away for years earning a degree – this title might not be real! Fortunately, to balance that small-thinking and unconscious program, there is a wild Goddess adventurer inside of me – a good thing!

The development of the Lemurian Sisterhood grew from listening and following the guidance and instructions from Kryon and my own Lemurian Akash. This profound information continues to surprise me! I am learning to trust that I hold the power of a sacred, magnificent spirit within me, and the voices that speak from my Akash are to be trusted. They are my voices – me – the ancestral, ancient me. The additional gift I have been receiving through my Akashic awakening is the gentle whispers of love and information from the Star Mothers, the Pleiadians. They are here with me now and ask me to convey to you their sheer joy and celebration that your own awakening has begun. You are sacred and magnificent and it's about time you know it.

My Pleiadian Connection

Through the Akashic Awakening of millions of Old Souls has come the awakening of the Divine Feminine energy in the world and a powerful energetic grid on the planet has been restored. The Pleiadian Star Mothers have told me that this reawakened grid is called the Goddess Grid. We have power grids all over our planet, those created by generating electricity, running it through wires and cables, bringing electricity into our homes, so why wouldn't we have invisible energetic grids?

When first revealed to me by the Star Mothers, they showed me what I assumed was their star cluster, the Pleiades, over 444 light years from Earth! Again I asked, "How could this have anything to do with me?" I was immediately given a magnificent light show! They showed me how our galaxy is interconnected with grids of light and energy, some visible and some invisible, but all interwoven. I watched as, from deep space, a line of light lead right to my door, or, more correctly, to my core! "Here, Mele'ha, this is what this Grid has to do with you. See it, feel it, and use its light to shine on all Beings," giving me another "sacred assignment" for the Lemurian Sisterhood. I believe this was the first realization that the worldwide Sisterhood would come into being.

Pleiadian Star Mothers Teach the Goddess Grid

With more specifics to anchor the light show, the Star Mothers presented the specifics of the Goddess Grid to me this way:

The Goddess Grid is an energy field that is visible and invisible and connects all feminine energy on the planet, reaching out beyond what we know into the limitless quantum hologram of cosmic, Divine Feminine energy. In other words, the Goddess Grid is a morphic field that interconnects and interweaves the whole of feminine energy *everywhere*.

Just as we are always connected to the Star Mothers, so the Grid of the Divine Feminine weaves all species of female together. Every woman is connected to the Goddess Grid – always, forever; some are more aware of that innate connection and some less. This is how enormous it is: *every woman, mammal, animal, plant that comes into being as female is interwoven into the deep, far, wide, and beautiful web of Goddess-ness.* Imagine your feminine energy is connected to the female deer nursing her fawn, the queen bee in the hive, the mother sparrow guarding her eggs, a woman teaching prayers to her children on another continent, and a gray whale lifting her calf to the surface of the ocean for its first breath. Let your thinking and your imagination expand to encompass this concept – a concept of limitless female interconnection – a precious grid of female energy – where we are never alone.

Teaching Us the Practical

Again I asked them, "Why are you showing me this in such depth? Is there something I should be learning and teaching here?" I tried to breathe and relax again, opening to what else might come through. This time, my third eye began to tingle and the light there literally came on where I experienced another "ah-ha" moment!

I call this explanation a "download" of information and knowing – where does it come from? From my Akashic awareness, of course!

We have learned that our thoughts are powerful, and each time that we have one (a thought), we connect to the object of our thought(s). Isn't this the way that multidimensional healing works? Isn't this what we were originally given by our Pleiadian teachers? The Star Mothers endowed us with the ability to make a deep and permanent connection to the Goddess Grid. They gave us the ability and consciousness to reach beyond time and space and create the miraculous. Why not use that power to unite with the feminine energy – the Goddess Grid – that is your legacy and link from the stars to the planet? Here's an idea – instead of thoughts of worry, fear, sorrow, or concern, think about any other feminine energy. Not only does this shift *your* moment, there is a ripple effect that changes the energy ... of the *cosmos*! Yes, really! Similar to adding a pinch of salt to a cup of water, the water is forever changed. That is your inherent power to change yourself and to change the world, one thought at a time, with the support of the Goddess Grid – all of the feminine energy *in existence*!

We are on the front of a wave of transformation right now, creating our future with the conscious connection to many energetic grids. Let us live each moment in the rekindled awareness of our Divine nature so that a grid of Light, healing, and spiritual Oneness covers the great Gaia Mother and all Her inhabitants. The time, and the teachers within, are awakening and WE are the Ones!

Given in love,
Amber Mele'ha Wolf, PhD

◊ ◊ ◊

Now that you have read Mele'ha's story about her Akashic awakening, there is another perspective that was given by Kryon during one of her Lemurian Sisterhood meetings. It's a beautiful example of what Kryon means by the expression, *"Things are not always as they seem."* It was mentioned earlier that this expression is about perception. There is also another meaning, which relates to soul planning, done on the other side of the veil. Part of soul planning is the orchestration of experiences for us to learn from during our Human experience. These learning opportunities can impact us deeply on an emotional scale, such as the death of a loved one. Even this is often designed to deepen our spiritual connection. This is exactly what happened for Mele'ha, and here is Kryon to explain:

I want to talk about something that is profound, today. I wish to do this, but I don't want you to misunderstand it. There are beautiful systems of the Akash for Old Souls. You might ask yourself in the circle tonight, *"What do I feel is the truth about myself? Who am I?"*

I want to help you answer this, and I want this to be about Akashic awakening. I also want to tell you about Mele'ha. It's difficult to give the history of Lemuria because it's so filled with profundity, with beauty. The entire reason Amber met her partner Sid [Wolf], was so she could be Mele'ha today. If you were to question her, as a woman, about the relationship she had with Sid, she would tell you that, against all odds, things opened up for them to get married and to have a partnership. She was already very knowledgeable, and he was a master teacher. He helped place her on a journey of discovery and, together, they were powerful and ... it was not an accident. I could tell you of a planning session they had as souls on the other side of the veil, where they put this potential together before they ever arrived on the planet. This potential was realized and, again, against all odds, they were married.

At some level, please understand that the appropriateness of Sid's passing was perfect. The appropriateness even has something to do with my partner [Lee], who is not listening at the moment [Kryon speaking of the fact that the Sisterhood channels are hidden from Lee while he gives them]. You see, Sid's soul is back, and he is currently growing up again, and I won't tell you where.

Some might say, *"Kryon, that's too quick. Turnaround time for a soul takes longer than that."* Dear ones, it's time to understand that the paradigm of past processes is changing. That is past. His turnaround had to be quick, because Sid will again be a master and his main student will be my partner. Dear ones, the plan is that the spiritual family stays together.

In order for the Akashic awakening to take place with Mele'ha, Sid had to pass. On time, he did. On schedule, he did, and it was a time of great sorrow. Now, after an appropriate time, there begins to be some understanding. Mele'ha had her Akashic awakening, and she is perfectly suited, academically credentialed, trained appropriately, and a powerful teacher. She was to lead women intuitively and, if you look at her credentials, many of them are specifically about leading women. The event was perfect, and her Akashic awakening took place on schedule.

All of you have the potential of remembering something that is very precious during the time you had the shamanic seed and used it [your time in Lemuria with new DNA for the planet]. Inside you is the potential for a profound awakening. Now listen to me, for this is very important. Every single one of you is unique in this awakening. Mele'ha had something that had to be accomplished a certain way for her life. The specific memory of being Mele'ha had to come forward for her to do what she does today. You also have the opportunity to remember your own awakening. What is *in there* for you? Why do you sit in the chair? Again you can ask, *"Who am I?"*

Can you ever remember feeling the power of Spirit being so accepted around you? Together, you are singing and celebrating and helping to guide the civilization around you into sweeter, more benevolent places. You were doing the same thing in Lemuria, helping the community to find food, and even guiding them when not to go to sea at all. Things were different, indeed, back then, but the very reason you are here today is that with the Akashic awakening, comes the softness and balance that is needed today.

Today, you become the *way-showers* under the tutelage of Mele'ha. Each one of you has the opportunity to awaken as she did. It won't be to a position like hers, but rather, to a remembrance of the preciousness of who you were, and what you did, and how you felt.

If you are able to study how to awaken this remembrance, you're going to leave this room with a greater self-worth. You're going to know that your place in history was significant, and that the Old Soul that you are, has a reason for remembering. You're going to be able to *take on that precious mantle again*, even if it's only being the Shaman of your life or your family.

It's got to start somewhere and, ladies, you are the only ones with the seeds [original Pleiadian core truths]. Did you realize that? This is where these truths are going to come from in this current culture. The softness of those who give life are women. That's where it has to come from. It has to make sense to all, and it will. There will come a day when the church counts on this and will ordain women. Believe me, it will be intuitive with the wisdom that is coming. The invitation is yours to awaken. Find the core inside and stand taller because of it. Know who you are. It's beautiful!

Kryon live channelling given during a Lemurian Sisterhood Meeting
in Kelowna, Canada – February 27, 2016

The Akashic Awakening of Women

Kryon has said that each of us has the opportunity to awaken to the wisdom of our Akash. In particular, the Akashic awakening of women is a return to their role as wisdom-givers for humanity. This role is something that men honored, supported, and counted on. In Kryon Book 14, *The New Human*, we discover that the new Humans are beginning to awaken to a remembrance of energy from their past lives that will assist them, instead of it being a blockage or difficult karmic energy. Kryon tells us that this is a new paradigm, involving a more elegant role for the Akash. This means that the Akash starts seeing the Human Being as an evolving spiritual part of the entire planet, and begins to deliver the things that he/she should *remember*, that are going to help his or her evolution and belief. These Akashic remembrances create pure wisdom, and for the women, there is a greater reflection of compassionate mother energy.

Chances are, if you're reading this book, you have already begun your Akashic awakening. Many of you have been living an awakened life for several years, if not decades! The awakening process is one of the grandest and most sacred paths you can take. It can also bring with it many challenges, especially if there is no one around to share your experience or guide you through it. The good news is the practical help we have from so many, including Kryon and the Lemurian Sisterhood.

Once you have awakened, what's next? How do we integrate our spiritual selves in our everyday life? This was one of the questions Mele'ha asked, and Kryon's response follows:

Spirit is genderless. It's really difficult for you to imagine such a thing in your planetary culture, since, in your reality, you're either one or the other. However, the *one or the other* comes with responsibilities and actions that are assigned or hardwired.

Your Akash is filled with remembrance, ladies, where you were the guiding-posts for everyone. The planet is literally filled with this, too. Many, many generations of humanity participated in a system where the female gender was the one that would be looked to for advice. I've said it before: It's intuitive that it would be this way, and it's natural and makes common sense.

It's unnatural the way it is today, and the unnatural part of it creates issues and problems. Common sense: Wouldn't it seem more natural to all humanity that the mother energy, the one that gives birth and teaches its young, would then be the one you also turn to for spiritual things? It's obvious and comfortable. It's so natural and makes so much sense, that all of the men would want it intuitively. However, it's not that way today.

What did men think about a society where women were the spiritual leaders? The answer is that they didn't think anything of it. It was intuitive and it was natural. This is a time that we want you to remember. We want you to remember it because this past time you experienced in Lemuria can actually empower you today. That's what I want to speak of – today.

We've spoken of the past so often, but that's what makes you come here and question whether you were part of a Lemurian Sisterhood of any kind. Perhaps you were just simply thinking you were and don't know? I want to tell you, what you have in common as you sit here, is a common *Akashic awakening*.

The Akashic awakening triggers your mind just enough to make you curious about what's going on with you. Listen: An Old Soul who is a woman today, in this energy, was a woman then. This is not a coincidence, but rather a plan. Although you might have changed genders over a long period of time, you were women long enough to have all participated in being a Shaman for those around you.

Now, this is in your remembrance and this is what brings you here. So forget the minutiae for a moment about if you were actually part of a Sisterhood in Lemuria or not. It doesn't matter. You were part of something greater than that. It was a time when your gender was looked to as the one to naturally guide all humanity in spiritual direction. It started this way, remember? We've also told you before: It's not a mistake that, when the astronomers decided to name a specific constellation, it became the Seven Sisters!

The gender was important to this name. It was not a random name. From the Seven Sisters, which are actually nine stars, came the Pleiadians – and the Pleiadians were women. They looked just like you, a little taller, but they looked like you. So the model was set and beginning humanity saw this. The model was that the women carried the wisdom and this is what you're awakening to right now. This awakening is going to go someplace eventually, and history will look back at this time of a shift and they will say, among other things, it gave balance to the planet.

It's not that women are again going take charge of all spiritual things. Instead, there will be a slow balance and a return of women to positions of common sense advice. The intuition of women will someday be measurable, and society will honor better intuition. But right now, you're awakening to something you were, all of you, and in the awakening, there is a bias, and that's what I want to talk about.

What do you do with the awakening? Before this channelling began, a question was presented by Mele'ha: Her question is this: *"During this new energy, when you begin to awaken to profound things and you know your life is changed forever, what do you do with it?"*

A true Akashic awakening is a realization that you didn't have before. It's normally one that is extremely profound, so you cognize it. You believe that you were, indeed, part of something grander and bigger, and this belief changes you. Now, here's the bias again, dear ones: In Human singularity, you go through a process that is extremely linear. You *straight-line* things. You normally go to a place that asks a linear question: *"What am I going to do with it?"*

When you graduate from college, or from high school, or from any other institution, there is ceremony. There is often celebration and music. Within all this, someone older than you will often come up to you and ask, *"Well, now that you've got all this, what are you going to do with it?"* And the answer is, *"Well, I think I will go over here; I think I will get this job; I think I will do this or that."* So the premise is that now that you've become wiser, you will do something with it. You're going to apply it.

I have another premise for you to think about. Back up with me and think of this: Some of you are having an Akashic awakening and some of you are really, really feeling it. Don't let your Human bias ask the question, *"What am I going to do with it?"* Let me present this to you: If you have an Akashic awakening, what are you awakening *to*, ladies? The answer is that you're awakening to a reality that you used to have, and it starts to change the very attitude you have – the wisdom that you have. So ... what are you going to do with it?

Understand that, with an awakening, what is going to change is the way you think about things in the future. It's not about what are you going to *do* with it. It's not about reading a book and applying information. Instead, it's about awakening to a different consciousness. What follows that is not how you apply it, but how you personally change yourself through the intuition of this realization.

Changing consciousness and thinking differently are core issues, not simply the application of information. The decisions you make after an Akashic awakening are totally different than if you had never awakened. You awaken and, in the awakening, you're different. The very awakening itself then creates a different you. I want this to make sense to you. Some things are just this way. You come into the fruition of another reality and the decisions, the questions, the answers you give, and the wisdom you have, are now different.

Mele'ha, you had an awakening, and here you sit today with what's in front of you. So I say, that's good enough! This came from your awakening. You made different decisions. You said *yes* when perhaps you would not have before, because of your awakening. You learned things because of your awakening. You don't ever have to ask, *"What am I going to do with it?"* Instead, it starts to develop itself through renewed intuition.

When you leave this place, having had an awakening, you'll know it. You can claim that you're different and you'll say different things. You'll spread a wisdom that you didn't have before and, down the line, this will change what happens – not just for you, but also for those around you. Proceed with the awakening.

Kryon live channelling given during a Lemurian Sisterhood Meeting
in Portland, Oregon – July 25, 2016

The Akash holds all the energies of past, present, and future life experiences. The Old Soul is someone who has had lifetime after lifetime after lifetime on the planet. Think about how many lives a soul has lived and experienced within a 50,000-year time frame. Modern history is filled with tragedy after tragedy of separation, conflict, drama, conquering, and war. The treatment of women and children has been vastly different than it was in Ancient Lemuria. This is why Kryon implores us to wipe away any Akashic memory that did not honor and recognize our sacredness. One of the attributes to assist us in the process is to rekindle the original Akashic imprint, which came directly from the Pleiadians.

This message comes from a place which you would call *The Creative Source*, and it's honoring you at this moment for who you are. Being female at this particular time on this planet is far different than what it was in the Sisterhood that you celebrate tonight. Many of you have just discovered it and wish to know more about something you may feel that you were part of.

Again, I tell you that it is not an accident that you sit here as women once again, awakening, after all these years, to something that pulls at your hidden Akashic memory. It whispers to you, *"Was I there? If so, can I create again what I created before with these other women?"*

I love to take you back to that Lemurian mountain, for it is so pure and simple, yet spectacular. The Sisterhood-type meetings were often given in the water. Often they were sunset meetings, and even more often, morning meetings. However, they were mostly given in the water.

Sometimes, you were standing and sometimes, your feet were simply dangling in that warm Pacific Ocean. Back then, there were trade winds like today, but slightly different due to the vastly increased size of the mountain. The gathering was so sacred! It was beautiful and the songs that you would sing remain clearly etched into your Akash. If you could hear them today, it would probably bring tears to your eyes because you would remember them at some level. What you would remember is softness and sweetness, appropriateness, and beauty.

Was Lemuria utopia? The answer is no, not even close. But it had something else that you should remember. You were first-generation humanity. The Pleiadians were your seed parents, and were not only responsible for your 23-chromosome DNA, but for the core truth of your spirituality. By the time you were participating in the Sisterhood-style meetings, your bodies were complete in the new chemistry [what you have today]. You were ready to be a part of that Akashic launching pad for the planet. Know this: There were other places doing this as well on Earth, but Lemuria was interestingly special because it was an island that was inescapable. It was a pressure-cooker of purity, and there was no interference from the outside. So it could remain pure for thousands of years, with almost no changes at all.

Now, I want you to start connecting the dots [logically connecting information]. Where did you come from originally? Let's say you were sitting there as a woman in Lemuria, enjoying a lifetime in a sacred circle. Through your shamanic training, you had helped set the cultural energies for survival and food, and even set the energies for relationships and spiritual celebration. You were constantly working the template of Lemuria. All of you. However, if you represent the beginning of the beginning, where did you come from?

Dear ladies, this may be confusing, but souls incarnate as souls throughout the galaxy. All of you had the interstellar Akash of a Pleiadian. In other words, there was no Earth Akashic record in the Sisterhood because you had never been Human. You were the first type of Human with the knowledge of God inside. Therefore, as you came into the planet as a woman, doing sacred things in this Lemurian circle, your Human Akash was blank! The only thing you had in that department was that which you were given by the Pleiadians.

So let's discuss something that is very sacred, and has not been spoken of before in much detail. What was the Akash of a Pleiadian? The Pleiadians were from an *ascended sacred planet [group]*. These are planets who had gone through a sacred evolvement over a vast amount of time, allowing them to almost become angelic. This is even the potential of the Earth in a distant future. They "knew" core truth about the Creative Source. You might say, they "knew God" as an angel would. They were the ones who gave you the songs, and who taught you what you [learned to] know.

How did you feel? The answer is, sacred. It wasn't hard to feel this way. It's far harder to feel that now. Without an Akash that would beat you up or give you any history at all, you were sacred and you knew it. You felt God inside, and the songs came naturally. The cheerful attitudes you had, came naturally. The applause after the birth of a child was more than just "welcome to Earth." It was that a new child was being born who was *first generation [divine] Human.*

There's a sacredness that you felt there in that place, which has not been repeated since those days. For a while, and specifically in Lemuria, you had an off-world remembrance – an Akash that was from a very advanced society. After being reincarnated a few times in other parts of the Earth, life after life, a balance set in and, slowly, the Pleiadian remembrance of sacredness that you felt was tempered by your own free-will-developed humanism. Soon, the consciousness of the Earth would be what Humans did with it, and the off-world remembrances were forgotten [as was the plan]. Slowly, the dishonoring of women would set in as low consciousness developed, and a readjustment of the genders set in as is common for an un-evolved society where one gender is physically stronger than the other.

Know this: This identical thing happened in Pleiadian history as well. Consciousness, no matter how high it might start, must seek its own level on its own world. It always has to evolve by itself. Therefore, know that all this happened before. You might wonder then, what is it that we're asking you to do about all of this today?

You don't receive actual Pleiadian remembrance today, but you still have remembrance of how you felt as a Human in those days. That becomes your beginning Human Akashic remembrance. Tonight, during the public seminar, we spoke of *filters* [referring to the channel *The Human Filters*]. What we tell you now is actually one of them for you, and it's part of your gender filter that we did acknowledge earlier. It wasn't for the men to hear, since it's not their filter. But it's for you to hear now.

The reason you are doing this meeting tonight is to try to recapture pure sacredness of Spirit. You see, it's still in there! Can you feel it? Old Souls who started as women in Lemuria carry this. Can you feel the sacredness of it? Can you wipe away, for just a moment, all the Akashic un-evolved remembrances? Can you take the other filters away and only remember the one? It's the one that was the *starting one*, the sacred one. The reason we ask this is that we invite you to rekindle it. We need you to stand from this place and go out more sacred than you came in. So, as a Human woman, you lived these feelings and worked the puzzle, back then, of a completely pure and sacred Akash. Can you remember that?

Let me tell you about the sacredness you can develop today: It's catchy. Other people will see it in you and they will want the same. They'll see what it does within you. They will see the softness in you, and the purity in you. There's more to this than just having been in many sacred women's gatherings. It's about eventually creating worldwide female remembrance in similar meetings.

Why the gender split? Again, it's because the true spiritual understanding for humanity, and the sacredness of the core truth of the universe always belonged to the women. As life-givers, women are equipped with a consciousness that is closer to the Creative Source. You are the ones who experienced the Love of God first, and can teach it. You're the guides for humanity. In order to do that in these next generations, a return to sacredness is the goal.

Kryon live channelling given during a Lemurian Sisterhood Meeting in Totowa, New Jersey – June 27, 2015

All over the planet, more and more women are awakening to their spiritual core and, in the process, the wisdom and knowledge held within their Akash is coming forward. It's the reason why so many women have felt the call to attend the Lemurian Sisterhood meetings. And yet, the Akashic awakening of women is planetary wide and affects women from all cultures and belief systems. Since the 2012 Shift, women are stepping into their power and claiming their mastery, and the energy of the planet supports this more than ever before. This is not about women's rights and the feminist movement, but instead, it's a return to the original role of women as the shamanic teachers and guides for humanity.

The Lemurian Sisterhood Today

Today's Lemurian Sisterhood is a result of Dr. Amber Wolf's lifetime commitment to holistic health care, education, spiritual transformation, and her Akashic remembrance. The Lemurian Sisterhood is a global community where many women from around the world are also hosting their own Sacred Circles under the guidance of Amber (Mele'ha). Many women connect with the Sisterhood because of their own Akashic remembrance of Lemuria. How is your experience in Lemuria relevant today? How does it help you and those around you? How does it help you live from moment to moment, and to raise your children?

Kryon has said that those in Lemuria had a shining seed within their Akash, which they remember. It is the epitome of motherhood and femininity. That Lemurian seed is very practical, for it is the truth and compassion of God inside. The Pleiadians were the Lemurian teachers from the stars and it's what those with a Lemurian Akash remember. The Sisterhood is about finding that Lemurian seed and applying it to your life and spreading the compassion of the original knowledge that was taught from the stars.

What about those of you reading this who don't feel a connection to Lemuria? What about those who don't feel a connection to the Sisterhood? What if you're not sure about any of it? What if you're a male? Here is what you should know: The spiritual seeds planted by the Lemurians all those years ago are now available to ALL souls on the planet. This means that everyone, Lemurian or not, female or not, has the potential to awaken to ancient Lemurian spiritual wisdom and knowledge. Here is Mele'ha to tell how this occurs in the Lemurian Sisterhood today:

The Lemurian Sisterhood today was created in response to my Akashic remembrance as Mele'ha. The evolution of this sacred mission continues to unfold for me with my remembrance; my communication with the Star Mothers and the women who come to my meetings from all over the world is continuously rekindled. Our global communities of Lemurian Sisters are recognizing each other from our ancient lives and sacred circles.

This feeling of remembrance and recognition is similar to the feeling of *déjà vu* (the feeling that you have been here before). Most likely, you've met someone in your life who you feel like you've known before, or you have discovered an instant kindred spirit. You don't even have to be metaphysical to have had this experience! Some people just feel familiar from the moment you meet them – a feeling of connection and a knowing that you have been with them before. The interesting part is that we never really know the exact time frame of when we knew them "before." We simply knew them!

However, for me this significant "before" time was in ancient Lemuria, a time where I was Mele'ha, the last Lemurian Priestess of the Sisterhood. I believe that many of us had interwoven lives in Lemuria. In addition, Kryon has told us that the Lemurian society lasted for over 30,000 years with the same Pleiadian teachers throughout that time. This is why it doesn't matter in what time frame you were in Lemuria, we all remember the experience. The Sisterhood has reemerged now to help create a healing and balanced community. Today, we are together again, bringing the Ancient Lemurian Sisterhood wisdom into the modern world. That is what the Lemurian Sisterhood is bringing forward today – the honoring of the Sacred Divine Feminine, a way of life from ancient Le-MU-ria that is valid for today.

What Now for the Sisterhood?

Women from all over the world have asked me, "How can we continue to have these uplifting meetings after you (Amber) are gone?" That was a question that found its answer in the creation of the Worldwide Sacred Circles. Here's how it all happened....

To ponder this question in a deep and meaningful way, I retreated to a cabin in the northern Arizona woods for a month. The purpose of this retreat was two-fold: 1) to begin writing a book about the Lemurian Sisterhood, and 2) contemplate the future direction of the Lemurian Sisterhood.

The first week went by and I wrote nothing! I had pages of transcribed and printed channels by Kryon at the Lemurian Sisterhood meetings for the past three years. They were in order, by subject and timeline ... still nothing. I had them underlined, tabbed, and highlighted – nothing! I was frustrated and feeling pressured to produce a book about the Sisterhood – so many people were asking! I felt like a failure – my favorite subject, my mission, and my passion would not come forth. I had planned this time and place for the book to unfold. "Spirit, why are you blocking this?" I asked again and again.

My turning point

Going into week two, I reached out to my dear friend and HeartMath® coach, Shamir Ladhani. I hadn't done any HeartMath processes yet, but I was desperate! He led me through a deep and moving exercise that brought peace to my heart and a feeling of trusting the process that was now unfolding. Even though I hadn't liked what wasn't unfolding (the book not being written), I was reminded that the evidence in my life shows that "Spirit has the perfect plan for me" – always. The result of my surrender opened a portal to the guidance for creating the Worldwide Sacred Circles – who would have guessed! And it was just that easy and simple – finally! I had to stop my timing expectations (I had only three weeks) and linear desire (creating the book) and surrender to what else might be waiting to come through. I needed to step back from the door in order for it to open.

The magic of letting go of the book concept was that a download of information came to create the Worldwide Sisterhood and all "her" parts. I was able to write and print the manuals, update my website, create a registered trademark, and an LLC corporation in those next three weeks. I had a waiting list of women ready to sign up and bring the messages of the Sisterhood to the planet in a bigger way, but I had needed those next steps.

And let me mention here that it was exactly 11 months later that Monika Muranyi approached me with a proposal to write the book together! Spirit always has the perfect plan, "Thank you, Spirit!"

Saying Yes to Sacredness

Each and all of the women who say "yes" to hosting the Sacred Circle meetings in their cities are talented, dedicated, and beautiful women who are as different from each other as you and me. I love and appreciate how they take their unique energy signatures into their meetings across the world. Some of them have facilitated meetings and circles before and others are first-timers. They have faced the possible challenges of getting the information into their communities (sometimes feeling daunted by the internet), finding places for the meetings and being authentically their Divine Feminine selves, by walking through the fire of judgment, self-doubt, or fear – much of that from past lives, when living our Divine Feminine selves didn't turn out so well. Now they are shining souls in their communities.

Every day, women are being called to honor their Divine Feminine essence and recreate the Sacred Circles from lifetimes ago. These Circles create community and help awaken the energy of the Sisterhood – a field of energy that connects all women as Sacred Sisters. From each one of us, a Goddess Grid is growing.

The Pleiadian Star Mothers and Kryon's messages have given me guidance, information, and remembrances of the ceremonies, celebrations, sacred songs, and meditations that we did in the ancient Lemurian Sisterhood meetings. These have been "translated" into modern language and use, where each Sacred Circle meeting is an opportunity for the Divine Feminine to be invoked, ignited, and celebrated. The women in the circle pray, meditate, sing, and celebrate together. A Sacred Circle is a place where women give themselves permission to feel and know their power ... their beauty ... and their perfection. It is a time to celebrate who we are. We are Sisters together in the greatest awakening of our Age and, together, we are supporting each other as we create a balanced planet and plant the seeds of peace on Mother Earth.

To conclude what the Lemurian Sisterhood is really about here is a beautiful channelled message from Kryon about what the Star Mothers want us to remember:

So we enter tonight and give you more information about the Sisterhood, and about the wisdom of the Sisterhood. Remember that this gathering is called the Sisterhood, but was not called that in Lemuria. But it's the closest thing you have in the concept of what happened then.

You've heard me, many times, talk about what happened in Lemuria, but I would like to say, yet again, that Lemuria was very different. It was different than any other place on the planet. What made Lemuria so different was that it stayed pure a lot longer than any other place. It stayed pure for thousands of years – unchanged. So the Sisterhood-like women's gatherings in Lemuria also remained pure for a very long time.

Let's review what we have taught about Akashic remembrance. In general, what Humans remember in the Akash, and what comes forward first, is NOT that which is the most recent. There is no linearity in Akashic remembrance. Instead, what is remembered most often and most dramatically are negative things, no matter how new or old. However, for you, the potential is vastly different due to what you went through.

You have the ability to literally focus on calling up the beauty and the wisdom and the shamanic energy assigned to your gender in those years. It was unusual then. It was unusual because the planet is not this way now. Again, the premise is that it's in you, all of you.

In this new energy, you are being asked to generate that which only you experienced as an Old Soul back then, and it's why you are awakening to this information. There is great wisdom here and the reason this Sisterhood concept has started to develop is that at no time in history has there been this kind of sacredness and purity since.

Your Pleiadian teachers remained and remained and they taught for centuries. As we have told you, ladies, you were not all part of the same gatherings. But, over a vast amount of time, you received the identical information and teachings, and felt it all. It remained pure. It might be hard for you to believe, but you also participated with the same teachers, for they're timeless. What do you think it was like to be taught by those who seeded the planet and changed the DNA of Humans? What would they say to you now?

Dear Star Sisters, they were not *above* you. You did not sit in a circle around them and have them elevated. You did not worship them. You loved them because they were one with you. Each one was like a mother to you, and all of them, women. The greatest teaching that ever occurred on this planet was from those from the stars, who knew God, and who knew the purity and sacredness of what had been placed within you.

Although the whole planet received these things within the same time frame, the Lemurian teaching was different, for it stayed pure far longer. So this is the difference between other groups and other circles, and your experience. The purity remained the same for a very long time. Even though you feel you may have been in female Lemurian gatherings [Sisterhoods], you probably didn't know each other, for you were not even within the same century. However, you had the same instructors! So you see, that's what makes the Sisterhood special. It's a coming together of women from the past, who have something very sacred in common.

What do you think would be the most needed attribute of all, right now? What can you remember from then that might change this planet today? The answer is poised in another question: What do you think a Shaman needs to know in general? What does a Shaman share that is the most valuable? Ceremony specifics? No, you can do that on your own. By the way, ceremonies came from Humans, not Pleiadians.

What does a Shaman need to know? The answer is the profound wisdom of guidance. Humans turn to a shamanic source for help. Wisdom for decisions of life is the most valuable attribute a teacher can have. A Shaman needs to know these things well so that they can teach others, not just give advice. All of this came to you through the Pleiadian Mothers and it's anchored in your Akash. This is the attribute which can change the planet.

So the Sisterhood is about regenerating some of the original wisdom from the original teachers who were Pleiadian. For you here, don't expect the remembrance of words. I want you to expect emotions and then, perhaps, new things in your dreams. There will be a maturity when you start remembering these things, and I want you to elevate yourselves and stop the poor self-worth issues that are here today. Don't be surprised if some of these things that you were taught are basics of motherhood.

When another woman comes to you in trouble, what would you say to her? The last time we asked that question, we said: You would quiet. You would listen. But eventually, there has to be more: Perhaps you would open up and start having spontaneous intuitive thought, which brings up the wisdom of the Pleiadian teacher? Perhaps this is channelling? If so, the Sisterhood then becomes a remembering-hood [Kryon laugh]. It's a place where you gather together en masse, sing the songs you used to sing, and begin a remembrance of the original teachers and Mele'ha, the Human who led you through these circles throughout the ages.

Kryon live channelling given during a Lemurian Sisterhood Meeting
in Grand Rapids, Michigan – July 19, 2016

CHAPTER FIVE

The Unexpected, Underground "Sisterhood"

Human divinity came from our Star Mothers, the Pleiadians. The original Shamans were, therefore, the women. For thousands of years, women guided society and were seen as the ones who were closest to the Creative Source. It was the women who were regarded as the ones with enhanced intuition, wisdom, knowledge, and spiritual intelligence. This was simply the way of life in Lemuria and other cultures, such as the Anangu in Australia.

Very slowly, over many decades, the bubble of magma that had pushed up the land, creating the mini-continent of Lemuria, began to subside. This slow sinking of the island was the catalyst for many Lemurians to leave, seeking other places to live. Although some Lemurians remained on what became the islands of Hawaii, the substantial departure of the majority of the population heralded the end of this culture. This event was in divine order, as the planetary Akash was now set, and the test of duality could begin. With free choice, humanity could decide where it would take consciousness.

In the thousands of years that followed, humanity decided to take the consciousness to a lower level than what was given to them by the Pleiadians. When it became obvious that Human consciousness was devolving, those who carried the shamanic wisdom and knowledge went underground. The original ancient wisdom of Lemuria became part of the most secret societies all over the Earth, and Gaia cooperated.

There are parts of the Earth that hide secrets very well. You might call that process a cooperative Gaia energy, or not. Whatever you call it, there are places on the planet that keep the deepest secrets possible. As Human Beings choose their own consciousness, what will they then do with it, within free choice? Where would they go with it? This is really the ultimate question for the survival of the planet. The answer is this: From the days of the creation through the thousands of years that followed, humanity decided to allow their consciousness to slip to a lower level than was given to them.

Things had to be hidden while humanity's consciousness went into the dark, and you know this. Often the things hidden were truths that were dangerous, or not ready to be seen. There are some of you whose Akash will resound with this next information, because you were there!

There are places on the planet that hide secrets very well. There are secrets at the bottom of the Mediterranean Sea yet to be revealed. There are secrets yet to be discovered in Greece, Egypt, Turkey, and especially here [UK]. When it became obvious that Human consciousness was sinking to a level where the light was in trouble, many of you went underground and had to take the secrets of the mystery schools [which included Lemurian information] and hide them – and you did.

The societies that were here [UK] were the ones who would do the best job in keeping them hidden. There have been so many names of these societies, dear ones. Some of them were false societies with false names, so people wouldn't go near them. Did you realize that? All of that, to hold the light and the precious core information of truth.

Today, the revelations of how you can reprogram the data in your DNA, how you can "mine" the Akash for your own past treasures, and how you can find "the God inside," were the profound secrets that could never be put forward to a low consciousness humanity. From Plymouth, in the south, to Wick, in the north, the whole island participated.

There are so many portals here – so much energy still here where the mysteries were hidden. You ask yourself about the purpose of Druids. You ask yourself about the purpose of the mythology in the 1100s of Merlin. Merlin was not a man, at all, but a combination of concepts about magic. What was the magic? It's what we teach today. It's metaphysics – something that goes way beyond the 3D of everyday life. To some, it's magic.

Kryon live channelling "Releasing the Hidden Wisdom"
given in London, England – September 14, 2014

Kryon indicated that the purpose of mythology and magic is to teach us metaphysics. Think about the past masters on the planet and their ability to create things out of nothing, or heal with a touch, or morph one object into another? These are all examples of what is possible for ALL humanity in a future time when multi-dimensional things are understood. Someday, it will be normal to manipulate physics with consciousness. However, in an older energy, this would have appeared supernatural and even dangerous. The consequence would sometimes result in death, hence, the need to keep the esoteric truths secret and hidden. Today, we call this newly revealed wisdom of metaphysics the New Age, but in truth, it's something that the Ancients understood. Kryon tells us more:

The Ancients Knew It All...

Let me speak of spiritualism in general. The Ancients, through their intuition, carried the "secrets of Spirit" that today you call New Age. There's nothing new about these attributes, for they are as old as humanity. In the Ancients' beliefs, they were not secrets at all. They didn't need to be. Nothing really competed with them and the Ancients openly acknowledged that there was an energy of the planet called Gaia, and that it worked closely with Human Beings. It fed them; it clothed them; it gave them wisdom. Humans celebrated the birth of their children around the energy of the Earth. They named their children for their ancestors for many reasons, including the belief that their children were their own ancestors! The circle of life called reincarnation was accepted as reality, and it was intuitive for societies all over the planet who had never even seen each other or knew the other existed. Yet, all of these ancient beliefs you claim today as part of your *New Age*.

Through history, these belief attributes matured until the energy of the planet was developed enough for the Masters to start appearing. These were Masters who came to show how humanity could take these intuitive attributes and make a difference for the planet. Masters taught mastery, but Humans wanted only to worship them. One by one, the Masters came and, one by one, they were eliminated by Humans. This martyrdom created new systems, for now there were prophets to be worshipped, and the belief systems of the world began to shift and change and the ways of the Ancients had to go underground. So what we speak of in this wisdom place is not really metaphysics and it's not New Age. It is *basic intuitive spiritualism*. It is what the Ancients knew and what they carried forward, yet now, the information had to be hidden and had become the "secrets."

The Secrets Began – The Preservation of Ancient Truth

I wish to take you to a place with me, metaphorically. This is a real place and a real happening in history. Let me take you to a place not that far removed from your time, for it is less than 300 years ago. I take you to a room filled with old men, seniors each, professionals each. Some were leaders in the government and some leaders in law, even one leader in the church. They were meeting in secret, sitting in a circle, in an important meeting that will not be identified by a

256

name or a place or a town, but it took place. The meeting was an agreement to continue the secrets in various ways, using social organizations as a front. This was the time when intuitive spiritual thoughts were becoming seen as evil, where basic Human nature was being taught as from the darkness, and where the gifts of Spirit were seen as the devil's work. They had to do something to preserve the simple truths of God that had been with humanity for eons but were being threatened. The birth of today's religious paradigms was taking hold, and it was beginning to teach that humanity was born dirty, not empowered, and that the prophets held the key to everything and, therefore, had to be followed and worshipped, even in death. Spirituality was being redefined in a package that was fragmented and impersonal. Men were beginning to write 3D rules of "how to follow and worship" and men collected the power from all of this. Humanity was beginning to slide into a spiritual darkness that would be filled with mythology, suffering, death, wars, and hatred, all in the name of God.

The first thing these old men did was to pull out what they felt were the "accouterments of energy" – the Crystallines. They placed these stones [crystals] in their circle in a very interesting pattern. That pattern is known today as the double tetrahedron, and was a sacred shape to them. On the floor in front of them the crystals went, and then the men started singing. They sang tone notes without lyrics because there was the acknowledgment that Human voice creates an energy of sacredness. God was seen as "in them" and they filled the room with tones to purify what they were about to do. They lit many candles, not because candles made it any more sacred, but because they didn't have electricity. [Kryon humor] It's odd, because you carry this attribute even to this day, like seed remembrance of this time when the truth had to be hidden.

The decisions in this room became the seeds of secret organizations that would go around the planet for decades, for centuries. Some of these organizations would flourish and be misunderstood, and others would morph and change into yet other organizations when the membership became greedy. Some wanted to use the secrets for power. Some of them called themselves, "The Enlightened Ones," [those who were illuminated]. But they were not, and others kept the secrets to themselves, said very little, and kept the purity of what was given.

One of those organizations is with your current society even today – the organization that you call Masonic [The Masons]. If they could give you the secrets that they hold today, these men would tell you the core information is that there is a prophet inside of each of them called God, and at the source of all wisdom, healing, and energy on the planet comes from inside. What a concept! It is what you study today and call the New Age.

Kryon live channelling "The Lineage of Spirituality"
given in McCaysville, Georgia – July 11, 2009

What was the role of women in these secret societies? In many instances, these societies only involved men – or did they? All of you have been both genders. If you have lived for thousands of lifetimes, you have the attributes of an Old Soul. Within the Lemurian Akash are profound energies of the core spiritual truth, taught by the Pleiadians. Now, what happens in the Akash of the Lemurian women when they come back as men? What happens to the groups of women who change genders, after carrying the torch of enlightenment for centuries? Does their shamanic knowledge go away because they are no longer women? Do these souls that have come back as men remember any of it?

These are great questions and the answers can be found in how the Akash remembers things. The Akash is alive with the energy of awakening. Therefore, the groups of shamanic women reincarnating as men have an Akashic remembrance of wisdom and knowledge that created the foundation of many secret male societies. Controversial? Very. Kryon explains how and why the role of men and women changed from the original beginning in Ancient Lemuria in this next channel.

Being a Human is specific to Earth. The test you've all gone through has to do with free choice, and when we say free choice, we mean an intuitive consensus of consciousness. We don't interfere, dear ones, but part of your test involves energy on the planet. Where the energy of the truth starts is one thing, and where it goes with free choice is another.

Now, we've said those things before, but I want you to relax with me just for a moment. Mele'ha [Amber Wolf] is again with us. Sisters, your Akash rings with the truth of what I'm telling you. You're interested in Lemuria and you should be, for it's in your Akash. More than just "in your Akash." Can you imagine how deep the etching is, metaphorically, of what you may have experienced at one of the first times you were on this planet? The energy of it is greatly enhanced since it was taught to you by those who seeded you from the Pleiadians.

You were actually with these other-worldly teachers, having the feeling of being comforted by them, and seeing the beautiful benevolence of everything that they did. To some of you, they seemed angelic. Their teachings were amazing and this is where you learned what you know even today.

Can you imagine bringing those feelings forward to today, rekindling them and continuing? That's what the Sisterhood is. There is a feeling of past remembrance because this is what you did, and it is where you were. Channel after channel, we have described you sitting in the alcove in a circle, with the stones and with the water, which is almost body temperature, doing the various ceremonies. You are birthing, singing, and participating in many other kinds of things. We've talked about the men as they go fishing, depending upon what you bring them through your prayers, and what you learned from the Seven Sisters. You actually temper the energy of the catch, and they (the men) know this.

Can you imagine being a male, being responsible for feeding the village *by chance* with fish – by chance? All hunting and fishing are like this even today on the planet. Ask a hunter. Sometimes, they return with nothing at all, as a family waits. But a male in Lemuria knew that the women had the intuition to direct you to the catch. It was far more than *chance*.

Once a small Lemurian boy, under the age of thirteen, asked his father, *"Father, no woman ever goes fishing, yet you listen to them to tell you where to fish. Why?"* The father looked at the boy and slowly told him this: *"The women don't fish. But somehow they ARE the fish. They actually know what the fish know."*

The men depended on the women for guidance, since what they received worked! They delighted in this, and were very proud of this "second sight" from their mates and loved ones. Not only were the women responsible for the spiritualness of the entire Lemurian continent, but they also raised all the children. Sisters, you had plenty to do then, just like you do now, and that hasn't changed.

Through thousands and thousands of years, and very gradually with free choice, things changed and you changed. Lemuria was the launching pad of the Akash. In other words, your lives, and all your children, only had one lifetime in Lemuria. The next lifetime, you moved on to a bigger continent, and for most of you, it was in what you now call Europe.

How do you think your Akash sees Lemuria and subsequent lifetimes? Now, follow the logic and the reasoning with me. You find yourself back on the planet, and you are now in "lifetime two." You only have one life experience to remember in the Akash, only one. However, it was a stellar one! It literally *sits* upon you. It sits upon you in a way that you can't shake. It's singular, and there was only one. You, then, naturally return to the ways that you had, and you develop a Sisterhood.

So, in this, you find yourself trying to emulate what you remember. It's a Sisterhood, not one that necessarily has the Pacific Ocean around it, but a modified one. As history goes forward, however, the intuition from the women is not seen as something that is necessarily needed by the men. They're going out hunting and gathering now. They're not fishing, and they don't have an Akash that is as active as you do. Wisdom is like that. The Akash carries the profound remembrance of wisdom, and tries to emulate it. It's energy, and that's what the Akash really remembers. But the Akash does not carry the remembrance of "who you got the wisdom from." Therefore, the men don't carry the remembrance of you being shamanic. This attribute has to be shown each lifetime.

Your culture begins to build buildings and have commerce and trade. There starts to be an entire shift in the way things work. Women's business [sacredness and shamanship] is then something that is suppressed. It is starting to be lost, not from your side, dear women, but from the culture. It is understandable that the energy would go in this direction first.

So, what eventually happened was that the idea of women's intuitive sacred guidance for all, never recovered. Instead, it got worse. This is free choice and what we talked about today as something slowly starting to reverse itself as the population of Earth sees and appreciates the role of women in a sacred place. You are recognizing that personally, and it's even in your news. You're waking up to, perhaps, the possibility that again there could be *women's business.* The idea that women can be spiritual leaders has got to start somewhere, and tonight, it starts with you.

You are not necessarily going to do the same thing you did in Lemuria, dear ladies, but the concept is there for you to meet, discuss, and celebrate. It has nothing to do with women's power, and everything to do with women's sacredness and leadership for all. There's a difference. Can you recognize the difference between gender power and wise leadership? Humanity is attracted to wise leadership. Everywhere it exists, it is appreciated and sought after. Do you understand that you are your own ancestors? That means you have the equipment in your Akash to awaken to these attributes.

What happened in history that changed it all? What took place? Where did it go? There is so much to discuss, but let me just give you a brief overview: Again, you are in lifetime two, and then three, and on and on. Now, you have had to place the Sisterhood underground.

You still have this in your Akash, to meet and work with all the core truths that the Lemurian experience and the Pleiadians taught you. It is still very alive in your Akash. But this is not there in the men. The culture and the consciousness have slipped, and there is a time when you cannot sustain what you are doing any longer. It is a threat to the men to have women meeting together and doing powerful things. It ceases to exist.

Get ready for something funny: Oddly enough, throughout history, the men take the mantle and they developed a secret brotherhood! What? What are the secrets? They are the same ones as the Sisterhood. Read on...

This brotherhood becomes many things over the years, including what you call today the *Masons*. You might say that the Masons are almost an exact duplicate of the sacred business that the women used to have. They took the mantle from women! Now the odd and rather funny thing is this: Where did they get the idea? Where did they get the information? Why would they do this? Well, here is the answer: You've got to remember that you do not return over and over as one gender. These gentlemen with the secret societies used to be women! The Akash of the soul does not change when you change genders, dear ones. So, as time goes on, all of you will remember the core teachings.

So, the men were able to plug into all of this, but they didn't remember it as though it came from women. They simply remembered truth, and knew it had to go underground. Now, think about it. That's funny! As men, they could plan this and work the puzzle that women could not do in the cultures that followed throughout history.

There's more. There was a resurgence, in many places on this planet, of what you would loosely call, the Sisterhood. These resurgences can be tracked back as something that was working in various parts of the Earth. Some of them were directly south of Hawaii.

Although many of you were reincarnated into Europe, many also went into South America. Today, you will find women's business [shamanship] there, and some remnants of what appears to be women's sacred ceremony in that land. It is a remnant of what you started in Lemuria that the West didn't step on.

In Europe, there was one place where the idea of women in a sacred role seemed to be ripe to continue, and it did. Whereas almost everywhere else in Europe changed radically, there was one place where it remained for a very, very long time, and that one place is going to be visited soon by Mele'ha, and it's called Greece.

There's women's business [shamanship] – Goddesses, in Greece. It never stopped. There was even an underground for it. There were some things even involving the Illuminati. (Remember, I told you not to judge the names given in secret). Women's business [shamanship] was there, too. We didn't say it was necessarily fair, but it was for "Sisterhood survival" and it's your history. As we told you, you were rekindling something that had worked before, almost at any cost. This is hard to describe to you – where something sacred would then be rekindled into something that, perhaps, had motives that were not. However, the wiser of you know that, with Human nature as it was, this is how life worked.

In these lifetimes, your Akash was remembering what you were able to do, not necessarily where you did it. This new energy is rekindling it today. Today begins a remembrance of the core, and where you learned it.

What did you do in Lemuria? Really, what did you do? How did you do it? But more than that, can you remember the feeling of pride that you were needed to do it? You were needed to do it! Humanity needs you to do it again, and to give you the space to remember it.

Mele'ha, when you return to Greece, you will be greeted well. The energy will remember you. There will be some intensity in some places, so just get ready for them as you remember that your seeds of teaching helped start it.

Mele'ha was the last leader of the Sisterhood in Lemuria before it started going under. We told you this. We also told you that she did not leave. She couldn't. She was ready to go down with the island if it had gone all the way down. She went to her favorite mountain-top to await that which she felt was inevitable for her. She had lived over three lifetimes longer than most of you, enhanced by the Temple of Rejuvenation at the top of the mountain. She waited there as it sunk and then ... stopped sinking.

So she was then stranded, if you wish to call it that, in paradise on the now island of Kauai. Mele'ha, why didn't you go to the Temple, or at least choose a higher peak while the mountain was going down? Perhaps she doesn't remember? As the huge mountain sank, it did so erratically, and almost without warning, certain areas were flooded that became lower than they had been. So, Mele'ha was actually "steered" to the Kauai mountaintop for her long retirement. She and a few others survived well there ... and the men fished for her all her life. This is her story.

So, what happened to you? Where did you go? Were you part of the Greek Sisterhood? Did you remember it? Most of you were those lifetimes. You are your own ancestors, dear Sisters! How many times did you go through this? It's all starting to work now in your favor, as you sort it out within the energetic memories of your Akash. As you figure it out, here are some things to know, for those listening, reading, and here in the chairs.

Number One: You were all there in Lemuria, but not necessarily together. That is to say, each one of you had one lifetime in Lemuria, but that one life may have happened within a very long time frame, which Lemuria was part of. So, the odds are not good that you knew each other, or that you were part of the same Sisterhood there. So, understand that you are not necessarily remembering each other as much as the concept.

Number Two: You had the original seed information and, believe me, you still have it. Time does not diminish the energy of the core teachings. The Akash is not linear, and feelings do not fade with time. So what does this tell you about what I'm saying? If you have any energetic feelings for this information at all, is it accurate or not?

Number Three: You were honored in what you did. The humanity on the mini-continent of MU needed what you had and freely gave. I want that to stick. Those are the three areas that I want you to cling to. Nothing else. Not what you did later, not what it became, but the original bliss of those wonderful beginning times.

There is a new beginning today. Remember.

Kryon live channelling given during a Lemurian Sisterhood Meeting in Chicagoland, Illinois – July 25, 2015

There are some who may consider the information from Kryon about the secret underground sisterhood controversial. Others will resound to this revelation with a strong feeling that they participated in it. Those who have carried the secrets are some of the original ones on the planet who had these ancient truths embedded into their Akash. So what's next? Kryon says that it's now time to release the hidden wisdom. Exactly how is this done? Kryon gives us the instructions on how to do this:

Dear ones, it is time to release all of the secrets of the mystery school [core Lemurian information]. It's hard because, for generations, you have been hiding things in your Akash. You've segmented all of these secret things, and you've compartmentalized them, given them labels, and you've stuffed them away so that nothing can be discovered and get you in trouble again. However, now I'm telling you that it is time to release all.

This is not your grandfathers' metaphysics, but rather, this is a New Age. This is the time the Ancients predicted and have waited for. You kept the secrets for a reason. Now, *secret keepers*, I want you to walk out of this place with a new concept of who you are and what you're here for.

It's time to share what you know, and the best way to do it is to live with the consciousness of a master. How do you treat people? Can you heal yourself with the shamanic information that you have kept hidden and sequestered for all of these years? Perhaps not yet, but you know you can! So release the information. Let those around you see the majesty in you. Let the secrets come out within the way you run your life.

Say the concepts out loud, if anybody asks: You can change your DNA; you can change your reality; you can change your life; you can change your life span! That's the concept of Merlin. That's magic to most people. It's all there in your Akash.

That's the message. Drop the walls. We said this last night, sitting while in another country. Drop the walls. Join with others who you would never have joined with before. Watch for the synchronicity of love. Is it possible that there are those around you who wear odd garb, and perhaps have religious beliefs or spirituality that are filled with God? Perhaps they have the same secrets you do? Watch for it, for perhaps they are ready to release it, too. The message that I'm giving you is not sequestered to Kryon. It is being shouted within the grass [crop circles]. It is being given to mediums everywhere. This is the time you waited for.

"Kryon, what is it we are supposed to do here, in this reality? What can we physically do right now?" I just told you: Walk out of this room and live like a master. Watch what you say. Watch how quick you are, or slow you are, to anger. Look for God in others. Start solving problems in your life so well that others will look at you and say, *"I don't know what you are into, but I want a piece of it!"* And if someone says that to you, you can say: *"Ah! It's magic."* And you'd be right. It is magic.

Imagine a Human Being who can extend their years on Earth with their mind. What about a Human, with the intuition they have, who can bring in energy from the past to change their present life? What about patience and lack of anger? It's done with metaphysical magic that is a light that has been kept hidden for centuries. Let it out.

Combine with those who you would normally never combine with. There are those from other beliefs who might say, *"You are doing it wrong!"* Tell them that you honor their ways, and that you believe that things are changing, and that it's time to drop the barriers of protocol and, instead, see God in all things. Don't look at their belief. Look at their heart. Dear ones, awareness precedes change. Someone in the audience knows exactly where I got that. That was for you, dear.

What are you going to do next? This is the awareness cycle. Next comes change. Leave this place differently than you came. We've said this already: This is the purpose of the meeting here.

Kryon live channelling "Releasing the Hidden Wisdom"
given in London, England – September 14, 2014

The admonition from Kryon is to "leave this place different than you came," for it was the true purpose of the meeting. What does that mean to you personally? Why have you chosen to read this book? Perhaps there is a deep connection to Lemuria and what you read is more about *remembrance* than new information. Perhaps it was mere curiosity, and you are simply exploring possibilities. Regardless of your reason, Kryon is telling us to claim the God inside and demonstrate this in our everyday life. In this new energy, secret societies are no longer necessary. We don't have to hide our truth; instead, we become a living example of our truth, when we discover the God inside, and realize the oneness we have with humanity.

Question for Kryon:
It was mentioned that there are secrets at the bottom of the Mediterranean, in Greece, Egypt, and the United Kingdom. Is this referring to Lemurian artifacts? Can you provide us with more information about this?

Answer:
This information was in reference to your immense past history, a history that is four to five times as old as any of the projections made by historians. The secrets you will discover are all buried by water or

dirt, and your ability to "see" them will eventually develop with your technology and let you observe many things that can't be justified with current-day thinking about how long you have been here as civilized humanity.

The final "Atlantis" is lurking in the depths of the Mediterranean, and will be discovered. It's not that old! You can still "see" roads on that small mountain, since it is very recent in your idea of Atlantis. It was covered quickly when the Mediterranean was not a sea, and when an earthquake let in the water at the "gates." As we have said before, "Atlantis" is a word that means "sinking island syndrome" to the Akash, and so many of you were involved in those events, that they all became your one "Atlantis."

In the areas of England and Scotland (and portions of Ireland), there are many secrets of former societies located under the ground. This issue was caused by waves of conquering over the millennia. They tended to cover up the cities they destroyed and build others in the same place. Eventually, city after city was buried, built upon, destroyed, and re-buried. It's quite humorous to see you uncover cities in Europe and give tours of them underground. You never ask: Was there another city below this one for the same reasons? Indeed, there are normally a few.

Any time you have a city built around a natural seaport, you also have the potential of discovery under the sea directly around the ports. Sea levels change over time, and erosion also occurs over time. You can be assured that, in the majority of older ports of your civilization, there are secrets hidden right under you.

The "secrets" are about what you knew about God, and what you knew about the application of science. It might interest you to know that everything from about 10,000 years ago was a total "restart" of Human knowledge. If, indeed, you have been here for more than 40,000 years (as we have discussed), it is possible you will find exceptionally ancient artifacts with etchings on them that show your solar system, and even mysteries about potential knowledge of your immediate neighbor objects in the sky.

If you follow this logic or this idea, there is another misconception: Scientific discovery always follows the same avenue or progression. You look for evidence of your own progressive technology in the ruins of another consciousness. This is actually quite amusing.

Let me give you an advanced axiom of thinking from other civilizations: Physics is physics, and the manipulation of the elements around it and within it have many roads to get to the same solution. One society may discover that air can support flight, if you go fast enough and use a "lifting surface." So, your answer to flight is to force air in a way that creates lift. Airplanes are born, and so, futurist-archeologists look for drawings of airplanes in the rubble of the Ancients to see if they found flight.

Another civilization before you may have discovered the secret to actually manipulating the mass of any object. It's not that hard, and with almost any kind of ability to create designer magnetics, it can be done. In fact, it shows itself immediately! Controlling it is done with patterns of *phasic displacement*. Tesla even knew that (but couldn't control it). The idea that this process belongs to some highly advanced society of the future is folly! It could have been any of you at any time. But you went another way.

A culture that can manipulate mass can fly almost anywhere, or lift almost anything. Speed is not needed to take off or land, or re-enter the atmosphere. The manipulation of basic physics is a staple of almost all advanced civilizations in the galaxy. You simply have not seen it yet. You sit here, believing that the laws of physics are the laws of the way things work. Instead, they are the baseline of where they default to, inviting you to change them all.

In summary, you will discover things that make no sense at all, and technology that you won't even recognize as technology. But when you find the *books*, it will change everything.

Rewriting the Future

Why does the future need to be rewritten? After all, the future is not known; it's simply a field of potentials. What affects the field of potentials? The answer is consciousness, and for thousands of years, the collective consciousness has been affected by humanity's predominant prophecy of an Armageddon scenario where we are all destroyed. That was supposed to happen at the turn of the millennium, or the year 2000. And when nothing happened, there was another big scary prediction that 2012 was "the end of time."

We have passed 2012 and yet, our doomsday clock keeps changing because of our fascination with drama, fear, and horror. Our history is filled with the expectation of destruction. Humanity carries a doom bias. Kryon tells us that every single Old Soul carries a *bias of remembrance* that says, *"Earth is doomed."* There are many who still feel like *something bad is coming*. They can only see the various problems we face, and feel despair because they believe these problems are unsolvable. There are several predictions that the economy is going to collapse, and there is real fear that we will have another major war. The world is expecting doom. That is why Kryon is asking us to rewrite what we consider to be our future.

It is only in the last few decades that humanity changed the *end of world* direction that we were headed for. The residual of this doom bias from the past, and what *might have been*, remains in our psyche. The residue of this old energy potential is dangerous because if enough Humans cooperate with the fear and drama it produces, the effect will be to slow down our evolution. Some of the things we fear most may even occur! It's almost like we attract them by our expectations.

What are your expectations? How do you feel about your personal future? Is it hopeful and exciting, and filled with benevolence? Do you expect good things coming your way, and that perhaps they may be even better than you expected? For many, it's tough to believe they have a bright future. Some are expecting the drama, problems, or challenges to continue and believe that it's *"this or something worse!"* Sending negative energy to a situation merely continues its production. Each complaint is like a confirmation of negative expectation. If that is you, then here is an opportunity to rewrite your future. Can you turn around your thoughts, beliefs, and actions, so that you create positive comments? What you say changes your reality and affects those around you.

Perhaps you know this already, and yet, there are old habits that get in the way. Or maybe, you find yourself sitting with family or friends that start complaining and, before you know it, you join in. Sometimes it's easier to be compliant and not offend. It can be difficult to move from dark to light in any situation; after all, we've only just emerged from the old energy of the past. These are the things that Kryon discusses as we move deeper into the new energy that is on the planet. The following channel from Kryon provides us with an opportunity to contemplate how we might rewrite our personal future.

Greetings, dear ones, I am Kryon of Magnetic Service. I want you to put a bubble around this place, blocking out all other sounds and concepts. There is an energy here for you, and for some of you, this day of teaching is an energy of "a-ha!" It's an energy that isn't new, for it's remembering.

Dear ones, for many of you, there will be many of these rememberings, and this is what you expected at this time. You are going to start remembering the things of ancient days that made sense. These are the things you learned and experienced as shamanic beings in your past. The Ancients were you, Old Soul, and there's a lot to remember.

You'll remember the various prophecies that even you, as Ancients, participated in – knowing at some level you'd actually be in that future someday – and now, here you are. All of these things begin to make sense within the feelings that you are now starting to have. This particular channel is one that asks a question, "How are you going to perform life now, going from the dark to the light?" When you, as an Old Soul, have literally been on the planet for thousands of years, from the very creation story, you are literally imbued with the knowledge of light and dark. You've been alive at some level, civilization after civilization. You've even been here in civilizations that history books don't know about yet.

That's how old you are. Yet, each time you were on this planet, you returned into a low consciousness. On a scale of one to 10, meaning one is starting consciousness and 10 is the wisest consciousness, Human civilization is still only at about three-and-a-half. That is as far as it has developed within any civilization on this planet. Be aware that some started with more, but devolved into what you have now. You have lived thousands of years within an older energy, and here you are with a changing energy where light is starting to show itself and where darkness is starting to flail in its dysfunction.

Low consciousness (darkness) is losing because the very attributes of what used to feed it are no longer viable. The systems that featured the lack of integrity and greed are going to start to crumble. Different parts of the planet will be affected first, and others will follow. However, they will crumble because light is winning. How are you doing personally? How will it be, walking into the light from thousands of years of darkness? What habits are you going to carry into this new era that will keep you in the dark?

I wish to share with you just a few attributes in these few moments. These will be what you call *food for thought*, Old Soul. You are the hope of the planet, the light of the planet, Old Soul. You are the experienced ones of the planet, yet, so many of you are still working the puzzle in the dark. How are you going to do it? I'm going to make a list of attributes, as I often do, and it's not a long one. The list will represent steps and insights into the process of moving from the dark to the light.

Belief

Like so many other lists we have given you, number one goes like this: Do you believe it? Do you really believe it? We've given channels about health and your ability to mine the Akash. We've spoken about you, talking to your cells and working with your Innate. In all of these, number one is always: Do you believe it? The reason that this step is primary and the most important is that, unless your consciousness takes it in as truth, the rest of your body hasn't got a chance. You are the boss of your cells and your consciousness talks to that which is your *Innate*, and you have to be on board with all of it. You have to make it your own. Do you believe it? Do you really believe a shift is taking place?

As you look around the planet and see all that is happening in business and government, you may see something odd. Although these things all happened regularly in an old energy, they are floundering in this new energy, or at least appearing to be inappropriate. You have never seen this energy, which has never been tested in your lifetimes. No Human has ever seen these coming attributes yet. If you take saltwater fish and put them into fresh water, they will die, unless there is a mechanism for them to refine their metabolism. They are aquatic, but not with that *type* of water. You're moving from dark to light, and although you have lived many lives, the paradigms are different. You will have to adjust. So number one is that you have to believe it.

Is this really happening on the planet, or is it something you heard at a seminar during a channel? Is it wishful thinking – something that you are not really on board with – or are you a part of it? If you are, then you have to say, *"I see it! Wow, it's really happening! I am in the right place at the right time and I am part of the shift. It's one of the grandest things that has happened on the planet. I am alive at the right time, and I came for this."*

Some of you may be super-analytical and say, *"I couldn't have come for this new darkness/light shift because I'm too old. This or that is wrong with me, so I can't proceed with something so different with so much change."* Dear one, the creation of light is something you do best no matter who you are, how old you are, or what's happening in your body. The creation of compassion and light is consciousness working in its most elegant way, and all of you can do this.

There are so many who have said, *"I'm not coming back. I've done my job!"* Yes, you are! I'll say it again and again. You wouldn't miss the party! Dear ones, you're not going to make the same mistakes you did this time. You will come in with freshness and an Akashic remembrance that will create wisdom that is new. That's what is going to happen later, but for now we need you, Old Soul. You are here now to literally win this war of light and dark while you're still alive, and that is why we offer you information for extended life when you start to understand how you can heal your body, talk to your cells, and create that which medicine has said is impossible.

Some are sitting here right now and you've already done it. I know who's here, and I know who sits in front of me. Miracles abound with you and synchronicities are here in the audience. I know what has happened in your life. Spirit knows. You are so ripe for this information! Once you have decided that it's real, and decide to own it for yourself, then you can begin the journey into the light. Next you have to ask: If it's real, what am I going to do to cooperate with it? What changes within me because I have cognized or owned the fact that there is a dark/light shift happening? This is the fulfillment of the prophecy of the ages, and you are in a time that is unusual and ripe with change. What is your next step? What are you going to do?

Old Consciousness Habits

Human, you contain old habits and this is nothing to be ashamed of or be guilty about. Habits are habits, and you've done what you've done to survive all your life, and now the fabric of what you are used to has started to shift. So what if you were to analyze your reaction to things? Are you a complainer? You may not even realize you are because it's so easy to chime in with other complainers without thinking about it. Did you know this is a habit? It's a cultural habit. You may not actually believe the things that you say, but it's a habit.

Do you have a positive approach to the future? You may say you do, but when others around you say, *"We're all doomed and it will never get better. It's all going downhill!"* Do you say nothing and nod your head, yes? That's easy to do.

Perhaps you are more proactive. Perhaps, without being contrary or antisocial, you instead think about the negative statements and say, *"Well, I'm not really sure. I've heard some good things. I'm a little more positive than that."* Perhaps you have learned to be more positive without stating something that would make your friends uncomfortable or wrong? Have you figured out the diplomacy of common sense and balance? Perhaps you have figured out how to go against the grain of the negative habits of those around you, yet not be seen as somebody who is out of touch, but rather one who is forward thinking and positive? There's a difference.

With what you now know about the shift, can you start looking at things differently? What thing is possible now, when before, you thought it wasn't? In your own life, will you start taking stock, perhaps, of what *might be* instead of that which you've already decided *can't be*? I'm talking to some here who have defined the planet and themselves, and feel that nothing will change it. That's just not true, dear ones. I gave a channel recently about the *delusions of the darkness and the great untruths* and one untruth is this: *Nothing will ever change; Human nature will always be the same, and history proves it.* Can you get out of the box of the past and start looking forward to something you don't expect?

When somebody says to you, *"Look, these are the facts. Cleaning this up just can't happen! Look, these are the facts! This is what happened in the past over and over, and it will continue to happen."* Can you then say, *"I don't know how it's going to happen, but I feel confident that we are not the same as in the past, and the future is not what we've been told. You see, we don't know everything, and you don't know what you don't know and, therefore, there is hope – not just hope, there's promise"?* Are you one who believes in the shift? How, then, do you change old habits to show it? That was number two.

Marketing the Drama and Unseen Truth

Number three: There are some very old energies in your society and in your culture that have always been the same and represent past Human nature, and you have to decide what to do with them. You may not be able to change them, but you have a choice on what to do with them.

If you believe in the shift and you are starting to think more positively, then let me tell you something that will help. There is light on this planet that is not being reported. There is the beginning of high consciousness ideas and new thought about the future of humanity in very powerful places. These are seeds of new thought that are beginning to grow, and some of them make so much sense and are elegant, yet you'll never know about them. The reason? Your media is filled with the old dark consciousness of *drama above all else* and many of you willingly create a platform to sustain it.

Some of you will come home from work and feel it's a nice idea to turn on the media and watch all of the horrible things that happened on the planet that day. Perhaps you don't want the news, so you go for entertainment, instead. So you turn on a program where you can watch families in drama, arguing and complaining. What I'm telling you, dear ones, is that your media is broken, and you watch it anyway.

Right now, it continues in the old energy and the management in charge thinks it knows best what you and your neighbors want. So it's going to deliver darkness on a regular basis, and if there's nothing dark, it will create it for you. That is what you're faced with. Here is my advice. Select the media carefully that you believe is true and accurate. Wouldn't you rather have fun things to watch? Perhaps you'd like to watch cute pets or animals doing fun things? How about children doing amazing and hilarious things, or great stories of heroism with uplifting endings? How about amazing nature or comedy that is hilarious? Right now, with new devices, you can see all of that as much as you want, without commercials. This is the newest trend and evolution of your media selection – personal control over programs in your home, without commercial interruption. Did you see this happening and wonder why now?

So the solution to drama-biased media is simple: Don't watch or listen to standard broadcast! Instead, find out about the alternatives and be selective. Select news that is less biased in bringing you full-time drama. Of course, you need to stay in touch with what is happening, but you don't have to accept a program that is dedicated to enhancing and promoting the drama of the day and making it worse – or that gives no news at all about the good things going on.

I say this because [the media] broadcasting is not only broken, it's dangerous, since it gives false impressions of the overview of the planet. They are stuck in the old energy and haven't caught up yet with the overview of what might really be happening on the planet. Not yet. Even the [media] channels that will give you supposedly good education and history are biased in ways that you would not even expect. They continue to believe in slanting even historic or documentary stories to be horrific and dark. They believe that is what people really want.

What would happen if these companies started programming [positive] things people really wanted to watch? What would happen is exactly what they want, and their revenues would go up! I hope they're listening. There will come [a day,] someday, dear ones, where there'll be more than one good news channel and you can tune in to hear the most heroic and heart-rendering things that have happened on that day on the planet. It will be balanced, perhaps with some other things that also happened. But it will be a balance that you have not seen yet anywhere.

Disabling Drama

Let me give you another: Dear ones, some of you have friends, family, and colleagues at work who are difficult to be around. Each time you show up, there is drama. It hurts your heart. Sometimes, it makes you afraid to be there, and it always makes you tired. It's not anything you can change. It's the nature of darkness.

I want to tell you something I've never said before. There are two kinds of situations here and two kinds of answers to these kinds of issues. One is consistent drama. If this is something that is happening where you now live, it would serve you, Old Soul, to find an avenue out of the drama, whatever that means to you. Disengage from the drama and, when you do, you're going to find that you're going to live longer, light is going to come in, and you're going to laugh more.

Lightworker, listen to me. Old Soul, listen to me. Get out of the drama. Don't let any situation go to a dramatic place over and over and over while you sit there and let it. If you cannot control it, if you cannot be part of changing it, then remove yourself. Why would you sit around poison? Why would you continue to ingest things that are going to kill you? Then why stay with drama?

Two is temporary drama. The hardest one? Drama often spins and spins in families and it's the reason that so many of you in this room and listening have disengaged from the core family. You have become the black sheep. Actually, you are the white sheep and what is black is the drama that the family spins within! That is why holidays are so difficult for you. It's a time where there is an obligation to visit and, in the process, you must *pop back* into the family drama for a day or two and it's very uncomfortable, often confrontational, and difficult.

When you go, don't let them push your anger or frustration buttons. Stay balanced and be ready for potential family drama. If they try to get you to be involved in their drama process, just stay balanced and show them what you have learned – how to be positive and not be affected by their process.

This is difficult, but if you can do it, they notice. They notice that they can't upset you, or frustrate you, or bully you with something that is very old, karmically not tuned to you any longer, or inappropriate. No matter how much they try, you laugh it off and, clearly, are not "taking the bait." You have no idea how empowering this is for you and how much light it creates in dark places. You just won't "play" drama with them. This is what mastery is really about.

Role of the Inner Child

I want you to invite the inner child back into your life. Can you remember, dear ones, a time where you had nothing to worry about? Can you remember when the biggest issue in your life was how long you could play and when you had to come back in the house? That wonderful feeling of release from life's issues is still inside. It's not an invitation to be irresponsible, but rather, it's an invitation to find the joy of the child and to paste it back upon your current life when you need to.

This creates a more relaxed Human and a kindness and balance that only the remembrance of the innocence of a child can create. This is a critical step to staying balanced and not letting the adult world dictate your depression or your clinical feelings toward life.

This actually may be the hardest of the steps because of what is around you and the situations you encounter and the increasing battle of light and dark. Within all of this, I'm asking you to find joy. In order to do that, you bring back remembrances of the most joyful things that have ever happened to you. This often has to do with your childhood. You create the feelings of the day before Christmas, or your birthday, or the day before some event that you've been looking forward to for so long. The excitement that you have for these things makes you want to jump up and down and smile. Life is good.

These things are all still part of the inner child within you. Dear ones, the evolved Human Being is the one who has the opportunity to have this as part of everyday life until the last breath. It doesn't just belong to children. It belongs to an evolved Human Being. That's what makes the difference between the old and the new.

Compassion will play its part here naturally. It becomes automatic and self-evident. Love will play its part naturally. Common sense will, too. Balance prevails with common sense. You don't have to try to love; you don't have to try to be compassionate; it's just who you are.

Can you cognize this? Is it really happening? Is the shift happening? The wind is finally at your back. We've said that before. This is the new energy. Welcome to the new Earth!

Go from this place changed. There will be some who listen to this and say that Kryon is crazy. *"There is no improvement or light coming."* It's not what they see on the news. Exactly! So why watch it? There are things on this planet that are beautiful and are happening now that are not being seen. I want you to cognize that and know it, believe it, and understand it. Light is winning.

And so it is.

Kryon live channelling "Going from Dark to Light"
given in Buffalo, New York – June 24, 2017

Groups of high consciousness individuals are starting to spread the possibility of a brighter future, which is important for the evolving consciousness of our planet. The evolution of consciousness, especially as it relates to women, is the purpose of the Lemurian Sisterhood, created by Dr. Amber (Mele'ha) Wolf. What about you? The fact that you are interested in reading about these things means that your consciousness is already onboard with a bright future. As you continue creating a bright future, watch it spill over to those around you. Love and compassionate action are contagious. Joy and laughter are contagious. It's about time we begin to saturate ourselves with love, happiness, peace and joy. When enough Old Souls do this, we will not only rewrite our future, but the future of the planet.

The Task of the New Lemurian

The New Lemurian is referring to you, regardless of whether you were in Lemuria or not. The New Lemurian is aware of their own sacredness, the sacredness of others, and the oneness of everything. Every single thing you do, knowing what you know from here on, makes a difference for those around you. The New Lemurian is able to erase the lifetimes of low self-worth and pull forward the Lemurian Akash, which was set for the planet. During a Kryon Cruise in Hawaii, as the ship was underway, Kryon reminded us what the task of the New Lemurian is today.

The Lemurian carries a specific attribute that most Human Beings do not, no matter how old they are. Lemurian, you went through the pure race. You went through that which we would call "the population center of divinity." That's where you received a pure imprint that others did not.

We've spoken over and over of those who seeded you, but we haven't yet given you much information except that they came from the other stars that you would call the Seven Sisters. We did not even give you their planetary names. We have given few hints regarding their solar system, or of the stars that connect them energetically, for we want this all to be something that they will give you again when the time is correct. But they carry the energy of the seven, which is divine. They carry the compassion of the mother, which is female, and this was the teaching in this very place [Hawaii].

Here is something you should know: These teachers stayed a very long time in physical form. They did not come and seed and leave, and we have given you this information before. Like the other places on the planet where they existed, in a multidimensional way they remained, and some of them never left.

One of them visited you yesterday just for a moment by the volcano. She took the form of a small, white bird. It was a sign that said, *"We're here and we always will be."* The bird was very rare to be in the area, and there have been those who live here who have never seen it before. Some of you felt this magic, and you met one of the *Sisters* that your DNA knows so well.

Dear ones, there were not that many Lemurians, really. I would venture to give you a number for reference: If you projected the amount of years of Lemuria, and include the number of generations possible in that time, you would come to approximately thirty million Lemurian souls.* That's how many passed through the Lemurian system, and that's how many Lemurians there are on Earth right now. It's far fewer than the one-half of one percent number that we mentioned before. We told you previously that this larger number was the number that must awaken as Old Souls to fully make a difference for the shift. But there were far fewer Lemurians than that.

Now, what does the Lemurian soul have that other Old Souls might not? You might answer, *"Well, we might have it easier because we got the pure information."* However, there were other places where the teaching was given, and they received the pure information also. So what's the difference between you and them? The answer is this: Although you received the same information, you were in a society that lived it, and you got to experience it far differently than the others. You got to meet and work with the Star Seeds.

Lemuria was isolated. It was impossible to leave, and impossible for others to come to you. You were in a *pressure cooker* of teaching,

---

* In a previous channel, Kryon mentions the awakening of three hundred fifty million Lemurian crystals in the Cave of Creation, and yet, in this channel, Kryon says that only thirty million souls had a one-time Lemurian experience. What is the reason for this contradiction? Three hundred fifty million refers to the combination of the one-time Lemurian souls (thirty million), and those who were their descendants!

and some of you even met the ones *whose names are not pronounceable [Actual Pleiadian Mothers from the Stars]*. You sat in front of the teachers from another Star System! You felt their love for you, and saw that they were real, looked like you, and had the core love of God within them like the masters of Earth you now study.

In your Akash, many of you can see their faces. You knew them better than anyone else, and that etches itself right into your Akash and stays there, dear ones. You know what they looked like and sounded like! It changes who you are. Most of the others didn't actually see the teachers at all. They were taught by the direct children of the teachers (the Pleiadian Mothers). This was the main difference between Lemuria and the other nodes where Pleiadian landings took place and humanity was changed and taught.

So now we tell you that the task of the Lemurian is to reawaken to the DNA that you had here under the shadow of the mountain. It's to recalibrate that which is in the DNA you have now. Your Akash is multidimensionally stored in your DNA and it means that it is available instantly. Years and millennia make no difference at all. Thousands of generations of your lifetimes are meaningless in a linear way. You don't have to dig down deep in this system to find the Lemurian that you are. Instead, it lays there in its sacredness and divinity looking at you, and is awakening because of the time capsules that are opening now.

The faces of the Sisters are there for you to observe again in that which you would call your quantum intuition, and you can feel that which is the purity that you received in this place, the one you sit in right now.

So the gauntlet is thrown [done] to you, Lemurian, because these thirty million of you who are all on the Earth right now must to do more than the rest. You have the memory that the rest do not. You knew the ones from the stars like no one else did. It brings you en masse to an awakening and a recalibration.

Sometimes, it makes you feel unworthy because of the task in front of you that you feel is huge. Sometimes, it makes you feel sick because of what is before you. It fogs the mind and the imagination because you can't quite understand it or figure it out. But that's why you came here to listen (and read).

There will be past Lemurians, even in this room, who don't want to go to this place of awakening, and won't. There is no mandate that supersedes free choice that says, just because you're here, you have to do this, or just because you're Lemurian means you have to do this. Many will hear (or read) this message and may or may not act upon it. However, let me tell you something: Although it sounds urgent, I'm telling you that you have time and there's no judgment if you wish to wait. Remember this: You're a Lemurian today, tomorrow, and for the life of the planet. Some of you will take up the gauntlet and awaken now, and some of you will wait until the next time. There is never any judgment. There is only love.

The more who awaken, the sooner the planet will be able to change. When Lemurians start to take their awakening to a level where they are like the masters who walked this planet, believe me ... they will be noticed. Wise leadership is lacking on the Earth at the moment, and when it starts to happen, everyone will notice and want to participate. This has happened before with other awakening societies. There is nothing like being with those who know what they are doing.

This is the attribute of awakening to a quantum reality, a multidimensional attribute of humanity that is seen and felt by many. When it begins to happen to the Lemurians here, you have help! The awakening signals an entire change in the planet, and you have help in a multidimensional way that you never had before.

Dear ones, listen: You do not have to do this by yourselves! Just be the ones to begin it. Intent is like an outstretched hand to God. It's like you reaching for that Higher-Self, and saying with pure intent: *"Dear Spirit, this is the hour under the shadow of the mountain that I have dreamed about. I take that which is the mantle of my responsibility to Gaia and I give permission to meld to that which I said I could be."*

Pause...

"Well, that's hardly specific, Kryon." Dear Human, why do you need to be specific in everything? Did you learn that in some class you took in 3D logic?

◊◊◊

One Human looks into the eyes of another with deep, apprecia-tive love and says, *"I love you."* The other one pauses and says ... *"Can you be more specific?"*

◊◊◊

Don't make up your mind what it means! It's you, awakening to the mysteries that you have hidden for yourself, being revealed at this time. The invitation is to shift in an appropriate way and start a process within this lifetime and the next and the next, which will rework your DNA to a higher percentage of efficiency. Each lifetime means longer life and better wisdom and health. We've said it before, dear ones: You will awaken in the next lifetime with far better intu-ition of the past, and never have to work through the issues you did this lifetime! There are those in the room who have even had this happen in this lifetime! It changes what you'll do in life and makes you wiser, as you begin to take charge of the very core attributes that were given to you in the shadow of the mountain that is next to you right now.

Use this energy in these days. I'm speaking to those in the room: Use this energy that you feel now, for, when you leave this place, you lose part of the catalyst. The catalyst is actually your energy mingled with this place. Your Akash remembers this place. The Crystalline Grid that you helped to set, remembers you. It resounds to the soul that you are, and between the two of you, an agreement is set to change the status quo.

It helps your personal healing, dear ones. Situationally, it helps the wisdom that you have, to work the puzzles you carry right now in 3D. Emotionally, it gives you the compassion to walk through life with a different perception of what is around you. Eventually, it gives you the Lemurian mind.

If I could take you into the future, you would see a number of generations go by, and something that no one expected: A special group of Human Beings who think differently. Civilization will see them as *the wise ones*. I speak now of what happened on the planets of the Pleiadians, and the ones before them. It's the way evolution works. Not all evolve at the same time. The "starters" evolve first (the Lemurians, on Earth). Those *wise ones* will be welcomed and seen as forerunners to the future.

I want you to go from this place with, perhaps, a different perception from the one you had when you came. Now, for the listener and for the reader: You are not excluded from this message, for the eyes and the ears that would come to this particular message are drawn here synchronistically [no accident]. Many of you are Lemurians and you are also awakening to these messages and will be touched by them. It's a homecoming, isn't it? It's physical; it's compassionate; it's mental, emotional, and it involves the entire blueprint of your DNA. You will change because of it.

Finally, do not pay attention to the things that happen on this planet that are reactions from the old energy. For the old guard is trying very, very hard to pull everything right back to the old prophecies. They want a war so badly! For they understand that war creates a good economy and control. If they achieve even a part of that goal, it won't be for long, for the ball rolls forward now and can't easily be stopped. The free choice potential of this planet has been set. More of you want peace than not, and that's all it takes. A large portion of this planet can now see each other clearly. You have begun a higher consciousness slide into a place that eventually will see no war at all, and this is what we see in this moment.

Kryon live channelling "The Task of the New Lemurian"
given during the Hawaii Cruise – August 15, 2012

Peace on Earth begins with each person remembering his or her sacredness. The planet gets enlightenment one person at a time, not with groups. You don't have enlightened groups where the entire group has an "aha" experience. Enlightenment happens one heart at a time. Perhaps that is why Kryon continually says that you are the hope of the planet in a system that is filled with the love of God, and it's beautiful.

The Lemuria/Hindu Connection

What does Hinduism have to do with Lemuria? At first glance, absolutely nothing! However, this unusual connection was revealed through one of Hinduism's foremost spiritual preceptor (teacher and leader), Satguru Sivaya Subramuniyaswami, affectionately known as Gurudeva. He was born in 1927 in Oakland, California, and as young man of 20, he journeyed to India and Sri Lanka where he adopted Shaivism. Shaivism is one of the major sects within Hinduism. He passed away in 2001 and was considered a living example of awakening and wisdom.

Gurudeva was venerated as one of the strictest and most traditional gurus in the world. He gently oversaw the establishment of more than 50 independent temples worldwide. He was the hereditary guru of 2.5 million Sri Lankan Hindus and, in 1979, he founded "Hinduism Today," an award-wining, international monthly magazine. In 2000, he received the prestigious U Thant Peace Award at the United Nations, New York (previously bestowed on the Dalai Lama, Nelson Mandela, Mikhail Gorbachev, Pope John Paul II, and Mother Teresa). Those who knew Gurudeva felt his great peace, presence, and centeredness. He was someone who inspired others toward their highest Self. He was an unfailing light within Indian spirituality and created a beautiful bridge between East and West spiritual philosophies.

In 1970, he founded Kauai Aadheenam, also known as Kauai's Hindu Monastery, on the tropical Garden Island of Kauai, Hawaii. In 1973, something remarkable happened to Gurudeva. Soon after placing a statue of Lord Siva Nataraja, purchased in India, at the Kauai Monastery, his inner eye opened and he saw an array of manuscripts in the inner library of Lord Subramaniam. His vision included a librarian that would open a volume in response to questions. These clairvoyant revelations occurred over many months in the garden restaurant of the former Coco Palms Hotel.

The librarian would present a volume, turning page after page, and Gurudeva would slowly dictate to a sincere monastic scribe, who patiently and accurately wrote down each word. For 25 years, he entrusted this information only to his cloistered monk order. Then, in 1998, Gurudeva published these scribed volumes into a book called *"The Lemurian Scrolls – Angelic Prophecies Revealing Human Origins."* Whoa! Here we have a Hindu guru writing about Lemuria. *"The Lemurian Scrolls**"* chronicles man's untold journey to Earth from the Pleiades millions of years ago, and the struggles faced in ensuing eras as souls matured into their ultimate destiny and Divinity. This is the connection between Hinduism, the oldest religious belief system on the planet, and Lemuria.

What follows are two channelled messages from Kryon, given at the Kauai Hindu Monastery, that further explains the sacred purpose of Gurudeva's vision.

Greetings, dear ones, I am Kryon of Magnetic Service. Once again, I say to you that I know where I am, for this is a place that has been created because of channelling [the channelling of Gurudeva at the Hindu Monastery], and that is what they call it here.

Before we speak of the brief lesson for today, I wish to let those who are not actually here know what has just taken place. We are on the Garden Isle of Kauai, a place that is known within my teachings as Lemuria. It is a place where Lemurians lived and worked, and that is why this spiritual adventure that you are on now has been called "The Lemurian Retreat."

---

* Authors' note: The Lemurian Scrolls were channelled by Gurudeva and represent teachings for those who follow Hinduism. The information within the scrolls do not necessarily parallel the teachings from Kryon, they merely demonstrate a connection that the origins of humanity are from the Pleiadians and involve a place called Lemuria.

We are here at the monastery on top of the hill, a place run by the gentleness of the Hindu. They are here because of Gurudeva and his channelling throughout all of these years that spoke of Lemuria, much the same as I have taught you.

Let it not to be lost on any of you, the similarities of the channelling that I have given you in the past about where you sit. For the Hindu Master Gurudeva knew it, and wrote of it in his books. We, again, ask you: Are you aware of your seeds from the stars? Is it possible that inside you is more than you think? Is it possible that the DNA you have has come from somewhere else? This is exactly what they believe here, right from the teachings of Gurudeva.

Did you hear earlier from the Hindu teacher the belief that there are some Lemurians still here? This is the very information we have given you about the Pleiadian teachers for years. Now you get to actually sit in Lemuria, and hear this ancient truth from a profound spiritual source. Indeed, these teachers from the stars are still here and they still exist.

Did you hear from the Hindu teacher about the Dispensations? He has his names for it, and we have ours. But they are just labels that accurately describe the four Dispensations of Humanity, moving into the fifth. Did you hear the teachings that a soul evolves? Did you hear the teachings that, when you first got here as a Lemurian, you knew more than you do now? Did you hear the teaching that told you things are beginning to change? This is year one (2014) of that change.

Some time ago, I said that the end of war on the planet will be the beginning of your evolution. Did you hear this same information a moment ago from a holy man who reflects the channelling that has built this place? All of this information has come from the Akash of the man whom we honor here as Gurudeva, profound leader of thousands of Hindus, and author of *"The Lemurian Scrolls."* Here is a man who was in touch with a very beautiful truth: The core teachings of humanity started here, in a place called Lemuria, taught by those from the stars.

In past channellings, we have used the letters of the word *Lemuria* as a teaching tool, and now we come to the letter R. Today, as I sit in a chair in this sacred place, that letter will mean several things. The first one is *Revelation*. The revealing of the truth is at hand, again. Here is a truth that has been hidden for eons. But now, you come into the fifth dispensation of time and it is beginning to be revealed.

The number *five*, in Tibetan numerology, means *change*. That was described, even today, from this platform, as given by the Hindu teacher a moment ago. This is a time of change; one you have been waiting for. *"Do not despair"* were his words, and these are the same words we have given to you over and over. What you hear and see on your media is simply "getting there." This change is a journey into an advanced consciousness, and change is often frightening.

We have told you that the evolution of Human spirit at the soul level has many stages of learning. We've also told you that Old Souls, the ones who are listening and reading, are the ones to whom this truth is being revealed. So, we honor the R for *revelation*, especially here. For, this place has been created at the right time and the right place for the planet, and actually holds an energy for Lemuria and the teachers from the stars.

It is appropriate and proper, and it needs to be here at this time. It is honored and there is deep appreciation for the dedication of those who work in the gardens here, for their Akash is filled with the history here. The temple of worship that they are finishing, the one you've just been in, honors the Pleiadian teachers who are still here. They're right.

Next, I want to use the R for *Responsibility*. You are responsible for your discernment, right now, about the truth of everything you have just seen and heard. Is this true? Can this really be – teaching from the stars? You can sit there and you can go to sleep and say, *"This is nonsense, so I'm turning off because I don't want to think about it."* This is your absolute free choice, dear ones. As the holy man said, some will see it and some will not. So, for those who are not asleep, I ask this: What is your responsibility to your own Akash? How many times have you been on this planet through the learning cycles, bringing you to a realization that there really is truth here?

What is it that some of you are feeling here in this garden in Lemuria? What could it be? Could there be divinity inside? Perhaps you are already aware of many lifetimes that you've lived, but did you ever consider that there might be a plan for all this? Could it be that the sweetness and the essence of the love of God actually knows your soul, and that you have been here on this planet through all the cycles? Perhaps you might even call yourselves Lemurian? If so, what is your responsibility for the discernment of this truth?

Based upon what you've been through in the eons you have lived, who are you now? Is there really is a plan and a "next step for you"? It doesn't matter that you are not of the belief system of those who built this temple. It doesn't matter at all. Truth is truth, and here, in this place, they are holding the energy of the ancient, sacred Lemuria. But you're the ones who go into the world to show who you are by how you act. Can others see the teachings in you? Can they see the God inside you? Can they see the ascended Human Being in your eyes or not?

You are the Lightworkers who go to work and have the children, doing all the ordinary things that they cannot do here, as they hold the light in this place. The responsibility of the truth is upon you, to spread through the consciousness of who you are in the world. It's profound what is going on now, and is about to go on in this planet. Yes, this is a difficult period, as the old energy tries to get a grip. It doesn't want to lose. You can see it on the news – it doesn't want to lose, and yet it will. This is because there are many who are awakening to the grandness of a truth inside, that a divine angelic spark from another place was brought to this planet by the Pleiadians.

This is what is taught here in this garden. This is what is channelled here. Gurudeva was correct to release this information to the public at the right time. I have been telling you these things now for almost thirty years. This is not a "new age." It is the revelation and responsibility that comes from an ancient age.

That is the message for this day. The R is revelation and responsibility of truth. What are you going to do with it? You are the ones who are going to get on the bus and leave [speaking of the excursion with the attendees]. The monks will remain, holding this energy and light for this island, as they should. Dear ones, this island is completely protected in so many ways that you are not aware of. They are part of it. They may not ever talk about it, but they know.

Go from this place and remember it. It's bigger than you think. The energy here is something that's beyond anything you expect.

Kryon live channelling "Kryon Lemurian Retreat"
given at Hindu Monastery, Kauai, Hawaii – August 14, 2014

Dear ones, as you sit here and as you listen and read this, I want to remind you where you are: You are in a place that has been dedicated to the growth of the Human Spirit. The knowledge that is in this garden paradise would tell you that every single Human on the planet is born with a magnificent seed inside. It's a seed that is waiting for the nourishment of Gaia and the oneness of all things.

The man who planned all of what you see (Kauai Hindu Monastery), and who channelled information that is represented here, is called Gurudeva. He actually channelled the message that this is Lemuria. This great Hindu master, representing the original, organized belief system of your age, tells you that you came from the stars. What do you think about that?

Did you ever wonder what humanity had as a belief before the "modern" doctrines changed it all? It was this: humanity was here on purpose; humanity had a chance, with free choice, to ascend; humanity goes through lifetime after lifetime after lifetime with choices to personally work with dark and light. This is original thought.

You sit in a temple, the grounds of a temple dedicated to the Lemurian spark. This is what Gurudeva had – the Lemurian spark. It hit him with an explosion of awakening, and he knew the truth. He actually channelled the information that this is Lemuria and wrote the book, *"The Lemurian Scrolls."* As a revered Hindu master, he gave the best information he intuitively received, about what happened right here on this mountain.

Dear ones, this is what the teaching of Kryon also represents: This is Lemuria! (Pause) Listen to it [referring to the sudden downpour of rain on the roof of the open shelter]. The presence of the conscious-ness of Gaia is speaking as well. *"Are you there listening, Lightworker? Why is it you were able to walk through these gardens without a drop of rain, where the sun came out so bright, and now we wait for you to assemble under the shelter for the downpour?"* Think about this.

Do you think that's an accident? This seeming synchronicity is Gaia smiling on you, saying, *"You're in the right place at the right time. Respect what happened here and all the seeming accidents and the syn-chronicity that would put together a place like this. It's no accident you sit here in a spiritual place, on holy ground, appreciated and respected."* The rain continues...

Dear ones, do you remember anything you see here in this gar-den? Has it affected you a little, or more than a little? It's a funny thing about Lemurians: Once a Lemurian, you always want to return to this place, or a similar place with these attributes. You're born with this. How many of you remember wearing the color of the Swami? [The Hindu guide for the day is wearing an orange robe]. How many of you, perhaps in other cultures, sought this information? How many became the kind of a person who might dedicate yourself and live alone? How many of you called yourself a Shaman? How many of you remember being so dedicated that you'd *sign off* on being com-mon in your culture in order to teach and meditate?

I want you to remember these things when they come forward in your Akash. This remembrance is an attribute of a Lemurian. How many of you were here on this mountain for any of this? If this expe-rience has affected you, I will tell you this: You're remembering it and it can hit you hard, emotionally. It opens doors that you didn't know you had, doors of allowance to look upon these things today. You see the statues, the beliefs, the man in orange, and even though you may not be Hindu, it affects you. You see God inside those who are here. It lets you open your heart to understand that there are no boxes with God.

This place smiles upon you now. What do you realize today in this place after spending time with the Swami? When you see who he really is, this gives you the invitation to realize the Lemurian spark, and to leave differently than you came because you saw some things you didn't expect.

Perhaps it will recalibrate that which is the consciousness of your culture? Perhaps you will go home a different person because you were here on this land? If you do, and you are one of those who are affected today, I tell you that the original one who put this together [Gurudeva] had the vision of you sitting here today, opening a door of realization. The realization: You're not apart from God. You are not born dirty, and you have magnificence within. This is a truth that is universal, but which has often been forgotten or rewritten.

The truth is like this. It starts to be remembered first, when light energies begin to swirl around you. It all epitomizes the Lemurian spark that is here. Take it all in, what has transpired here, the timing of it, and what has been said. Go from this place differently than you came. That was the plan of those who built it.

Kryon live channelling "Kryon Lemurian Retreat"
given at Hindu Monastery, Kauai, Hawaii – August 18, 2015

The connection between Hinduism and Lemuria was through the Lemurian Akash of Gurudeva. Get ready for a similar connection ... between Lemuria and His Holiness the 14th Dalai Lama, Tenzin Gyatso. During 2017, many Old Souls joined Lee Carroll on a Kryon Tour through India and Nepal. In a series of synchronicities, the group was profoundly surprised by an opportunity to have a private audience with His Holiness, at his home in Dharamshala. The beautiful system of Tibetan Buddhism and the lineage of His Holiness were discussed by Kryon later that year, during a Lemurian Sisterhood meeting. Here is what Kryon said:

I want to tell you a little bit about the system that exists within your humanism, which is starting to evolve. The system that I want to tell you about is one of the revelation of the Akash. It's a system that will absolutely let you know who you've been and where you've been. Is that a possibility?

I turn to something that was given to my partner so he can then describe it. He has been in a place where this particular sacred attribute works and resounds with truth.

When he was in India, he was told about a remarkable attribute of the culture. Dharamshala is where the leader of all the (Buddhist) monks lives. You call him the Dalai Lama. Under his tutelage, there is a system of hierarchy which is the position of the monks, who they are, why they are there, and how important they are in a very sacred system.

Now, in a traditional organization in the West, leaders would normally rise through a pre-determined system of achievement or, perhaps, be appointed. The senior ones would be elevated, and so on. That's a linear, logical system that you know very well. However, that's not how it works at all in the hierarchy of this holy leadership we are discussing ... not even close.

Get ready for something beyond linear thinking: At a very young age [of the children], the elder monks are able to "sense" that some of the children in the area are different. These children are sent to monasteries to be examined, but not tested as you might think. Instead, the examination is done by a shamanic-like monk who "reads" their Akashic record! Now, here in your land, you call this a "past life reader." However, in this land, they are not readers at all, but past life examiners.

What they are looking for is very, very detailed and specific. There are certain small children who have had lifetimes of enlightenment, and have been leaders of many Buddhists in the past. They expect that the karmic system would place them in Dharamshala so that they would be found. Indeed, they find them, and a very few are selected.

The selected ones are immediately removed from their families at the age of eight, and they remain in the monastery to begin their advanced training. By the time they are in their late teens and into their twenties, they are often sent overseas to be immersed in other cultures and learn multiple languages.

Right away you can see that, if the shamanic monks make a mistake with their selection, you would have young people without these aptitudes or intelligences, and they would fail. But they don't! Instead, they all rise to the occasion, and you start to see that the monks were right. These young people begin to ascend to the important positions in Buddhism, almost like they were originally bred for it. Against all the odds of logic or chance, they are revealed as highly intelligent, esoteric, charismatic men.

So let's rewind this whole picture. The Akashic examiner: What is he really *looking* at? Is there a system he knows that works? Does he do it all through his intellect or intuition? What is he looking at? Indeed, there is a system and I wish to, again, reveal it.

All Humans have a field around them, which is esoteric but also multidimensional. It has been seen and identified with a Hebrew word: Merkabah or Merkaba. It is the field that you literally *ride* within as a Human. It would seem to "carry you in life." The word in Hebrew actually means "to ride."

This field is a large one and it is filled with information. Because it isn't totally esoteric, it has substance in a multidimensional way. This means that you could say, it's in a physical world of reality. Because of this, humanity may actually see it someday when instruments are developed that can see multiple-dimensionality (things in quantum reality). However, because this field is actual physics, there are certain Humans who can see it and "read" it now. This is what past life readers sense and read, and it's also what medical intuitives are able to read.

So, I have just revealed that this seemingly strange and unbelievable shamanic ability is very real, for it's something that exists in physics and the ones who "see" it are simply before their time. It will eventually be discovered and will be identified by science. So, here is a profound question: What if these "Merkabah seers" could look at yours? What if the Buddhist examiner looked at yours? What might they see first?

Dear ones, if you were Lemurians, believe me when I tell you that this would show. It wouldn't just show, it would glow! What it would mean is that you were one of the first souls on the planet, and the ones taught sacred core information by those from the stars who seeded Humans with the 23 pairs of chromosomes you currently have.

Anyone who can read a Merkabah would see that first. Because you were the ones who actually met and were taught by the ones from the Stars, there are not that many of you. However, any Lemurian soul is also classified as a very Old Soul, and those are the ones who tend to gather at places like this to listen to channelling in this age of the shift.

Next question: In this new energy, do you think it's at all possible for Old Souls to sense this attribute in the Merkabah? And the answer is yes. Some of you are sensing not only that you were Lemurian, but that others around you are as well. What would that actually mean if this is the case? First of all, it's validation of your history and spiritual lineage. But what it really indicates is that you are ready to participate helping become the leaders of light within the shift that is taking place on this planet at this time.

By the way, this is what the monk "'examiners" were looking for – Lemurians! As the selected children grow and become monks who ascend to a higher place, they might even be in line, someday, for something much bigger. So let's go further: Are the selected ones later able to "see and read a Merkabah" as well? Yes, they are. In fact, some become the examiners. If they would examine you, they would know who you were. Indeed, I see you and I know it!

Congratulations, ladies, you've done well to even be here. Because seated in front of me, indeed, are many Lemurians. They're all over the world, you know? Lemuria was there a long time. There are many souls who were born there and who met the Star teachers and, later, moved on with many other lifetimes. However, the *select* ones of interest today are the women. The reason is that the women of Lemuria were designated to be trained as the Shamans and spiritual leaders of the land. Therefore, they hold the seeds of core truth, and the potentials for the evolution of Human consciousness today.

There are some facts and attributes behind all this "Lemurian remembering" that we've given many times. We've given it over and over and wish to say it again. The system of genders goes back and forth. All of you have been men, and all the men have been women. However, as we've said before, the shift – the precession of the equinoxes – carries no error or mistake that most of the women who started in Lemuria are alive now. If you were a woman in Lemuria, you are a woman now.

This is part of a benevolent system that would allow you to begin to recognize your lineage and take the power of wisdom that is actually within your Akash. However, there are also men on this planet who used to be part of Sisterhoods that happened directly after Lemuria, but their gender was as a woman then. There are a few of them and they stick out. They stick out because of the magnificence and wisdom of their messages and the gentleness of their countenance.

In India, my partner met one of these and he held his hand. It was confusing, for my partner felt that he was holding hands with a shamanic Lemurian woman – however, it was the Dalai Lama (His Holiness the 14th Dalai Lama). It takes something like this intuitive experience to really bring it home, and to understand that the shamanship of humanity originally belonged to the gentle gender, and that was the plan all along. It was an acknowledgment that the best teaching on the planet will come from the mother.

The Human Being wants to hear the gentle, compassionate, benevolent voice of the mother. It's what you all grow up with, no matter what the gender. It's only natural that these would also be the ones to be the spiritual leaders of society on Earth. They would be the guides, the priests, the pastors, and the intuitive ones who you could go to for help and good advice.

This is the message of why you're here. The practicalness of it asks you to grasp the full understanding of it and begin to live that which you were taught. Dear Sisters, you carry a mantle of responsibility for compassion to the planet. Not just for your children. It's a responsibility and a "cloak of wisdom" – a compassion for the humanity on the planet. You were born with this, mom. Those of you without children experienced it with your mothers, especially in the original years. You were born to understand compassionate action and benevolence. That's who you are.

There are many of you Lemurian Sisters on this planet, and as the Sisterhood grows, you will meet together mostly as strangers. Also, know that most of you were not together in one generation because Lemuria lasted thousands of years. You came and you went and you came and you went, but what you have in common is that you were actually there on the continent of MU. It became the launching pad for your Akash, and the core truth you were taught is still within your Akash.

The Star Mothers who taught you remained there, and they didn't die. That's simply part of that which is a system of biology that you don't have yet. In fact, many of them are still here on this planet! But think of this: Although you may be strangers now, and were, even then, you are rekindling the compassion that you learned in Lemuria, from the SAME TEACHER. This is what you have in common and that is profound. The same Star Mother taught you all.

Kryon live channelling given during Lemurian Sisterhood
in Philadelphia, Pennsylvania – November 18, 2017

This beautiful message from Kryon reminds us that love and compassionate action are changing the planet, one Human at a time.

The Lemuria/Hawaiian Kahuna Connection

The chain of islands called Hawaii was the dwelling place of the Ancient Lemurians. Approximately 15,000 years ago, the Lemurians took to their canoes and the Pleiadians left their corporeal bodies, with many becoming part of the Earth. In the Hawaiian culture, Na Huihui o Makali'i refers to the cluster of stars known as the Pleiades. The Makali'i is much revered in the Hawaiian tradition because it is the place from where the first Hawaiian people came. When the Pleiades constellation appears in the night sky (usually in late November), it signifies the beginning of the Makahiki, the most important holiday or festival of the year. It is a time of celebrating the great harvest and a time of personal rest and renewal. All wars and battles ceased, and festivities commenced. Several of the rigid kapu (regulating religious and social laws) were temporarily relaxed to allow more freedom for celebration.

The kahuna would preside over the Hawaiian ceremonies. Kahuna are highly respected as master practitioners of their art or craft. They are the official keepers of the ancient wisdom and knowledge of the early Hawaiians, and there are many kinds of kahuna experts. There are several ways to analyze the word kahuna. The word Kahu means keeper, custodian, guardian, or someone who takes care of persons, property, or knowledge, and na means to care for, or belonging. The word "Ka" means "the," or "light," and "Huna" means "secret," or "hidden" (in reference to hidden esoteric knowledge). In essence, the kahuna were the high priests and priestesses, Shamans, healers, and ceremonialists, who could directly communicate with the spirit world and their ancestors, accessing wisdom and knowledge that would seem mystical to those who could not.

Despite the suppression of kahuna wisdom by Christian missionaries in the nineteenth and twentieth centuries, there are still traditional kahuna that can found in Hawaii. Previously, the sacred spiritual knowledge of the kahuna was rarely shared with outsiders.

Thankfully, the shift of consciousness on the planet has resulted in several kahuna sharing their hidden knowledge with those of like mind. One of the first to do this was a full-blooded Hawaiian man known as Hale Kealohalani Makua.

Kahuna Hale Kealohalani Makua

Hale Kealohalani Makua was born on the Island of Hawaii (known as the Big Island) as the seventh-generation direct descendant of King Kamehameha Nui from his mother's lineage, and as the seventh generation direct descendant of Kamehameha's cousin, the High Chief Keoua Ku'ahu'ula from his father's lineage. Many knew him simply as Makua.

For many years, he served with the United States Marine Corps, until he was severely wounded during his last tour of duty in Vietnam. It was this injury that became the catalyst for him to transition from a physical warrior to a spiritual warrior. For five years, Makua was in a hospital in San Antonio, Texas, dealing with bone infections and repeated surgeries. Makua claimed that his final recovery was due to his ancestors. His ancestors would visit him and help him deal with all his anger, pain, and grief. Through his ancestors, he gained a new sense of freedom and the responsibility of the kahuna.

Kahuna Hale Makua was highly regarded throughout Polynesia and beyond. He was the council elder of the Hawaiian Spiritual Warrior Society, *Na 'Ao Koa o Pu'ukohola*, and played a pivotal role in fostering deeper connection and enhanced communication between the peoples of the Pacific. As an indigenous elder, he was continually traveling to international conferences, including the United Nations in New York, sharing the stage with His Holiness the 14th Dalai Lama. He was also a member of the International Elders Council and devoted his life to being in service to humanity, sharing his wisdom, knowledge, and divine light through the guidance of his ancestors. Hale Makua left his corporeal body on March 27, 2004, due to an automobile accident on the Big Island of Hawaii.

Before Makua passed away, he had written a manuscript that held the knowledge of his ancestors. Copies of this manuscript were given to Lee Carroll, Kahuna Kalei'iliahi, and his close friend, Dr. Hank Wesselman. Dr. Wesselman, an American anthropologist, shared a very special relationship with Makua that extended beyond the bond of friendship. This unusual connection between two visionaries resulted in the publication of *"The Bowl of Light."* This book is filled with the powerful teachings of Makua's Hawaiian ancestral wisdom, via Dr. Wesselman's personal story of their journeys together.

The following extract from *"The Bowl of Light,"* by Hank Wesselman, directly relates to the new paradigm that is emerging – one where women once again take their place as shamanic guides for humanity, just as they did during Ancient Lemuria.

In a discussion at the gathering soon after our visit to the Pu'uhonua, a tall elder woman named Sandra with short blonde hair asked the chief [Makua] a pointed question.

"What does it mean for women to reclaim their power?"

The room went silent. This was, in fact, a major area of discussion in our gatherings, and if it didn't come up on its own, Jill [Hank's wife] or I often brought it up. For we are all in agreement that it is time for women to take back their power. And there is little consensus on exactly what this means. We looked at Makua beseechingly. He appeared serious, and after a few long moments, he turned to us and unfolded his thoughts for us.

"It is time for all the women to come together to generate a new vision. They must dream a new dream – a new vision that must be about what they want for their grandchildren and for the next seven generations."

"And what about the men?" replied Sandra, who was clearly wanting to hear more. "We cannot simply exclude them from the dynamic. As you have observed, the energy is rotary."

The chief smiled. "Women are the keepers of the culture, the family, the home, as well as the foundation of the world. The lesson that the women have to teach the men is how to be gentle.

"It's the women who are going to change the world now, and so the men have to protect them." Makua smiled again, then added, "The men need to follow the women for a change, because in doing so, men will become more selective. It's about discrimination, about learning discernment."

The women in the group were utterly still, their eyes glowing with focused attention. The men looked supportive, yet their eyes shifted uneasily. This was new to most of them.

"This is Mother Earth," Makua went on. "It is not Father Earth. The energy of the Earth is feminine, about Haumea, and the lesson for the men is about gentleness. The job of the women is to teach the men how to be gentle. So, it's time for the men to sit down and listen, and it is time for the women to stand up and speak."

Jill caught Makua's attention, and he waited for her to speak. "If I've got this right," she began, "when you say that the energy is rotary, this is not simply about altruism in which we are selective to whom we extend our support in hope of reciprocation. It's not about a unilateral direction in which the women continually give, and the men continually take. Rather, it's about authentic and unconditional reciprocation, in which everyone extends support to everyone else, with nobody keeping tabs on who owes whom what. This alone would be truly rotary ... and this alone is the feminine impulse."

Makua smiled at her in agreement. "That's it precisely. The universe is always in balance. We are the ones who are out of balance. Yet the paradox is that to establish and experience balance here on this level, it always begins with us – with ourselves. And to establish this balance, this harmony, within yourself, you have to be in love. And when you are in love, you can offer yourself that love as well.

"This energy, this tapestry of aloha, is the most powerful of all the forces in the universe. And only when you are in the state of aloha, only then you can truly touch the universe. Only when you are in a state of love and practicing kindness, only then will the universe, as well as the ancestors, respond.

"This is why the greatest discovery that you will ever make," the kahuna continued, "is the discovery of yourself, and particularly the discovery of your relationship with your Higher Self, your 'Aumakua. This is the godlike being who really listens to your prayers, responds in ways that are mysterious, and sends occasional messengers to Earth – you – who usually get treated very badly." Makua burst into laughter, and we all joined him.

"There is no great messiah out there who is going to return to save us all," he offered. "That is a myth, and yet this fiction contains an eternal truth – one that even a child can understand. Each one of us carries the potential to be a messiah. We carry this energy within us, but we have to choose it. It will always and forever be about choice.

"And when we understand this, when we understand who we are and where we are, then each one of us, both male and female, has the potential, as well as the kuleana – the responsibility – to become a world redeemer. This is what is meant by the statement that 'each of us must become the change that we wish to experience.' There simply is no other way. If we wish to create a new and better world, we must dream our new world into being … and then we must act on our dreams to bring them into manifestation through ourselves."

What a divine message from Makua. Many of Makua's teachings mirror the messages of Kryon, and it is no accident that Makua befriended Lee Carroll. Makua often performed ceremonies for the Kryon group at the rim of the Kilauea Caldera, in the Hawaii Volcanoes National Park. Since Makua's passing, another Kahuna, who has known Lee and Kryon for over two decades, has come forward as Ambassador of the Ancestors, and her name is Kahuna Kalei'iliahi.

Kahuna Kalei'iliahi

Kahuna Kalei'iliahi was born and raised in the lush Kalihi Valley on the island of Oahu. Her ancestral roots trace seventy-five generations, all the way back to the stars, to the Makali'i (the Pleiades), to Papa (Earth Mother) and Wakea (Sky Father), and a long line of Royal High Chief Priests and Priestesses (Kahuna). Within the Hawaiian culture, each family has their own 'Aumakua, which is their own personal Ancestral Spirits, their personal God and protector. Kahuna Kalei'iliahi's 'Aumakua is Lono – God of peace, fertility, abundance, and agriculture, and uncle to Goddess Pele. Pele is the goddess of fire, lightening, wind, and volcanoes and the creator of the Hawaiian Islands.

One of the interesting attributes of Kahuna Kalei'iliahi is that she calls herself a kahuna. Traditionally, a true kahuna would never do this! To do so would be considered arrogant and ego driven. Authentic kahuna and Shaman have great humility and their power comes from the loving, benevolent source of the universe and the cosmic field, often accessed through their ancestors. However, adopting the title of Kahuna is another example of the great shift that is occurring on our planet. Here is the explanation from Kalei'iliahi as to why she has chosen to identify herself as a kahuna:

"The ancient kahuna did not call themselves kahuna ... they didn't need to. Everyone knew who they were, and the elders knew them when they were born. The kahuna went into hiding when it was forbidden to practice their spirituality and therefore when they walked amongst the people, no one addressed them to identify them. My ancestors have told me that it is now safe for the kahuna and indigenous Shamans all over the world to share the wisdom and knowledge to those seeking it. People from across the globe have been seeking them out and, by addressing myself as a Kahuna, I am thereby making it easier for them to find me. My ancestors have told me it is time. I usually address myself as a Hawaiian Priestess. Many Hawaiians may not agree with me, but I must trust the guidance of my ancestors. When I say I am Kahuna, it is to honor these grand ones, the Ancients of my lineage who went before me to light the way. All that I have inside me comes from them ... I hope to make them proud, for, in this moment, I am the reason they existed."

The connection that Kahuna Kalei'iliahi has with her ancestors is obvious to the Old Souls who meet her, or encounter her chants and channelled messages. When Kahuna Kalei'iliahi was asked how the ancestors communicate with her, this is what she said:

"When I hear my ancestors from the distant past speak to me, it's very different than the recent past. I am able to hear the ones from the recent past very clearly, and we share a wonderful dialog. However, the ones from the distant past – Lemuria – I have to be so still, so quiet, it's almost a whisper, how they speak to me. I have to go into the silence to hear them. It's like a whisper and they say things that are so beautiful. They are so ancient, much more than the ancient Hawaiian history. The voices that I hear from the 'Aumakua I ka Pō,' it's a holiness with a language all of its own. It's translated all of its own. Kryon speaks about the third language of the gods. That's the one. That's why I resonate so strongly to the Kryon teachings ... they match the teachings of the Ancients.

And so, I'm a keeper of the Lemurian Truths. Within my cellular memories is all of it, because I'm a very ancient soul on this planet. I was a Lemurian Priestess then, and I am one now. Inside of my DNA, inside of my Akashic Records is everything that is stored that I have experienced. If I get quiet enough, and peaceful enough within me, and ask with a pure heart, I will get information about that time and they (the Ancients) will transfer it to me and I will channel a message for people to hear."

Kahuna Kalei'iliahi has accompanied Lee Carroll and Kryon around the world. She has also attended many international indigenous gatherings to share the wisdom of her Ancestors. One of the highlights is when she joins Lee Carroll for a Kryon retreat in Hawaii. It was during 2015, at the Hikinaakala Heiau (Hawaiian Temple) on the island of Kauai, Hawaii, that Kryon identified why those around her feel the deep connection she has with her Ancestors. Here is what Kryon said:

I speak to a select group of people who are here by intent, standing on the beach of Lemuria. [Hawaii] Those who are listening or reading cannot hear the sound of the waves, as the ocean is so close! It is soothing to the ones who are with me now as you literally sit at the gateway of one of the many heiaus on this garden island. [A heiau is an area that is part of ancient sacred history in Hawaii]. Listen, for even the trade winds through the trees are speaking to you now.

There is much to be said about this area, and there's much history here. Be aware that what you study here at this protected sacred area cannot actually be something that happened in the time of Lemuria. Not really. You are looking at the sacredness of a time much later than Lemuria.

First of all, the actual land you sit on was a mountaintop that few could even visit! It was very high, and was extremely cold! However, now it's the shoreline and what you call the Ancient Hawaiians built the heiau that you stand before. Although this artifact was not Lemurian, it is still filled with the energy of the beginning.

The Lemurian spark is here. The only real way to feel what took place on this island is from the ancestors of the land, and that is why Kahuna Kalei'iliahi is here. [Kahuna Kalei'iliahi is with the Kryon Hawaiian excursion as a shamanic guide to the Ancestors – her Ancestors]. She is the "missing bridge" between those guides who might stand in front of this sacred Hawaiian heiau and give you the history of it as a temple, but nothing else. Kahuna Kalei'iliahi is the bridge who will not only give you the current history, but also translate that back to beginning Lemuria, because the ancestors flow through her today. You will see the compassion of these ancestors imbued within her, for the ancestors give her information that is current, based upon the past.

Listen to the ocean, for the sound really hasn't changed that much. It's the same sound that the Lemurians heard when they were at the base of the mountain joining the shoreline as you are now. The sky has not changed, either, and the rising sun has not changed. These are your connections with the ancestors and through Gaia to three things that we are going to talk about. Today we're going to call them the three R's, and the first one is *Respect*.

You stand here and respect what has happened on this mountain at any age in history and at any time at any civilization. It's sacred to all of the Ancients and to all of the ancestors, even to the Lemurians. This part of the Earth called Lemuria was sacred and special, and you respect that. You respect later what the Lemurians did, and later what the ancient Hawaiians did. Were you here?

That's the next R, and it is *Remembrance*. Are you able to remember, at some level, anything that is yours here? Forget the fact that the land might have been different, or the civilization might have been different. You're in Lemuria. Do you remember the land? Does it talk to you? Is it trying to get through to you to say, "*Forget the everyday life you have, and all the problems you came with. We're speaking about a remembrance of the God inside, and of the seed biology that you are, and of the beauty of Creation.*"

The third R is, perhaps, the most current one, for it is *Realization*. The word realization can mean many things, and it's based on one derivative: – *real*. Can you realize that this is all real to you? That is to say, can you cognize all of this today as pertinent and real in your life? Perhaps it's not a vacation, and not just a time for fun in the sun. Realization: How much can you remember, realize, and respect. Are you starting to feel the Lemurian spark while you are actually in the dirt at this sacred place?

That's the challenge of this week. Perhaps you're having a good time, relaxing and on vacation, enjoying the sights and esoteric energy? However, I challenge you to look at the three R's and what you're actually doing here. The examination of respect, remembrance, and realization may bring you to a whole other reality of who you might have been in this place.

Kryon live channelling given during the "Kryon Lemurian Retreat,"
Kauai, Hawaii – August 17, 2015

Now that you understand the connection between Kahuna Kalei'iliahi and Lemuria, we come full circle as we conclude with her connection to the Hindu belief system from India. Earlier, we revealed a connection between Hinduism and Lemuria, established through Gurudeva, who intuitively founded a Hindu Monastery on Kauai, Hawaii. Within the grounds of the monastery the construction of the San Marga Iraivan Temple is taking place. Gurudeva selected this particular place, because he recognized the spiritual power that was originally felt by the Hawaiian ancestors. The Hawaiians had called this place *pihanakalani* (where heaven touches the Earth).

In the Hawaiian tradition, whenever a heiau was being constructed, the kahuna would perform a blessing before the building was completed. In 2015, during the Kryon Lemurian Retreat, Kahuna Kalei'iliahi was visiting the construction site of the Iraivan Temple in Kauai. Immediately, as she walked the grounds, her ancestors started talking to her, but the origin of this story actually began a few weeks earlier in India. Here is Kahuna Kalei'iliahi to tell us how it all unfolded:

"India was not a place I had on my bucket list. It was never a place I felt drawn to go to – yet, there I found myself. I went with my sweet friend, Vanessa Murray, as a stopover on our way to and from

310

Africa. It was on our return trip where we were resting in India for a few days that we met up with a friend we had made, who introduced us to two wonderful healers. They invited us to visit a Hindu Temple, which we looked forward to seeing. The Hindu religion is one I knew very little about, but I did know its origins were ancient ... however, it was far more ancient than I understood.

I didn't recognize the deities in the temple, nor knew their story, but I felt the sacredness of this place. A Swami was giving a blessing of some kind to the multitudes of people coming and going. He was placing a gold cup-like object upside down on the heads of the devotees. Our host was explaining the meanings of the paintings on the walls throughout the temple. I could feel a powerful draw as my Ancestors directed me to go to the Swami to receive the blessing.

People rushed up in the crowd and I found myself easily slipping into the throng that was eagerly awaiting the Swami's blessing. Within seconds, I felt the gold object on my head. Vanessa was still laughing at how odd it had felt on her, until she looked at me carefully, sensing that something was happening. I was filled with emotions as cosmic light came pouring down into my crown chakra. I suddenly knew everything there was to know about this ancient religion – all of the gods, all of the meanings. I began to see the profound connection of these people and their religion and Lemuria.

In 2014, during the Kryon Lemurian Retreat on Kaua'i, we visited a Hindu Monastery. It was there that the Swami showed us a book called *"The Lemurian Scrolls,"* channeled by a great Hindu Master long before and only recently put into a book. We were so completely blown away with the fact that they believed they came from the Pleiades and Lemuria, and that their creation story was similar to that of Polynesians – we were seeded with our Divinity by our Ancestors from the Makali'i (Pleiades)! When I first heard there was a Hindu Monastery on that island, I really wondered why that was. Now, years later, I know why. They belong there and recognize it was 'home.'

What my Ancestors told me was this: I was the bridge between India and Lemuria (Hawai'i) ... a rainbow bridge. We Hawaiians

(Polynesians) are known as the Rainbow Children of MU – Le-MU-ria. They showed me that I was blocked from having any attraction to go to India because the time was not right, till now. They said that this was the preparation necessary before I went to the Hindu Temple on Kaua'i again, a few weeks later. There was a cosmic design to all of this that was far greater than I understood, but I felt it.

It was related to the publishing of *"The Lemurian Scrolls,"* but also with the new construction of the Hindu Iraivan Temple being built on Kaua'i! In August 2015, I went to that monastery and met the kind and loving Swami again. This time, he showed us the new temple that was under construction. There, I saw the spirits of the Na Koa (Warrior Protectors) in an outer ring around the temple. Inside the ring behind them were the Ancients from the Distant Past ... the Pleiadians. There was a holiness that we all felt and as the Swami took us to view the temple closer and share more of its meaning, my Ancestors told me that in Ancient Lemuria, it was the site of the Ice Temple (a metaphor for it was the Ice Ages), a sacred spot. They also said every one of us were there at one time doing ceremony ... a ceremony that honors the divinity within.

I was shown that our presence there was necessary and part of the blessing that was needed as protocol, before its completion. The Ancients always blessed the land and any structure. It is a practice we Hawaiians still continue. I asked the Swami permission to do the blessing ceremony and he graciously honored the tradition. It was very emotional for almost everyone. I write this in awe of the grandness of what occurred, something that could only be orchestrated by this benevolent Universe we call God."

After Kahuna Kalei'iliahi's blessing ceremony, the Swami invited the group to enter the temple. As the group wandered through, the Swami pointed out various features within the architecture. It was then that someone noticed an interesting carving within the foundations and asked the Swami to tell us about it. The Swami very casually responded, "Oh yes, that's a Hawaiian Menehune.

They are intentionally placed there to be a part of the temple." Wow! What a beautiful honoring of the Hawaiians.

In the Hawaiian culture, the Menehune were a mischievous group of little people, or dwarfs, who lived hidden in the forests and valleys of the island before the Polynesians arrived. They were known for being extremely strong and excellent craftsmen, using their skills to build temples (heiau), fishponds, roads, canoes, and houses. The Menehune have been credited with building Kauai's Alekoko Fishpond, as well as the Menehune Ditch, which is a historic irrigation ditch that funnels water from the Waimea River in Kauai.

A beautiful explanation from Paramacharya Palaniswami regarding the presence of Menehune in the Iraivan Temple on Kauai is given below:

"Each Hindu temple has a special stone, called the Gomugai, which brings the sanctified waters from the puja held in the inner sanctum out to the devotees, who receive blessings from sipping the water.

This stone is supported by a dwarf in traditional architecture. For Iraivan, we thought there is nothing more perfect for this than to have our own Kauaian Menehune hold up the stone, with his two hands above his head. The Menehunes are a race of stone builders who once inhabited our island, said to have been here before the current-day Hawaiians. They were of tiny stature, Lilliputian people, yet stout and strong. In fact, they were the stone masons who built large stone water ponds and walls on Kauai. We felt they would be at home in a stone temple."

Source: www.himalayanacademy.com/blog/taka/2005/9/21/

The Menehune are considered to be the Hawaiian counterpart to Hindu bhutas. Bhutas are small elemental devas that are benevolent and protective beings. Elementals are also known by other names such as fairies, elves, pixies, gnomes, sprites, brownies, leprechauns, Earth angels, nature spirits, and others. Regardless of the name, all of these beings are multidimensional energies that are the helpers for planet Earth – Gaia, and they are in service to humanity.

According to Kryon, the role of elementals is important to help humanity reconnect with Gaia. Why is this important? As humanity begins to become aware of Gaia's life force and consciousness, it means that the planet will begin to matter in a way it hasn't before. It will bring about new attitudes and solutions to some of our current environmental problems. The way we treat animals will also change, so that they are given respect, honor, and love. All this is a return to the way of the Ancients and their wisdom, and something that was inherently understood in Lemuria. The Lemurians were intimately connected to Gaia, and when you honor Gaia, you honor the ancestors and God.

Communicating with the Ancestors is Kahuna Kalei'iliahi's specialty. In her role as a wisdom keeper she is able to offer readings, blessings, and sacred journeys. She also channels messages from a multitude of holy beings of light. If you would like to connect with Kahuna Kalei'iliahi, please visit her website:

www.kaleiiliahi.com

Question for Kryon:

It is believed that the Native Hawaiians are Polynesians who arrived from other islands in the Pacific approximately 1,500 years ago. However, the mass exodus of Lemurians from what is now modern-day Hawaii occurred over 15,000 years ago. Did any Lemurians remain, and, if so, are some of the descendants in Hawaii today? What happened between 15,000 years ago and 1,500 years ago?

Answer:

Dear ones, when the continent of MU started to sink, and Lemuria eventually became the Hawaiian Islands, it was immensely frightening for the Lemurians. Although it was slow, there was no thought, whatsoever, that it would eventually stop sinking, with the tops of the mountains remaining as islands in the Pacific. Consequently, most of the population left, over time.

The sinking created earthquakes, and the gentle settling of the weight itself into the crust of the planet created great upheaval. On the big mountain, there was lava almost everywhere and nothing was stable. Water regularly poured into fissures and cracks that were open to the core mantle of the Earth, and violent explosions took place. Only on the extinct volcanic portions of the hotspot was there any safety at all, and that's where the few Lemurians fled to and remained. This was at the north end of the mountain range, and is now Kauai, the oldest of the peaks of the previous Lemurian mini-continent. It was the most stable during the sinking-island years.

This is also why Kauai became the home of Mele'ha and others who refused to leave, thinking that they would go down with the mountain – an honorable death in their precious Lemuria.

So the Lemurians, the real Hawaiians, stayed on Kauai and were the oldest and most shamanic descendants of Hawaii. One of these real Lemurians is responsible for the existence of the *magic ones*, called the Menehune, in the sacred valleys on the rugged coast of that island. The one I speak of is Mele'ha, for she was the only Star Sister to stay on the mountain. All the rest left, as well as the Star Mothers, who knew that they were finished there. Mele'ha lived an exceedingly long time after that, and her essence was eventually imbued into the land, along with her body.

Of all the islands of Hawaii today, Kauai carries the real spiritual lineage of Lemuria. This is also why the Akash of the Shaman from India, Gurudeva, demanded that he build his sacred temple to the Pleiadians on Kauai. Does this information begin to ring true to you?

All the current ideas of who migrated where, and when they did it, are only currently perceived truths from only a thousand years or so. The Polynesians, indeed, found Hawaii, but they were not the first to come. The truth is that Hawaii has been inhabited for almost 50,000 years, and the Shamans [kahuna] currently living there will claim that specific truth, even today, for everything we have told you has been written in their history. Did any Star Mothers return? Why don't you go to Kauai and ask?

In Closing

Our journey about "The Women of Lemuria" has come to an end, and yet, it's really just the beginning! Our ancient Akashic Remembrance of our original spiritual enlightenment is moving us into higher consciousness, which brings greater wisdom. The evolution of Human nature has begun and, eventually, we will have a peaceful planet that no longer has war. Our galactic ancestors have trod the same path that humanity now faces and this is cause for celebration! Against all odds, we [humanity] have passed the marker that the Ancients told us we could.

Thousands of years from now, it will be our turn to "seed" the next planet of free choice in the galaxy, and perhaps, someday, they will write a story about it, if they make it past their marker. Until then, we have work to do. We have a responsibility to claim our divinity, and not only believe we are sacred and magnificent, but to become it and live it! Let these final practical instructions from Kryon carry you forward as you step into your mastery and beyond.

What kind of power do you take from here? Power? Yes, I used that word. What kind of power do you take from here? Can you see anything to change?

You are all travelers to this excursion, so I'm going to give you a phrase: *"Repetitive consciousness and action create synchronicity and reality for the planet."* Again: *"Repetitive consciousness and action create synchronicity and reality for the planet."* Now, what does that mean?

Old Soul, let me give it to you straight: What are your habits? What do you repeat over and over? What's your demeanor? You're on the airplane or you're in the airport or you're at home. Is a smile something that happens automatically when you walk from place to place, or look around? Is it there when you see others or not? Is it joy or is it not? Whatever it is, if you repeat it and repeat it, it's a very powerful habit that will stick and stay. Does that affect people around you?

For many, if you lose your luggage, it's *"Woe is me"* or worse! You become the victim of the day because your luggage didn't make it. Perhaps something is too heavy or something hurts when you travel? What is your "demeanor of the moment?" What is normal for you? When you see a certain difficult situation, do you have immediate compassion for how it may have developed or do you complain about it? What is your repetitive habit? Here's what I am going to tell you, Old Soul: You are a very powerful person, and listen to this – all those listening and reading should know this: *Whatever your repetitive habit is, becomes your reality. Period.* How do you like it so far?

This is how powerful you are. We have spoken about this so many times, yet today, you are in Lemuria for the last time on this trip. Today, you can examine all of this in light of knowing what you know is the purpose of why you are on the Earth at the moment.

You can create whatever you want to. You are powerful and you are here in this amazing energy, so perhaps it's time for you to take the Lemurian spark, dear ones, and carry it with you as you go. Let it change the habits that, perhaps, you're not even aware you have, which can diminish perception of the love of God inside you. Did you get that? Your habits can diminish everything you may think you believe in, just because they are habits.

How do you look to others? Have you thought of that? Does it matter to you? Are you carrying the Lemurian spark of compassion and wisdom, or are you proud of being an odd New Ager? These are also habits. Some people might look at you and say, *"Well, I don't really want to be with that person too much because they're a little strange."* So, Lemurian, Lightworker, is that what you really want to show others – "a little strange?" How is this helping the planet? Instead of being a little strange, why not practice compassion and mastery?

Understand that this group before me will never be coming back in the same configuration of energy. These are the last moments for this Lemurian family. So we wish you to take away the concept of the ability to create mastery with your power. Examine the habits that are everyday, but which may be blocks along the way.

There's no goodbye here, and we want you to understand that, when you finally disperse, there is an energy which can stay with you. The one next to you goes with you, even if you don't know them that well. The camaraderie of the Lemurian spark and what you experienced goes with you. The beauty of Gaia and the synchronicities of the trip all go together with you. They repeat and repeat in your mind, showing you your magnificence. Don't let this escape you.

Here is an assignment for you: Take what you have learned here that has been elegant and elevated and advanced, and apply it to your life and change your habits. That's why you came. That's why you're here on the planet at this moment.

Some of you had tremendous synchronicities to get you here. It's the kind of synchronicity that yells, "It can't happen." Yet it did. Dear one, that means there was purpose to get you here, and that means there is a whole entourage looking at you right now, saying, *"Make it worth it. Make it worth it."* It's beautiful, isn't it? It couldn't be more beautiful for you to sit here knowing that there is no accident that got you here.

We have presented some synchronicities to you all week long so that you could admire them, and so that they would take your breath away. Don't forget them, because they were examples to you, for you can create the same kinds of things when you leave this mountain. You can take others' breaths away by the creation from the synchronicities you create for them – the healings, the love, the compassion, and the solved problems. It doesn't matter how old you are or how young you are. That's the beauty of who's here and who is reading this. That's the message for the week, and it is always the message when I'm on the mountain of Lemuria.

And so it is.

Kryon live channelling given during the "Kryon Lemurian Retreat,"
Kauai, Hawaii – August 22, 2015

Final Question for Kryon:

Do you have any additional information about "The Women of Lemuria" that we should know?

Answer:

The Old Souls who were the women of Lemuria have a dual purpose on the planet. The first one is obvious and we have shared it throughout these channellings and questions. It's the second purpose that is just now occurring, and the reason for this entire book.

This shift, past the 2012 precession of the equinoxes, is the beginning of the remembrance of the core information, as taught by those from the stars. The only ones who have this firmly implanted into their Akash are the former women of Lemuria. No other persons on this planet had it given to them in such a pure form, over such a long period of time, by the original teachers and seeds of Human DNA.

So, the entire reason why many of you are reading this is to know this fact, and to start remembering this information. You have time, ladies! For, you and your children and their children will begin to respond to what you teach, and how you teach it. Generations will begin to absorb what you were taught, and create a new form of wisdom on the planet.

We do not speak about still another religion or belief system. Instead, we speak about a return to core truths, which carry the love and compassion of the Creator, which can be taught and spread throughout the Earth. No membership – no buildings – no doctrine is needed for this. It can be celebrated within any religion, and any current belief, for it's a return to basic integrity of Human to Human, and brings with it an understanding of the preciousness of life, and the oneness with Gaia.

Priestesses arise! Let your love show in ways that are gentle and pure. The changes you make will be from taking the high ground and being the compassionate ones of the future. The system of old energy will crumble at your feet, while you send light that breaks up the very foundation of old systems that say one thing, yet do another. Let your presence be known as the ones whose light will remain pure, while established religious systems show their dysfunction. Be the Shamans of the future, and show the way. Let the planet know that the female is equipped to bring guidance and teaching and love to all humanity – a return to the way in which it was designed.

Connect with the Lemurian Sisterhood

The purpose of the Lemurian Sisterhood is to allow women to rekindle their remembrance of their Lemurian lifetime and the wisdom that they learned from their Pleiadian teachers and the priestesses of the ancient Lemurian Sisterhood. Whether you were in Lemuria or not is not important. If you have been drawn to this book, you are an Old Soul and, at the very least, you are a descendant of Lemuria. Your Akash still rings with the original truths given by the Pleiadians – the Star Mothers. If you would like to become part of the growing global community of Lemurian Sisters, please visit Dr. Amber (Mele'ha) Wolf's website:

www.amberwolfphd.com/lemurian-sisterhood

About the Authors

Monika Muranyi

Monika Muranyi has always had a deep affinity and connection with our planet Earth. She has a Bachelor of Applied Science degree with Honors, obtained at Southern Cross University, New South Wales, Australia. For over fifteen years, Monika worked in various national parks within Australia and New Zealand. She is an accredited Electro Magnetic Field (EMF) Balancing Technique™ Practitioner (Phases I to XIII).

Monika is the consummate archivist and researcher of the Kryon material, as channelled by Lee Carroll. Through Ariane Editions (Montreal, Canada), she has published a special Kryon trilogy that features subject-driven books that bring us new understandings about Gaia in *The Gaia Effect*, the Akash in *The Human Akash*, and the Soul in *The Human Soul Revealed*. With dozens of new questions answered by Kryon, this series is a profound addition to the Kryon library.

Monika frequently travels with Lee Carroll around the world, helping to bring the messages and teachings of Kryon to the planet. The inspiration to write and produce this book is a result of Monika's passion to ignite the Lemurian spark within the Old Souls who are awakening on the planet.

www.monikamuranyi.com

Dr. Amber (Mele'ha) Wolf

Dr. Amber (Mele'ha) Wolf has been a committed and practicing holistic health care and education professional since 1982. She is an internationally known teacher, facilitator, author, recording artist, healing intuitive, channel, and the originator of the Lemurian Sisterhood. She is a past member of the 3HO Foundation, a 35-year active member of the Self-Realization Fellowship, co-producer of the Kryon Discovery Series, and a member of the Kryon Team, frequently presenting two-day workshops alongside Lee Carroll.

Beside her healing practice and her travels throughout the world with Lee Carroll and Kryon, Dr. Amber (Mele'ha) Wolf is the creator and facilitator of the Lemurian Sisterhood Seminars. Her sacred assignment to help reawaken women to the core Lemurian seeds within their DNA, and recreate the Sacred Circles of the Lemurian Sisterhood. She continues to receive and channel information and guidance through her ongoing connection with the Pleiadian Star Mothers. Each initiation and activation she receives helps her lovingly steward the evolution of the Lemurian Sisterhood to help bridge ancient wisdom with modern knowledge.

Raised in rural New England, Dr. Wolf spent her youth in nature, always feeling drawn to the "spirit in nature." This continued into adulthood when she moved to the Alaskan wilderness, where she lived for 12 years. Surviving amidst the beauty and harshness of the elements, Dr. Wolf learned indigenous healing remedies and midwifery, while deepening her relationship to the natural world.

Moving to Colorado in 1989 opened more doors in the health and spiritual fields, as she began her full-time career as a health practitioner in cranial sacral therapy and "transformational" healing. A near-death accident in 1994 brought severe head and body injuries, but also the gift and ability to experience a heightened source of energy and wisdom. The foothills of the Colorado Rocky Mountains have been her home and sanctuary for 28 years.

Completing her Ph.D. in 1995 in Holistic Science and Alternative Therapies, Dr. Wolf is a Certified Cranial Sacral Therapist, Certified Somatic Therapist, trained Quantum-Touch practitioner, licensed minister, a Yoga Instructor and Pilates Instructor, a Matrix Energetics practitioner, and Certified Laughter Yoga Leader. She is a member in good standing of the American CranioSacral Therapy Association, the International Association of Healthcare Practitioners and a member of ABMP, Associated Massage and BodyWork Professionals.

www.amberwolfphd.com